Ride, Red, Ride

Also available from Continuum

An International History of the Recording Industry
by Pekka Gronow and Ilpo Saunio

Arranging the Score: Portraits of the Great Arrangers
by Gene Lees

Buddy Bolden and the Last Days of Storyville
by Danny Barker, edited by Alyn Shipton

The Essential Jazz Records, Volume I: Ragtime to Swing
by Max Harrison, Charles Fox and Eric Thacker

The Essential Jazz Records, Volume II: Modernism to Postmodernism
by Max Harrison, Stuart Nicholson and Eric Thacker

I Guess I'll Get the Papers and Go Home: The Life of Doc Cheatham
by Adolphus 'Doc' Cheatham, edited by Alyn Shipton

Marshall Royal: Jazz Survivor
by Marshall Royal with Claire P. Gordon

Preservation Hall
by William Carter

Song & Dance Man III: The Art of Bob Dylan
by Michael Gray

Teddy Wilson
by Teddy Wilson with Arie Ligthart and Humphrey van Loo

Who's Who of British Jazz
John Chilton

RIDE, RED, RIDE
The Life of Henry 'Red' Allen

John Chilton

With a Selected Discography
compiled by Brian Peerless

CONTINUUM
London and New York

Continuum
Wellington House, 125 Strand, London WC2R 0BB
370 Lexington Avenue, New York, NY 10017-6550

First published in Great Britain by Cassell by arrangement with Bayou Press Ltd.
Reprinted in paperback in 2000.

British Library Cataloguing-in-Publication Data
A catalogue record for this book is available from the British Library.

ISBN 0-304-70407-5 (hardback)
      0 8264-4744-9 (paperback)

Library of Congress Cataloging-in-Publication Data

Chilton, John, 1932
    Ride, Red, Ride: the life of Henry 'Red' Allen/John Chilton: with a selected
discography compiled by Brian Peerless.
        p.   cm.
    Includes bibliographical references (p.   ), discography (p.   ) and index.
    ISBN 0-3-4-70407-4 (hardcover) — 0-8264-4744-9 (paperback)
    1. Allen, Henry, 1908–1967.   2. Jazz musicians—United States—Bibliography.
I. Title.
ML419.A56C54 1998
788.9'2165'092—dc21
[B]
                                                                98–43703
                                                                CIP
                                                                MN

Designed and typeset by Ben Cracknell Studios

Printed and bound in Great Britain by Biddles Ltd, Guildford and King's Lynn

CONTENTS

ACKNOWLEDGEMENTS

Grateful thanks are extended to:

Henry Allen III, Richard B. Allen, Jeff Atterton, Cuff Billet, Ray
Bolden, Jack Bradley, Michael Brooks, Jack Cicolla, Derek Coller, Bill
Crow, Stanley Dance, Kenny Davern, Frank Driggs, Alan Elsdon,
Allan Gatward, David Griffiths, Marty Grosz, Mike Hazeldine, Karl
Gert zur Heide, Franz Hoffmann, William Ransom Hogan Jazz
Archive (Tulane University, New Orleans), Institute of Jazz Studies
(Rutgers University, New Jersey), Al Kennedy, Terry Lightfoot,
Humphrey Lyttelton, Barry Martyn, Dan Morgenstern, National Jazz
Foundation Archive (Loughton Library, Essex), Jane Palmer (Algiers
Point Library, Louisiana), Brian Peerless, Art Pilkington, Michael
Pointon, Ralph Porter, Dr Bruce Raeburn, Claes Ringqvist, Alyn
Shipton, Johnny Simmen, Keith Smith, Richard Sudhalter, Eddie
Taylor, Les Tompkins, Mike Tovey, Françoise Venet, Barbara Vaughn,
Joyce Wallis, John Whitehorn, Al Williams, Roy Williams, Val Wilmer
and Laurie Wright.

The photographs in the plate section are reproduced by kind
permission of Henry Allen III (1–6, 9, 11–12 and 14–15), Jack
Bradley (17), Teresa Chilton (7–8, 10, 16), Gladys Dobell (18) and
Barry Martyn (13).

For George Melly and the hundreds of gigs we've shared

1

NEW ORLEANS JOYS

The difference between Red Allen's onstage and offstage personality was remarkable. Anyone witnessing the tall, burly figure hollering at an audience and blowing daredevil phrases on his trumpet could be forgiven for thinking that Red Allen was an extrovert for all of his waking hours. But if one met Red away from an audience he was a model of courtesy; a quiet, considerate man who was both affable and reflective. The link between the two contrasting aspects of Red's character was the enormous presence that he always exuded. He was clearly a proud man, but his pride was never blemished with haughtiness. In social exchanges Red's soft, husky voice was full of old Southern charm, his pronunciations faithful to his Louisiana childhood. The word 'nice' entered many of his sentences, and he usually referred to himself as 'yours truly'. His terms of endearment for musicians he admired were 'my man', 'my ace boy' and 'champ'; he was, as writer Dan Morgenstern observed, 'a kind and decent man'.[1]

Red's lifelong wife, Pearly May, said to him in their early years, 'Allen, you're too quiet. You don't belong in this business.'[2] This was not meant as an admonition, but as a loving observation. Nevertheless Red took it as guiding advice and gradually developed an onstage charisma that was unforgettable.

Red Allen in action was an object lesson in personality projection. He could get the most blasé audience enthusiastically applauding a soloist by jovially commanding them to 'Make him happy', 'Make… Him…Happy!' Red often told his listeners how lucky they were to be hearing a performance by 'six princes of jazz', no matter how skimpy the talent was in the band that day. He made sure that nobody dozed off by yelling 'Wamp! Wamp!' at the start of each number, and at any point in the proceedings he was likely to shout 'Look out!' to the assembly. The people always laughed and Red joined in with them, never quite losing the V-shaped frown that was a permanent part of his creased features. His way of acknowledging the crowd's response was to give them a verbal pat with his all-purpose phrase 'nice'. This was Henry 'Red' Allen, the master showman, who frequently replaced his glistening Cadillac, parking the new model close to where he worked so that everyone could see it. This was also Henry 'Red' Allen, one of the greatest jazz trumpeters who ever lived.

Red was not a crusading visionary who patterned his bold improvisations on a system involving advanced harmonies. Nor did he consciously use his uncanny rhythmic sureness to break what has been called 'the tyranny of the bar-line', which ensnared many early jazz soloists into playing phrases that were in rigid two- or four-bar segments. With no revolutionary goals in mind Red used his remarkable, natural musicality to create phrases that sounded right to him. In doing so he introduced new possibilities (harmonically and rhythmically) to a succeeding generation of jazz musicians.

During the 1930s many jazz listeners were convinced that Red Allen's trumpet playing offered a serious challenge to Louis Armstrong. But despite Red's brilliance, Louis's genius continued to stand him in good stead during that era, and throughout subsequent decades he remained unchallengeable. Red's playing never overshadowed Armstrong's, but he always retained a superb gift for creating innovative solos. Of his own style Red simply said, 'I like to improvise in a different way'. Armstrong's work had its effect on the formation of Red's style, but from quite early on he showed that he was one of the least predictable of all jazz musicians, and many still believe that Allen retains a place that is second only to Armstrong in the pantheon of jazz trumpeters.

Like Armstrong, Henry Allen was born in Louisiana, of African-American parents, but the backgrounds of the two musicians were quite dissimilar. It would be an exaggeration to say that Henry was born with a silver spoon in his mouth, but he endured few hardships during his early years; he said, 'My father was never rich, but he tried to give me everything I'd think of'.[3] Henry Jr was the only child of parents who lived in a comfortable house, complete with a garden, at 414 Newton Street, Algiers (now known as West New Orleans), on the opposite side of the Mississippi from the city of New Orleans. Henry Jr was born at that address on 7 January 1906;[4] from quite early on in his career he gave 1908 as his year of birth. Later the family moved to 824 Lamarque Street.

Henry Allen Sr worked as a longshoreman on the Mississippi river docks, but devoted all of his spare time to playing the trumpet and organizing one of Louisiana's finest brass bands. More important to Henry Allen Jr than any silver spoon was the silver-plated trumpet mouthpiece given to him by his father on his tenth birthday. Previously Red's blowing had been done on an upright alto horn (shaped like a very small tuba). Originally the choice of instrument was made by Red's mother, not his father. 'My mother wouldn't let me play trumpet as she thought it was too strenuous for one of my years. She'd see the guys blowing with their necks all swollen out, and she said I was too young for that. She told me to play an easier instrument and got me a violin, but although I took a few lessons from Peter Bocage I was never keen on it.'[5]

The alto horn was a compromise. Red's father wanted his son to play trumpet, and eventually Red's mother (Juretta, born in 1883) agreed to her husband's wish, but initially she watched the youngster carefully while he practised, to make sure that he didn't suffer any undue physical strain from overblowing. Red said, 'So it came along slowly, and that is perhaps why I don't have the ball in my cheeks that some trumpet players do. I played trumpet, but I took to it easily and slowly.'[6]

Red was a respectful and obedient son who listened both to the advice his father gave him on the art of playing the trumpet, and to the biographical details and anecdotes of the life that his dad had encountered before he settled in Algiers. Red's father was born in Lockport, Louisiana, in 1871. He soon left that town with his parents and moved to Morgan City, Louisiana, where his father had found a job; there the youngster worked in the fields and ran errands for a grocer. Next the family moved on to Bowie, Louisiana. Henry, by now a teenager, began work on a local farm, then, after considerable deliberation, he ran away to Algiers where he eventually got a job on the docks, thus he became part of a highly organized workforce, with its own union.[7]

On a working trip to Thibodeaux, Louisiana, Allen heard a five-piece black band playing at a dance and was greatly impressed by the group's syncopations. He persuaded one of the band, Ed Paines, to give him lessons on the cornet, and soon became a competent player. On a visit to his birthplace he sat in with the local Excelsior Band at a picnic, his first experience of being part of an improvising ensemble. He felt that the band was 'altering the melody in spite of themselves',[8] inserting sudden stops in the music, the like of which he had never heard before. He admitted that he had difficulties in following the tempo, because the 'fakers' (as he called them) played faster without warning and made melodic alterations as they pleased. Also in Lockport he enjoyed hearing the more organized Claiborne Williams Band (from Donaldsonville), which he later classified as being the first ragtime band that he ever heard; this band featured Williams's daughter singing 'plaintive sounds like the blues'.[9]

Returning to New Orleans, Henry Sr, his musical imagination greatly stimulated, went out of his way to hear any emerging young black musicians. He was particularly impressed by the playing of trombonist Jack Carey (from Hahnville, Louisiana), who had recently settled in the city. According to Henry Sr, 'He was very rough, wild, and lived according to his inspiration.'[10] Carey was musically and socially dissimilar to Allen but this did not prevent the cornet player from joining Carey's Band, where he played in the ten-piece ensemble alongside up-and-coming young musicians including baritone horn player George Sims and cornettist Oscar Celestin. Henry Allen Sr often impressed on his son the importance of Jack Carey in the emergence of the new style of music that would later be called jazz. The oft-repeated tales of Carey's musical prowess sank deep into young Red's memory and over 40 years later he often introduced Carey's name in a stage routine that listed great jazz musicians.

Henry Sr did not stay long in Jack Carey's Band, for in truth he was happier in an ensemble that relied on printed music rather than inspired improvisations. Red was well aware of this: 'My father wasn't a great jazzman, but he had lots of power and was a fine musician as far as reading and organizing was concerned, in addition to being an outstanding conductor'.[11] Possessing these qualities made it inevitable that Henry Allen Sr formed his own band. The Allen Brass Band soon established an enviable reputation. Two of Henry Sr's brothers were founder-members of the ensemble: George (who played the snare drum) and Samuel (who played the alto horn and the tuba); later Jack Carey himself played regularly with the band. Looking back Red said, 'My father's band was what they call these days "a marching band", but they had a lot more than just 6/8 time. They could really swing. This band had probably more great musicians in it than any other I have heard of, such guys as Buddy Bolden, King Oliver, Big

Eye Louis Nelson and many others. My father used to hold rehearsals in our home, so I had a chance to hear anyone that was coming up.'[12]

But music-making was never allowed to interfere with young Henry's school studies. 'My father used to give dances to collect enough money to get the band its uniforms. When they had these great dances I would be there all night, now and then nodding off for a few minutes, but going straight on to school the next morning.'[13] Henry Jr's first school was the James Lewis Elementary on the Algiers side of the river; later he moved on to high school at McDonogh 35 on South Rampart and Girod in New Orleans, catching the ferry to cross the Mississippi (a one-cent journey for schoolchildren). He occasionally had to put up with taunts from young white kids when he walked home from the ferry via Homer or Newton Street.

McDonogh 35 High School was the only public high school for African-American students in New Orleans. Founded in September 1917 on the site of the previous (whites only) McDonogh 13, it was situated in an unsalubrious area two blocks from the Eagle Saloon and close to the old site of the Funky Butt Hall. As Al Kennedy has pointed out, 'When the legalized prostitution abruptly came to a halt on 12 November 1917, much of the activity moved across Canal Street to the McDonogh 35 neighborhood.' Nevertheless the 600 high school pupils benefited from the skills of a remarkable teaching team that included Edward Belfield Spriggins, a pioneering writer on jazz history, who was the first to publish an article on Buddy Bolden (in 1933).

Algiers was quite dissimilar from New Orleans proper in those days – the relationship between the two areas was likened by Henry Jr to that between the Bronx and Manhattan. Writer Martin Williams described Algiers as being removed from 'the poverty of the uptown Negro section of New Orleans, and from the particular snobberies of the colored Creole section'.[14] Certainly there was nothing like the old Storyville district in Algiers, though a few lively ladies plied their trade around the Brooklyn Street area. At the time of Henry Jr's childhood neither Newton nor Homer was paved, and though the African-American dwellers who lived in that locale still encountered racial prejudice and restrictions, there were few signs of overt retaliation. Most white people got their entertainment at segregated dance halls, but the black public had their own dance venues in Algiers, two of which, the Odd Fellows and the Ladies of Hope, were close to the Allen home. Mixed bands were unheard of in Algiers, or in New Orleans itself. Besides the racial prejudice of old Louisiana there were also district rivalries; Red Allen told fellow musician Garvin Bushell that as a youngster he would not mix with people who came from nearby Gretna.[15]

Red loved talking about his early days, but was disappointed that so few people asked him specific questions about the music he heard as a young man. In 1966 he said acidly, 'I guess they think I'm a New York musician. But I've still got the bass-drum from my daddy's band, to this day.'[16] Red really disliked it when critics lumped together all New Orleans jazz as Dixieland. He believed that New Orleans music was a style of playing and not an instrumentation. If the company was right he would point out emphatically that being a musician in New Orleans meant that you were expected to play in all sorts of line-ups, of which the trumpet/trombone/clarinet front line was only one example. He chuckled sarcastically when it was mentioned that saxophones were not encouraged in New Orleans, pointing out that most of the dance-hall and riverboat bands where he worked had saxophones, sometimes whole sections of them. Line-ups were flexible; if people could not afford to pay for six pieces they got a quartet, or a trio (sometimes even a duo – drummer Baby Dodds remembered gigging with just a trombonist). While admitting that he had no positive ideas as to who started jazz, he was dismissive of the white cornettist Nick LaRocca's claim to have 'originated jazz', and was also distinctly annoyed by the suggestion that recording company talent scouts could not find any black jazz talent in New Orleans when they visited during the 1920s.

At high school Red was not immune to the various fads and fashions that stampede teenagers. Playing the ukulele was one craze that caught hold of thousands of youngsters, including Red, during the early 1920s and his prowess on the instrument was outstanding enough to be remembered years later by guitarist Narvin Kimball, Red's junior at the McDonogh 35 School. Red attributed his skills on the ukulele to 'having good wrists and the ability to pick up chords very quickly',[17] but his interest in playing it was short-lived and he soon resumed practising the trumpet for hours on end. Nevertheless when he returned home from high school he still found time to play baseball with his pals, who as a tribute to his powerful hitting, nicknamed him 'Biffly Bam'. One of Red's contemporaries in these sand-lot games was Mel Ott, who later played for the New York Giants.

But baseball heroes took second place to Red's favourite brass players. Red never heard trumpeter Charles 'Buddy' Bolden play (he was incarcerated in a mental home in 1907). Nor did he hear Freddy

Keppard, who left New Orleans in 1912 to work in California with the Original Creole Orchestra; but from the age of ten he often listened admiringly to King Oliver, and a little later he became a fan of Oliver's protégé, Louis Armstrong (who was five years older than Red). But Armstrong was not the only source of inspiration in a city area that boasted dozens of fine trumpet players. Red listened to, and admired, Chris Kelly, Buddy Petit, Emile Emanuel 'Manuel' Perez, Henry 'Kid' Rena and Ernest 'Punch' Miller. Years later, trumpeter 'Doc' Cheatham, commenting on this plethora of talent, said: 'All of them had different ways of playing New Orleans music'.[18] Red Allen never heard the white bandleader Nick LaRocca live, the Original Dixieland Jazz Band having left New Orleans in 1915, but he admired the work of another white cornettist, Emmett Hardy, who died in 1925 aged 22 (and is said to have influenced Bix Beiderbecke). Red and Emmett Hardy went to the same music teacher, Manuel 'Fess' Manetta. Red described Hardy as 'a great jazz trumpet player … I was coming up in those days and probably listened to everybody, and Emmett Hardy impressed me more than most. A kind of lyrical player, it was a pity he never made a record.'[19] Red also listened carefully whenever he passed the home of the white Brunies family, where five brothers could be heard practising on various brass instruments. George Brunies became a star jazz trombonist, but in those days there was little social contact between him and Red Allen.

Besides receiving musical tuition from his father and from Manuel Manetta, Red also took lessons from Amos White. Red called Manetta his 'second father' and White his 'third father'. His coaching was supplemented by what was known as 'bandstand tuition' which Red willingly took from Punch Miller and others. The youngster had an enquiring mind and was always asking questions about trumpet technique, mouthpieces and practice routines. At the McDonogh 35 High School Red was able to further his knowledge of musical theory. In the annual report of the New Orleans Public Schools 1917–18, J.W. Hofman, the principal of Red's high school, wrote:

The Department of Music has made an excellent showing in view of the fact that there is no special teacher for that course. Nevertheless the musical ability of the pupils has shown a pleasing development and the chorus singing has received favorable comment.

During the early 1920s Narvin Kimball and Red Allen linked up at McDonogh 35 in an unofficial school band, which also included trumpeter Percy Humphrey. Kimball gave Al Kennedy the background:

Sometimes in the afternoons we would have an opportunity to play. I can only remember one time we were being presented. We played up on the platform where the teachers were. They had officials who had come from the School Board.[20]

The band did not play jazz on this occasion but performed 'some kind of a march', which, as Kimball recalled, was 'just something that would have been ordinarily expected to be played and timely for the situation. He went on to say, 'We had a very highly trained glee club... we used to broadcast over the radio'.[21]

By this time Red was a regular member of his father's band. The sight of the small figure among the grown-up musicians was a talked-about gimmick, but Red had gained his place in the Allen Brass Band strictly on merit. Before he was officially allowed to join the band he went through a sort of apprenticeship, carrying out various mundane tasks and errands. 'I used to pass the music out on parades. We used to carry the parts in little sacks, and I had those on my shoulders.'[22] Red's father was watchful that his young son did not overtire himself. 'Those parade jobs with my father meant a lot of walking. At first he'd arrange for me to meet the band at some corner, and then I'd come in and play a number, generally getting a lot of applause, though whether for being good or just because I was a youngster is something I don't know.'[23] One of the numbers regularly performed at the street corners was 'What a Friend We Have in Jesus'. If Red's father sensed that his young son was getting over-tired, he carried him home on his shoulders.

The parade routines gradually increased the youngster's stamina, and stood him in good stead at high school where he became a good cross-country runner. As a teenager he was tall, thin and gangly with a mass of freckles which embarrassed him then and continued to bother him somewhat as an adult. Red felt that the testing physical challenge of long parade marches was a factor in producing so many strong brass players in New Orleans:

You'll notice that most of the guys from New Orleans have power because we walked and played on rugged streets, and that builds up your embouchure. The roads were rough and if you stepped into a hole you had to hold on to that horn not to break your notes. After a while I went all the way in the parades, walking miles and miles, and I just grew up in this setting. At one time Louis Armstrong and I happened to be in my father's band, on a parade. I just realize now what a brass section that could have been with Louis, my father and myself. Already Louis was great, and because he squeezed me, I played as well as I could. Louis was already coming up to top them all.[24]

Louis Armstrong was one of the many great musicians who worked in the Allen Brass Band; Sidney Bechet was another (both on clarinet and on trumpet). New Orleans brass bands had a different instrumentation to European brass bands, who literally only used brass instruments in their line-ups. The New Orleans ensembles featured clarinets (and later saxophones) and could thus be considered to be more like the European military bands, which always have a reed section.

The Allen Brass Band usually consisted of 11 pieces: three trumpets, two trombones, an alto horn, a baritone horn, a tuba, a clarinet, a bass drummer and a snare drummer (sometimes two clarinets were used). This line-up was reduced or augmented depending on the type of engagement. The band fulfilled bookings at celebration parades, funerals and 'bally hoos' (where they marched and played to advertise an event or a product); they also occasionally played for dances. Music was truly an everyday part of New Orleans life and Red explained that it was not unusual for the band to be booked 'if someone was building a new home', or at a dedication ceremony when the cornerstone was laid for a new official building or clubhouse.[25] The USA's entry into World War I in 1917 also brought a series of engagements for the Allen Brass Band and the Excelsior Band. Harrison Barnes, then a trombonist, recalled, 'The boys was going to camp. You used to have parades and carry 'em to the train in Gretna.'[26]

This era marked a decline in the use of horses to draw funeral carriages, but even when the vehicles became mechanized, the marching tradition and repertory remained unchanged, with melodies such as 'Sing On', 'Over in Gloryland', 'When the Saints Go Marching In' and 'Bye and Bye' invariably being played. Red Allen spoke of the New Orleans tradition of playing dirges on the slow march to the cemetery and joyful themes after the interment, stressing

These funerals went according to the Bible, sadness at birth, rejoicing at death. They went in for big parties when someone was dead, and everybody would have a band for a funeral. If you belonged to four or five societies or clubs, you had four or five bands. If you didn't belong to any, they would put a saucer on the deceased's chest and others would walk in to view the body and contribute five, ten, fifteen or twenty cents, or a quarter, whatever could be spared. Now, whatever was raised, you got a band to coincide with this amount, musicians getting three dollars for a parade and the leader four dollars.[27]

The Second Line walked on the sidewalk, which we called the banquette. The band walked in the middle of the street. A guy used to get a dollar for carrying the banner, and a quarter for holding the tassel, and there had to be a proud stepper.[28]

Despite receiving a large number of four-dollar fees during the course of a year, Red's father had no intention of quitting his day job, having been promoted to a foreman longshoreman, a position that provided a degree of security that music-making could never offer. In general, pay rates for musicians in New Orleans were on the low side compared to what was normal in other cities, probably because there were more good musicians than jobs, even in this hive of music. In 1915, drummer Paul Barbarin's day job as an elevator operator at the St Charles Hotel paid $12.50 a week.[29] During this same era, trombonist Kid Ory, leader of the most successful club bands in the city, paid his musicians $17.50 a week.[30] Yet musicians based on Mississippi steamers earned between $40 and $50 a week. Small wonder that so many New Orleans musicians made an exodus to places where they could greatly increase their incomes.

For Red Allen, his earnings as a teenager meant little to him. His trumpet teacher, Amos White, recollected that the young Red was so keen to play that he often marched with a band as an auxiliary 'twelfth man', 'not even caring about getting paid'.[31] He was pleased to earn what was then abundant pocket money, but his real delight was in being part of a band. Looking back, he said, 'I loved it. I didn't have the least idea I would still be in this profession, for my father and all the others had their jobs, longshoremen, plasterers, slaters, cigar makers, and painters. Most of the guys had other trades, the music was mostly for kicks.'[32]

Red was delighted to point out that a photograph of his father's band published in *The Pictorial History of Jazz* showed him as a small child, peering out at the camera alongside trombonist Jack Carey (Red's Uncle George was one of the drummers in the photograph). Red never tired of describing how much rivalry existed between the various New Orleans marching bands. He himself often took part in these battles for musical supremacy, and liked to recount how rival bands counter-marched in and out of each other's ranks, playing different tunes. The band that kept rhythm and melody intact throughout the manoeuvre was judged the winner. It is not unlikely that the complicated cross-rhythms that enriched Red's later work and his ability always to know exactly where he was, even while creating the most daring improvisations, had their origins in these musical combats. Red described any such clash as a 'buck'.

Henry Allen Sr found that running a busy band took a good deal of time and effort, and he was delighted when his son became old enough to assist him. From an early age Red learnt the ropes and helped his father with the administration of the band. He collected up and re-distributed the music parts and made sure that each musician knew when and where to assemble for the next engagement. When Red first played in the band they wore a military-type uniform, with peaked caps (the leader's headgear having ornamental leaves) but, not long after the end of World War I, the Allen Brass Band, like most of its rivals, adopted a standard parade outfit consisting of dark trousers, white shirts, ties and peaked caps with ornamental silks. Red explained, 'You'd wear colours for regular parades and black for funerals'. Sometimes the band was booked to play in church for religious festivals. This was not a new experience for Red: at an early age, accompanied by an aunt who played organ, he had occasionally performed hymns in church.

While he was still in his early teens, Red was often sent out on horseback by his father to book musicians in outlying districts for engagements. Usually his father was still at work in the docks when Red got in from school, so he would take the horse and ride it over to Louis Kohlman's poolroom for an afternoon game. One day his father asked Red to share the saddle with him for a lift to the ferry, but the horse had got so used to his afternoon journeys to the poolroom he stopped abruptly at Louis Kohlman's door. Red's father immediately surmised what had been going on, but as Red said, 'he smiled and I knew I was off the hook'. Red told Whitney Balliett, 'At one time I even had a couple of horses – a pacer which puts down two feet at a time, and a racer, which puts down one foot at a time'.[33]

Because Red was too young to drink alcohol he was usually given the task of acting as 'watchman' on the band's engagements. During a funeral ceremony, while the rest of the band dispersed into the nearest bar, it was Red's job to watch for the first signs of the mourners coming out of the church at the completion of the service. He would then race over to the tavern and call out the musicians to re-assemble. He described the scene:

> The snare drum player would be the first one I'd call, he'd then make a roll, until everyone comes out of the bar. When everybody's there, the bass drummer would hit three beats.[34] We'd march along – first the bass drummer, laying on that offbeat cymbal with a coathanger, then the snare drummer, rolling up a storm, and behind him the three trumpets, two taking the lead together and one slipping in that second part, and so on: trombone, peck horn (alto horn) and the rest. Sousa was never like that![35]

2

A TRIP TO THE NORTH

The young Red Allen gradually developed a reputation for musical versatility. He could read music proficiently and, unlike his father, he could improvise solos with nonchalant ease. He could also quickly work out the harmonies for a second trumpet part without having to resort to a printed orchestration. Red's father realized that his son, like most of the young musicians in New Orleans, was fascinated by the sounds and structure of the new music – jazz. When the Allen Brass Band was strutting back to base at the conclusion of a parade, Henry Sr was all too well aware that his son was itching to cut loose so he would shout 'Take it, Sonny!' Red needed no second invitation. His auxiliary skills as a drummer often came in useful for the Allen Brass Band, where he could temporarily forsake the trumpet in order to play the drums. Red was passable on the snare drum, but he was a magnificent performer on the big bass drum, so much so that some veterans mentioned him in the same breath as the legendary 'Black Benny' Williams, a prince among the New Orleans percussionists. Drummer Paul Barbarin went as far as to say that Red was better than Black Benny.[1]

Leaving school gave Red opportunities to be available for engagements with other bands further afield. His father raised no objections, providing that he (Henry Sr) knew the bandleader. Speaking of his father, Red said, 'He was a serious man, a strict man',[2] but he also pointed out, 'My father wanted me to be a musician and nothing else'.[3] So Red began playing in various line-ups in what he described as 'a three mile radius' of his home. He recalled one such early opportunity:

Henry 'Kid' Rena used to use two trumpets, that's where I got a start playing in the smaller groups. They didn't have parts written out, you had to play a second part by ear. You had to play the harmony, it was good ear training. Kid Rena didn't need me to play, but used to add me to the band sometimes because I knew what was popular on records, and they weren't interested in that. They played the way they played, but I listened to everyone. This man Rena was a great inventor. His records, made at the end, don't show what he could do at all.[4]

During the early 1920s Red Allen played in many New Orleans bands. Later, when he became a celebrated jazzman, several musicians claimed to have given him his first regular work away from his father's band. One of those who had a good case for the claim was clarinettist George Lewis, though even he realized that Red had played various gigs before Lewis booked him to play at a party (around 1923, apparently). According to Lewis, Red's father brought his son to Lewis's house astride a horse and turned him over to the bandleader's care with 'gentle, implicit instructions as to what his son was – and was not – to do'.[5]

Although Red was a mature musician in terms of performance skills, he was still a youngster, a fact that was underlined on his first gig with George Lewis:

The very first night I played with George someone fired off a pistol in the place we were working and the police raided it, as a result the whole band was taken down to the station. Fortunately they didn't keep us in prison long and released the whole band.[6]

I asked George Lewis about the incident and he gave further details:

Well, Red was still in knee pants then, and as they took us away we all laughed and shouted out jokes. It was kind of an adventure, but when they put us in a cell, Red stood there and started to cry his eyes out for his mummy and daddy. We heard him play so fine we forgot that he was still a kid.[7]

Lewis went on to discuss Red's musical prowess and reliability:

I was a little older than Red, and I had the job of getting the money from whoever had booked the band. You've heard those stories of the man collecting all the cash at the door in a cigar box then disappearing while the band were still playing... well, that often happened, so someone had to watch things carefully. If I got off the bandstand to check up on things I knew that Red would be conscientious and wouldn't let me down by neglecting his playing.[8]

Red's father and mother accepted their son's explanations of events that led to him being taken into the police cell, and thereafter he played a series of gigs with George Lewis's band in a line-up that consisted of Lewis on clarinet, Arthur Mitchell on string bass, Albert Martin on drums, Clarence 'Little Dad' Vincent on banjo and guitar, and Harrison Barnes on trombone (later replaced by Ernest Kelly). Pianist Walter Decou was occasionally added to the personnel, but generally a piano was not used. Red later offered a reason for this:

Few of the bands used a piano. The dance halls didn't have one, so you'd need to borrow a piano from someone's home in order to use it. Now it was easy to get 30 or 40 guys to help you take this piano out of people's home up to the hall, but it was getting it back. After the dance they had trouble getting anyone to haul it back.[9]

Red also gained early experience with another reed player, Paul 'Polo' Barnes, whose Black Diamonds (also known as The Original Black Diamond Jazz Band) was a forerunner of the Young Tuxedo Band. Barnes (born 1902) specialized on the alto saxophone, an instrument that was something of a novelty in New Orleans in the early 1920s. He said, 'I was playing the clarinet but I wasn't quite up to playing in a band. I was the first one that made the saxophone popular in New Orleans.' Looking back over his career he spoke candidly when interviewed by Val Wilmer in 1971:

Dixieland is the style of the white boys. Dixieland is 'The South'. But we weren't interested in the South, we were more interested in New Orleans. Dixieland was taken from traditional New Orleans jazz, but New Orleans jazz actually didn't have any name. We had ragtime music first and traditional came right after that.[10]

In Paul Barnes's Band, Red replaced the promising Sam 'Bush' Hall, who died young. Red worked alongside Josiah 'Cie' Frazier on drums, and two cousins of Barnes, Lawrence Marrero on banjo and Eddie Marrero on string bass. When a piano was used it was played either by Mercedes Fields or Jeanette Salvant. Various trombonists worked with the band including Arthur 'Yank' Johnson, George Washington and Bob Thomas. This was certainly one of the first bands that Red worked with regularly according to bassist Eddie Marrero who said, 'We got Red Allen started',[11] though trombonist Bill Mathews (who lived near the Allen family on Newton Street) maintained that he, Mathews, 'was the first one to give Red Allen a break'.[12] Later Red also worked with Paul Barnes, Lawrence Marrero and Cie Frazier in the Golden Rule Band, whose other members at that time were trombonist Raymond Brown and occasionally another of the Marrerro brothers, Simon on double bass.

Red played a huge variety of jobs in a number of bands during his late teens, including being a 'sub' (deputy) in Sam Morgan's Band and briefly playing second trumpet to the celebrated Chris Kelly; Red had good reason to remember his gigs with Kelly. In those days it was a general rule that anyone who hired a band in New Orleans provided them with food, usually a choice of gumbo or ham. Chris Kelly always let Red have his share of the food on offer, and the youngster took full advantage of this and had both gumbo and ham. Kelly was, according to Red, 'superstitious … I mean he always had the feeling that somebody would poison him or do him wrong, so he always brought his own meals.'[13]

Red was thrilled to work occasionally with various jazz pioneers, including trumpeter 'Manuel' Perez and trombonist Willie Cornish. He also deputized for trumpeter Peter Lacaze in bassist Eddie Jackson's Band at the Sans Souci Hall, and sometimes played with the resident band at the Elite Café. Besides all his dance-hall and cabaret engagements, Red also continued to play in parades, sometimes with the Excelsior Band (on trumpet or bass drum), with the Eureka Brass Band (on bass drum) and with the Imperial Serenaders (on trumpet). For a while he regularly played funerals as part of George McCallum's Band (McCallum had a contract to provide music for ceremonies covered by payouts from the Eagle Eye Benevolent Association). From the time Red was about 17 he rarely played in his father's band; his absence was with the approval of his father, who realized that his son's future was likely to be in ensembles that encouraged improvisation.

Although he was still in his teens, Red decided it was time he formed his own band. Because of his lack of experience he utilized the services of a senior musician, clarinettist John Casimir, as manager of the group. Casimir (born 1898), who had played in the Allen Brass Band, organized the administrative side of the enterprise from his home on Tulane Avenue, New Orleans. Contract forms to be used for the band's bookings were printed (or rather mis-printed) 'Kid Allen and Casimi's Jazz Band', and although Red as a minor could not sign them he gradually began acquiring experience that was to prove useful when he led bands in later years.

According to John Casimir, Red was still in short pants when the band began. As Red himself explained, 'You weren't allowed to wear long pants until you were 18. Leonard Bocage would bring me home at night, or my father would come and get me.'[14] Guitarist and banjoist Bocage (nine years older than Red) regularly rehearsed jazz numbers with Red. Bocage, a cousin of the eminent trumpeter Peter Bocage, was also from Algiers. He did not begin playing until he was over 20, but after buying a guitar for five dollars he made rapid progress and was soon sitting alongside Red learning by rote what they heard on King Oliver's recently released 1923 recordings. Interestingly though, the first tune they learnt together was Nick LaRocca's composition 'Sensation Rag'. According to Bocage they made a private recording of this number 'in a house', but unfortunately the disc became 'broken up'.[15]

The original Allen-Casimir line-up operated as a four-piece group, with the co-leaders being joined by string-bassist Albert Glenny, and Leonard Bocage on guitar and banjo. Glenny (born 1870) was by then in his early fifties (he had been part of Buddy Bolden's Band) and his place was soon taken by Sanofer Mitchell. The quartet soon became a sextet with the addition of Albert 'Loochie' Jackson (aka Leonard Albert) on trombone, and Johnny Thomas on drums. The sextet proved to be a success, first at local house parties, then at picnics and playing aboard trucks for advertising assignments. They then rapidly gained enthusiastic followings at various venues including the Cooperative Fraternal Hall, the Turtle Back Hall, the Sacred Heart Hall and the Ladies of Hope Hall. By this time Leonard Bocage had bought Red a pair of long pants, as he explained, 'Red got tired of people talking about him in short pants'.[16] The band began working further afield; as John Casimir recollected, 'We used to play all them jobs to Delacroix Island'.[17] In fact the Allen-Casimir Band could have played even more engagements but for the fact that Red was continually being asked to work in other bands (sometimes for more money than he earned with his own group). Casimir summed up the situation, 'He got better than us, they kept hiring him'.[18] Eventually the increasing demands for Red's services made the joint leadership impractical and Red left.

Red's reputation as a trumpeter was growing week by week, but he was also recognized as a fine all-round musician. As an aftermath to singer Ethel Waters's visit to New Orleans many local bands began playing her big new number, the 1922 success 'That Da Da Strain'. Unfortunately they played it with a wrong harmonic progression, but Red's ear enabled him to find the correct chord changes. Years later he smilingly told writer Martin Williams, 'overnight I became a celebrity'.[19]

By this time it was not unusual for Red to work with four different bands during the course of a week. His gigs varied from fish fries (usually held on Saturdays) to lawn parties (usually on a Sunday); he also played for funerals, dances and picnics. People were continually asking if he could bring his own band and he began leading pick-up groups, using a big pool of musicians, but this was not entirely satisfactory. After guitarist Clarence 'Little Dad' Vincent played in one of these ensembles he told Red that he had 'a rotten band'. Vincent was a senior musician (born 1892) so Red heeded his words and asked for his help in booking better players for future engagements. Vincent did this by contacting several ex-members of George Lewis's Band including Lewis himself. As a result, Lewis on clarinet, Albert 'Fats' Martin on drums, Julian Barnes on trombone and Alex Scott on double bass were drafted in to work with Red and Vincent on guitar and mandolin. Red did not forget Vincent's helpful advice and kept his place open in the band when the guitarist went to play in Mexico for three months. Vincent tried to persuade Red to work outside Louisiana, but he was unsuccessful, commenting 'They couldn't get Red Allen to leave his Daddy'.[20] However, Red was gradually becoming aware that big opportunities awaited New Orleans musicians who were prepared to travel. Vincent observed that Red Allen's style gradually changed during this period: 'Buddy Petit was the first to "run" diminished chords. After a while Red Allen, and some other fellows picked it up.'[21] By this time the young Henry Allen answered to a variety of names; fellow musicians called him 'Sonny', 'Son', 'Kid', 'Biffly Bam', 'Henry Junior', or, most often, 'Red'. He explained the derivation of this last sobriquet, 'I was light skinned and my face got red when I blew'.[22] Later his father adopted the same nickname and billed himself as Henry 'Red' Allen in advertisements for the Allen Brass Band.

Originally the young Red Allen's Band didn't have a regular piano player, but, on being offered a residency that demanded a pianist, they soon got one. Albert Fernandez Walters (later to be a trumpeter) got the job. 'Henry Allen Jr and Albert Martin came looking for a piano player. They came to my house on St Claire Street and hired me to play at the Radio Café, on the corner of Decatur and Toulouse.' By then Edward Johnson was playing alto saxophone with the group, George Lewis having left. Red's memories of working with George Lewis were mostly happy ones, but he surprised me one day by saying, 'When I played alongside George Lewis he sounded very much like Johnny Dodds, quite naturally he later developed his own personal style.'

Red began to feel restless with the local music scene, and his growing discontent was stimulated by news of former colleagues achieving success in Chicago or in New York. The achievements of a Crescent City musician in the North was a matter of civic pride among players who remained in New Orleans. The progress of King Oliver, Louis Armstrong, the Dodds Brothers, Sidney Bechet and scores of other ex-local musicians was followed with avid interest. Decades later Red Allen could reel off, in sequence, when and where New Orleans expatriate musicians had played during the 1920s, simply because the details had been talked about so often during his formative years. Red stressed how keenly he and other young musicians awaited new recordings made by New Orleans players who were in the North, particularly those by Louis Armstrong's Hot Five. Red learnt every nuance of these performances by playing the recordings over and over again. A friend of his had a record player with a speed regulator, and Red used this device to alter the tempo of the recordings; he then played along with it and thus learnt the piece in a different key. From then on there was no such thing as a 'difficult key' for Red, and years later he instantly mastered the notoriously awkward arrangements devised by bandleader Fletcher Henderson in obscure keys. Red never forgot his 'studies' of Armstrong's work: 'We got Louis from records like jazz musicians all over the country, except of course we knew where his music came from better than others.'[23] But Red's admiration of Louis's playing existed alongside his own highly individual concepts: 'I can't explain who was the cause of me playing the way I do. I was just playing like I felt, but I liked anything Louis did.'[24]

Playing aboard the Mississippi steamers was a regular source of income for many New Orleans musicians. Several of the big riverboats wintered in New Orleans and while there sailed on brief evening excursions on which various bands played for dancing. Observance of Lent invariably meant a quiet period for musicians in New Orleans, thus many musicians were attracted to riverboat work, which continued through the seasons. Before Red did any long journeys on the riverboats he played for a series of evening sailings out of New Orleans. He remembered these gigs in some detail:

> There was a dance floor and food and some of the people standing about listening. You played from about 8 p.m. until midnight. The boat pulls out at 9, goes up the river and comes back at around 11 to 11.30. There's fourteen dances and every fourth dance is a waltz. When you get to fourteen it's 12 o'clock and you're playing 'Home Sweet Home'.[25]

The most important steamship line, as far as the musicians were concerned, was owned by the Streckfus Steamer Company, whose headquarters were in St Louis, Missouri, but boats owned by rival companies also offered live music, and it was on one of these, the *Island Queen* owned by Captain Scholz, that Red first played the excursion sailings from New Orleans. After a series of these brief journeys the riverboat prepared for its spring cruise which involved sailing up to Cairo, Illinois, stopping at various ports on the way, playing for afternoon cruises and midnight excursions. Thus Red experienced his first view of life outside Louisiana.

On the *Island Queen* Red joined a band led by Sidney Desvigne, a native of New Orleans, who had previously played in many ensembles, including the Allen Brass Band. He was some 13 years older than Red, not quite senior enough to be a father figure, but someone in whom Red's parents could place their trust. Desvigne, light-skinned enough to pass for white, was neither a virtuoso on the trumpet nor an inspired jazzman, but he was a proficient musician and a capable leader. Among his band (usually billed as the Southern Syncopators) were several players who later made names for themselves, including string bassist George 'Pops' Foster, sousaphonist Al Morgan and pianist Walter 'Fats' Pichon. Pichon, who had blown alto horn in various parade bands alongside Red, also had the task of playing the calliope up on deck (a series of steam whistles tuned to different notes, covering just over two octaves, and operated by a piano-like keyboard). Louis Barbarin (Paul's brother) was on drums, Bill Mathews on trombone, and a three-piece saxophone section consisted of Adolphe Alexander Jr, Henry Julian and Eddie Cherie.

A Trip to the North

Red enjoyed his stint with Desvigne but was happy to get home to tell his parents about life afloat. His time at home was soon curtailed by a message from King Oliver, who (on the recommendation of drummer Paul Barbarin) invited Red to join his band in St Louis, Missouri. By this time King Oliver was one of the leading black bandleaders in America. In 1922 Louis Armstrong had left New Orleans to join King Oliver in Chicago, a move that virtually launched Armstrong's spectacular career. Now, five years later, in April 1927, Red Allen was about to replicate Armstrong's career-enhancing move, except that he was joining Oliver in St Louis for that leader's first real assault on the musical bastion of New York City.

Red left New Orleans and journeyed to St Louis with two musicians he knew well, saxophonist Paul Barnes and guitarist Willie Foster (older brother of bassist Pops Foster). At a late stage in departure plans Red almost changed his mind: 'I was leery of leaving New Orleans. I'd heard of too many New Orleans musicians getting stranded in the North.'[26] Bassist Simon Marrero was supposed to be the fourth member of the travelling party, but he declined King Oliver's offer, making Red waver. However his confidence soon returned, and, knowing Oliver from the days when the veteran trumpeter had worked in the Allen Brass Band, he set out in good spirits to play his initial gigs with the band at the Capitol Palace in St Louis.

With the new men installed in the band, King Oliver's troupe made its way to New York by train to begin a two-week engagement at the recently opened Savoy Ballroom on Lenox Avenue. They began their residency on 10 May 1927, and were warmly received by the crowd, despite playing opposite a spirited orchestra led by drummer Chick Webb; the *New York Amsterdam News* review said, 'You simply must hear this band of bands'. King Oliver's Band achieved its success in spite of being exhausted by a train journey that Barney Bigard remembered as being on 'the cheapest and slowest train to the Big City'.[27] En route the trunk carrying the band uniforms went astray so the musicians had to make their Savoy début in what Bigard described as their 'dusty travelling clothes'. Even so the band settled down and played a stomping opening set that delighted the dancers.

New Orleans bands had been playing engagements in New York for over a decade, but by 1927 the importation of musicians from Louisiana to New York had slowed down considerably. King Oliver's band redressed the balance. Of its twelve members, eight were from New Orleans and its environs: King Oliver, Red Allen (trumpets), Kid

Ory (trombone), Omer Simeon, Barney Bigard, Paul Barnes (reeds), Willie Foster (banjo/guitar) and Paul Barbarin (drums). Pianist Luis Russell was an honorary New Orleanian, having lived there for some years. Red felt as though he was on familiar musical ground, and his confidence was given a boost by the number of features that the bandleader gave him: 'King Oliver's teeth had gone bad by then and he wasn't playing much so I'd take most of the solos at the Savoy'.[28] But despite being surrounded by friends from his native city, Red soon began feeling very homesick:

> I was an only child and I'd had a lot of care. I wasn't accustomed to taking things to the laundry and making my own bed. I couldn't get used to it. I lived in a boarding house with Omer Simeon, Barney Bigard and Paul Barbarin; New Orleans friends and all in Oliver's Band. Then I moved in with Oliver and his sister (Mrs Victoria Johnson). Oliver and I stayed together like father and son. I used to kid with him all the time and imitate the grand marshal in one of the parades back home and he'd laugh so hard he'd cry.[29]

Great musician though he was, King Oliver was not in the front rank of strategists when it came to dealing with band business. His band's stay at the Savoy Ballroom was a success, so much so that the management there wanted to extend the booking, but Oliver asked for a large increase in salary, which the owners would not agree to, and negotiations broke down completely. Through the late 1920s and 1930s the Savoy Ballroom maintained a strict policy of paying only the minimum union rate to musicians, they realized that the accolade of playing the prestigious venue gained bands publicity, radio exposure, big audiences and increased record sales. King Oliver might have enjoyed all of these in New York had he been more reasonable in his demands. As it was, the Oliver band found themselves with an empty date book, though there were prospects of their becoming the resident band at New York's Cotton Club, one of the top night spots in Manhattan. Again Oliver misjudged his quotation and asked for too much money, with the result that the young Duke Ellington gained the booking and took a huge step up the ladder of success.

The Oliver band scuffled around the New York area playing a series of unglamorous engagements. The experienced trombonist, Kid Ory, saw all the signs of a sinking band and told drummer Paul Barbarin,

A Trip to the North

'I'm going some place, can't stay around here, because there is nothing doing'.[30] The band picked up some bookings in Newark, Philadelphia and Washington, DC, by which time Jimmy Archey had taken Ory's place. Other dates materialized, but not enough to encourage optimism and Omer Simeon and Barney Bigard left. By pooling their money the remainder of the band narrowly avoided being stranded and made their way back to New York.

Other than some bookings in Baltimore the engagement list was bare. During this depressing period King Oliver, to keep up Red Allen's spirits, recommended that Clarence Williams use the young trumpeter on a recording date, thus in June 1927, Red made his début on wax. Pianist and vocalist Clarence Williams (from Louisiana) was well known to all the musicians in New Orleans. Red had childhood memories of Williams going from door to door selling sheet music: 'He was good at it, he'd even get people who didn't have a piano to buy the music'.[31] Later, when Williams became a successful composer, he began earning substantial royalties and decided to leave New Orleans to open a publishing house in Chicago (in partnership with the New Orleans bandleader Armand Piron). From Chicago he moved to New York, where he became a pioneering black music entrepreneur, running his own publishing company, composing and leading his own pick-up bands on record and on radio.

Red recalled his first recording:

Making my first recording was a big day for me and I was quite keyed up. When we were rehearsing I heard Clarence's wife, singer Eva Taylor, who was visiting the studio, ask her husband for a nickel to buy a doughnut and some coffee. He looked at her as though she had asked for a mink coat and spluttered, 'What do you want more coffee for? You had three cups at breakfast, do you think I'm made of money?' I knew that Clarence was a tight man with the buck, but it still made me smile. Of course, I didn't let Clarence see I was amused.[32]

Red didn't feel it was an appropriate time for him to ask for any sort of drink. Coffee was well down on his list of priorities during his stay in New York,

I couldn't get used to the food and I hated the coffee. It may seem a small gripe, but, as I didn't touch anything alcoholic, I usually loved my coffee back home, but the New York stuff gave me headaches, stomach aches, the lot.[33]

Red got on with the business in hand and made a satisfactory start to his recording career, blowing confidently on two versions (one vocal, one instrumental) of 'Slow River' and 'Zulu Wail'. Evelyn Preer's low-register singing on 'Slow River' sounds pleasant, but her high notes tend to quiver. Red plays a leading part in the proceedings, blowing plaintively on the opening chorus prior to fashioning an effective two-bar break. He mis-pitches a note on the vocal version of 'Slow River' but carries on undeterred and is bold enough to fill his next two-bar break with an elaborate trill. He sounds equally confident on 'Zulu Wail', growling his way through the opening phrases, then storming in after Charie Irvis's lachrymose trombone solo. Interestingly, one can hear traces of King Oliver's influence in the manner that Red plays during the final ride-out chorus, a trait that does not figure in Red's later work. Despite Red's commendable contributions to the session, the overall sound of the band is unattractive and disorganized to the point of cacophony. Soon after playing for these recordings Red set out for Louisiana, tired of living a hand-to-mouth existence: 'I'd saved my fare money – kept it in my shoe, so I didn't have to send to my father for money. I was only gone two months and I was happy to get back.'[34]

Apparently The Missourians, one of the leading bands of the period, were interested in having Red join them. He realized this but was so eager to get back to New Orleans that he did not follow up the possibility.

Red arrived back in New Orleans to discover that his old friend pianist Walter 'Fats' Pichon (with whom he had worked on the *Island Queen*) was about to take his own band into the Pelican Club on Gravier and South Rampart (the Pelican operated on two levels: a sidewalk café and a dance hall on the floor above). Pichon offered Red and his recent colleague in the Oliver Band, drummer Paul Barbarin, jobs in the band. They accepted and worked alongside James Cobert (alto saxophone), Raymond Brown (trombone), George Augustin (banjo) and veteran Henry Kimball on string bass. Barbarin left after four months and his place was taken by Alfred Williams; by then Bat Brown had been added on second trumpet and Sidney Carriere had joined on alto saxophone.

Pichon's Band played a four-nights-a-week residency at the Pelican, working opposite a band led by trumpeter Oscar 'Papa' Celestin, a former member of the Allen Brass Band. Like Henry Allen Sr, Celestin was happier when playing written orchestrations. One of his sidemen, saxophonist Joseph T. Rouzan, summed up the situation by saying 'Celestin was not really a jazz musician in my estimation. He was the type of guy who played a muted trumpet with pretty good rhythm.'[35] In order to compensate for his own lack of improvisational skills, Celestin hired one of the city's most promising young jazz trumpeters, Edgar 'Guy' Kelly (born in Scotlandville, Louisiana, in 1906). Red and Guy Kelly (both the same age) had taken part in various musical combats since their teen years, and had also played alongside each other in the Allen Brass Band; on these occasions, Harold Dejan recalled, 'they would really "tonk"'.[36] Their 'carving sessions', where each musician tried to top the other's solo efforts, became the talk of the town. The observant Joseph T. Rouzan spoke of Kelly, 'I believe he was capable of playing a style of his own, but he was taken over by Louis Armstrong's style and at that particular time Red Allen was too, but Allen, who didn't have quite the chops that Kelly had, had the nerve'.[37] Because they were working in different bands their musical 'battles' took place in jam sessions, mostly at a downtown gambling house known as 'The Alley'. On one such joust they chose to work out on Louis Armstrong's composition 'Cornet Chop Suey', each of them testing the other by creating spectacular variations. Apparently Red won the day because Kelly forgot part of the set coda. This particular duel was discussed and written up for many years. As early as 1936, when there was little interest in the history of jazz, *Down Beat* magazine spoke of this encounter as being one of the most celebrated cutting contests in the annals of New Orleans musical history.

There was no lasting ill-feeling between Allen and Kelly; it was simply that one New Orleans trumpeter seeing another with an instrument in his hand felt it a matter of honour to blow him into the next parish. One of Red's earlier musical skirmishes was with the powerful trumpeter Kid Thomas. This was an organized contest, with the prize for the victor being a leather satchel music case. Ill-feeling did surface on this occasion, and passions ran so high the police had to be called to restore order. Red never forgot that day:

> It was kind of hard for Kid Thomas to win a contest with me in Algiers, because all my playmates that grew up with me were there. Well I won it but one of the policemen came and took the prize from me and gave it back to Thomas. We couldn't do

anything about it because we had no business in the place, on account of our age.[38]

Guitarist Leonard Bocage, recalling the events, said that Red's group on this occasion chose to 'mostly play by music, including a waltz'; he added that all the older musicians present thought that Red Allen won the day.[39]

Years later Red could look back and smile at this one-off fracas, realizing that his encounters with Guy Kelly were much more significant, both for his development and for Kelly's:

> He and I became the drawing cards, with a lot of people coming to hear us blowing against each other, though Guy and I became very good friends anyway. The funny thing was that my friends and Guy's friends felt that there ought to be more saltiness between us just because we were playing against each other, but after a while Guy and I got fed up with this and we decided to go to Chicago together. Guy did go but I had another offer and made up my mind to stick around the home area a little longer.[40]

Red's decision to bide his time in New Orleans was not totally connected with musical endeavours – he had fallen in love. Pearly May Wilson, a secretary with a New Orleans insurance company by day, worked in the evenings as a ticket-seller at the Pelican Dance Club. A former student of New Orleans University, she was from a highly respected Creole family, which included her cousin, trumpeter Alvin Alcorn. As the only female on the staff of the Pelican Dance Club, she was used to being flirted with, but something about Red Allen's gentlemanly behaviour and his unfailing courtesy greatly impressed her. Years later she told Richard Sudhalter of her early impressions: 'A very nice person, very quiet. Very soft. Not at all like you'd expect some musicians to be, especially in those days.'[41] The friendship eventually blossomed into marriage.

With matrimony in sight Red determined to build some financial capital and began working almost every night of the week. On his nights off from the Pelican, he joined a band led by John Handy at the Entertainers' Club on Franklin Street. Clarinettist John Handy had moved into New Orleans from Pass Christian, Mississippi. He played with local bands, and worked in Texas and in Baton Rouge, Louisiana, before taking up the alto saxophone. He recalled, 'I bought a Conn alto and got myself going. A few weeks later I was using it at the Entertainers' Club'.[42] Red never spoke with much enthusiasm about working with Handy, perhaps because Handy seemed determined to take the lead on saxophone during the ensembles. Handy admitted to this strategy: 'When I got the sax I played like I was phrasing on trumpet'.[43] From 1930 John Handy adopted the rank of Captain for his billing, and when I asked Red about this he almost growled, 'He was no captain when I worked with him'.

3

RIVERBOAT DAYS

Pianist Fate Marable is justifiably given credit for his pioneering role as a bandleader on various Mississippi steamers. Marable was not from New Orleans; he was born in Paducah, Kentucky, in 1890, and by the time he was 17 he was playing on the steamboat *J.S.* in a duo with a violinist. The ensemble was soon enlarged and was, for a while, called Fate Marable's Kentucky Jazz Band; later it became Fate Marable's Cotton Pickers. All the various steamers that Marable worked on were owned by the Streckfus Steamboat Line (based in St Louis) which was founded by Captain John Streckfus in 1884 (his initials graced the Line's first steamboat). When Streckfus introduced his four sons into the business, Joseph, the eldest (who became known to everyone as Captain Joe), seems to have been the one who actively encouraged the employment of bands (black and white) on the various steamers. Captain Joe, an amateur pianist, loved music and played as big a part in selecting the musical repertory performed on the boats as any of the bandleaders, though his brother Verne (who played the violin) also took an interest. Captain Joe was a strict disciplinarian, but he always showed his appreciation of fine musicianship. Louis Armstrong, who worked on the Streckfus Line as a youngster, recalled:

> I had heard so much about how mean Captain Joe was that I could hardly blow my horn the first time I played on the steamer *Sidney*, but he soon put me at ease. But he insisted that everyone attend strictly to business. He loved our music, as he stood behind us at the bandstand he would smile and chuckle while he watched us swing, and he would order special tunes for us.[1]

Fate Marable was a competent pianist and an extremely capable musical director, so much so that when a musician joined his band it was said he was 'going to the conservatory'. An eyewitness described Marable in his prime:

> Fate had a magnetic personality. He was a handsome man who sat at the piano with great dignity. He moved the band with his eyes, every section, every soloist, every accent rarely escaped his gaze. He was respected by all his men for his leadership and his really great musicianship.[2]

Marable not only gave Louis Armstrong his first big opportunity, but was also an early employer of brilliant musicians including Baby Dodds, George 'Pops' Foster and Zutty Singleton. His knack of finding promising talent for his band continued through subsequent decades and he gave chances to many brilliant youngsters including saxophonist Earl Bostic, trumpeter Clark Terry and bassist Jimmy Blanton.

Usually two of the Streckfus Line's steamers, the *Saint Paul* (a side-wheeler) and *The Capitol* (a stern-wheeler, with six decks), spent their winters based in New Orleans, where from October to April they either sailed on short excursions or held open days and evening dances while anchored in port. Thus Fate Marable spent several months each year in New Orleans where he was able to contemplate a treasure trove of fine young musicians playing locally. Captain Joe often asked Marable to check out various promising players – he also occasionally vetoed Marable's own selections, in his position as chief director of the company (his father died in 1925). There was no argument between Captain Joe and Marable over the advisability of securing the services of Henry Allen Jr. Marable called into the Pelican to hear, in person, the trumpeter who many were citing as a possible contender for Louis Armstrong's crown. Marable, whose light complexion, reddish hair and mass of freckles were his trademark, was instantly recognized by the musicians on the bandstand at the Pelican. The set soon ended but Marable had already heard enough to offer Red a job there and then.

Red was able to ease himself into the new job by playing casual gigs with Marable ashore in New Orleans, and at dances that were held while the boat remained in the docks. Not everyone fancied a life afloat, and drummer Cie Frazier would only play aboard a riverboat if he was certain that it wasn't going to sail. When April came, the *SS Capitol* prepared to leave New Orleans to sail up the Mississippi, it spent part of the summer based in St Louis, Missouri, but also sailed on the upper Mississippi from St Louis to St Paul. En route from New Orleans it stopped at various riverside towns and cities (Donaldsonville, Baton Rouge, Natchez, Memphis etc.) where the musicians played on local excursions. For the musicians, pay was in the region of $45 a week, with a $5 a week bonus that was paid at the end of the season if the musician's behaviour had been satisfactory.

Once again Red found himself working with several New Orleanians, including trumpeter Albert Snaer, bassists Al Morgan and Jimmie Johnson and (briefly) Willie Humphrey on tenor saxophone and clarinet. Fortunately the cook was also from New Orleans, so Red didn't encounter any of the problems he had experienced with the food in New York. The boat's passengers, who could either listen or dance on the maple-wood floor of the ballroom, were all white, but on Mondays (in some locales) so-called 'coloured excursions' catered for black customers. The musicians lived aboard the boat when it was in transit, sharing cabins that housed two or four berths. The lucky ones were berthed on the 'Texas deck', which was situated high in the boat and was generally cooler. The steamer's arrival was well advertised at the various ports of call during its month-long journey to St Louis. At around 9 a.m. the customers for a daytime excursion assembled on the quayside; the band usually began playing at 9.45 a.m. and performed for an hour while the excursion passengers came aboard and settled down. The musicians took a short interval just before 11 a.m., then returned to play a three-hour performance, breaking the full band down into small units so that all the musicians had time for lunch. Then the entire band played again from 3 p.m. until 4.45 p.m., concluding their performance as the boat docked back at the original sailing point.

For evening sailings, or moonlight excursions as they were called, the band played from 7.15 p.m. until 7.45 p.m. for the embarking customers, who paid 50 cents to board. From just before 8 p.m. until 11.45 p.m. the band played for dancing, stopping in time to allow the passengers to disembark at midnight. The band often played for afternoon and evening sailings on the same day, and Red was the first to admit that working on the riverboats increased his range and his already considerable stamina. He never attempted stratospheric high notes but his surety in the upper register was exceptional, even though he used a slightly unorthodox embouchure, holding his trumpet at an angle that meant only the tip of his mouthpiece touched his upper lip. Like many another brass player, Red achieved wonderful results without observing a trumpet manual's advice about correct mouthpiece placement. He was not exactly touchy about this subject, but nor was he slow to air his feelings:

> Those books, they say to play the trumpet one must place the horn right in the centre of one's mouth with so much upper lip showing here and so much bottom lip there. Well that's what I've read and while I have nothing against what it says I know a trumpet player by the name of Oscar Celestin and a trombone player, Russell 'Big Chief' Moore, who can only play their instruments from the side of their mouth – and they do pretty well at that![3]

When the *SS Capitol* was berthed in New Orleans, Red gave twice-weekly lessons to an aspiring trumpeter, Bob Watts. Although the going rate for such lessons was 30 cents a time, Red never charged Watts. According to Watts, Red preferred showing him how to play by ear rather than from music, and part of the lessons consisted of the two trumpeters playing along with recordings by Louis Armstrong.[4]

The *SS Capitol* usually remained based in St Louis from 15 June to 15 September each year. Recalling those days Red said, 'We stayed in St Louis for about three months, and though we played on the boat we lived in the city. You had to go out and find a room – which was called "every tub on its bottom" or being on your own.'[5] On the rare occasions that the Marable band had a night off in St Louis they found a lot of good music being played by local jazzmen. Red gave details:

> I would get around and hear different people, and I remember listening to Johnny 'Buggs' Hamilton, who later became well known when he played with Fats Waller. At the time there seemed to be so many great players around St Louis. Others I remember are Nat Story – a really fine trombonist – drummer Floyd Campbell, and pianist Burroughs Lovingood. When Dewey Jackson, a great blues player, ran over his horn to warm it up, the people would start screaming. Then Charlie Creath would hit just one note and draw attention – his tone was so big and wide that he would pull everything together, I thought that both were great trumpeters.[6]

Lovingood, Story and Campbell worked alongside Red in Marable's Band. Others on the *Capitol* during various stages of Red's stay included Norman Mason, Willie Ford, Horace Millinder, William Rollins (saxophones), Jacob Frazier, (trombone), Armand 'Red' Brown, Emmanuel Sayles (banjo), Earl Martin, Theodore 'Bucket' Crosby, Eugene Hall (drums) and Carl Woods (violin and vocals); Burroughs Lovingood played piano while Fate Marable conducted the band. It is odd that Red's name was not included in the Fate Marable Band personnel published in the *Chicago Defender* of 9 June 1928, where Albert Snaer's partner in the trumpet section was given as Louis Aceheart. For whatever reason Red was temporarily absent from the band. The only clue came from banjoist Emmanuel Sayles who told me in 1977 that 'Red had a girl on his mind' at this time, so it seems quite possible that he had a rendezvous with Pearly May in New Orleans before beginning the three-month summer season in St Louis.

Captain Joe Streckfus took a keen, if, at times, dictatorial interest in the music that was played by Fate Marable's Band, even sending away for orchestrations of tunes he felt the public wanted to hear. He also designated the tempo, insisting that the St Louis dancers liked their music faster than the New Orleans patrons. Looking back to the 1920s, he said (in 1958), 'St Louis tempo was 20 beats per minute faster than New Orleans'.[7] Discipline for the musicians was strict, both on and off the bandstand, and though the Streckfus Brothers were generally respected their word was law. Marable simple acquiesced to the regime. While he could rehearse a band expertly, he was not particularly interested in fostering improvisation and once an arrangement had been mastered he was happy to repeat it without variation for the rest of the season. Throughout his long career Marable only ever recorded two titles (in 1924 as Fate Marable's Society Syncopators), and the overall results illustrate that Marable led a dance band and not a jazz group. From time to time the arrival of a brilliant musician, such as Louis Armstrong, gave the band new impetus, but by the time Red Allen joined, Marable was more interested in gambling and sipping bourbon than in making musical history.

One of the *Capitol*'s regular ports of call was Memphis, Tennessee, where their arrival was usually noted in the local press. Nathaniel Story had the foresight to keep a scrapbook of such cuttings, including an item from Frank Mitchell's *Musicians' Chatterbox* in the *Saint Louis Argus* which mentioned, 'Henry Allen, featured cornetist, melophone and entertainer', another report said 'Henry Allen, who is serving his second year, has shown considerable improvement and has a series of features that makes all "reel and rock". Aside from playing cornet Allen is the writer of a novelty foxtrot hit "This Way Out" – the band features this number.'[8] Red's memories of his days on the riverboats were more realistic than romantic:

> A lot of people think, when you mention riverboats, that you had to check your pistols when you came on, and that the boats were full of women good-timing, but I didn't find it like this. I do know that everyone had a good time, but it wasn't as wild as some writers say, and I can't remember ever seeing any gambling on board. This was Prohibition, so there were soda fountains for the people. Just in case things got out of hand there was usually a bouncer close by. I had happy times with the guys in that band because I was learning by experience and getting to the stage where I was able to sight-read any new arrangements that Fate put up. My lip got stronger by playing long hours day-after-day, but as time went on I knew that I was never going to better myself further no matter how long I stayed. The Streckfus Brothers were good people and had raised my money a couple of times. I wasn't unhappy but I was at an age when I felt restless.[9]

During one of the Marable Band's two-day stopoffs in Memphis, Red was heard by Loren L. Watson, who ran Watson and Co in Memphis, acting as a record distributor, freelance talent scout and occasional a-and-r man on local recordings, initially for Paramount, later for Victor. His main area of operation was in recordings made by local blues artistes, but mindful of the big sales that Louis Armstrong was enjoying on the rival Okeh label, he offered Red the chance to make some recordings under his own name in New York City. This was an exciting prospect, but the memories of Red's previous uncomfortable stay in the Big Apple were still fresh, so he told Watson that he would think it over. Coincidentally a letter came from Red's pal, Paul Barbarin, who was drumming with a band that pianist Luis Russell had formed in New York.

> Paul told me in his letter that I only needed to make the journey and a job in Luis Russell's Band was mine. This was quickly followed by an offer to join Duke Ellington's Band, where another friend of mine, Barney Bigard, was playing. This made my mind up about leaving, so I went to Fate Marable and explained my position, he in turn said he would have to discuss it with the Streckfus Brothers. While all this was going on, word came from

New Orleans that my grandfather had died and my family thought it right that I should return home for the funeral. So naturally I did, but when I got back to the boat, the steamship company thought I was deliberately breaking the agreement which I'd entered into when I started working for them. First Captain Streckfus took a stand and ordered me to stay, then he offered me more money to remain, but I said I was leaving to go to New York, so I lost a fifty dollar bond which I had deposited when I joined.

Fate Marable, who remained friendly throughout all this, was determined to get some mileage out of my leaving, so he took it upon himself to announce to the band that I was going. He said 'I have some important news. Young Allen here has worked hard at his music and has greatly improved since joining the band. I feel that he's about ready now, so I've decided to send him to New York to make some recordings. Now, if you work as hard as Allen has, then I'll try to do the same for you.'[10]

Recounting the incident, Red said 'I had to keep a straight face, but I didn't contradict Fate, because he was such a pleasant man'.[11] Red's talents left a lasting impression on Marable, and years later, when the bandleader was asked to select an all-star trumpet section from ex-sidemen, he chose Red Allen, Louis Armstrong and Irving 'Mouse' Randolph.[12]

Red now had to decide whether to join Luis Russell or Duke Ellington. He chose the former because several of his New Orleans buddies were in the band: Paul Barbarin, Pops Foster, Albert Nicholas and Russell himself. In contrast the only New Orleans musician in Duke Ellington's band whom Red knew was Barney Bigard (the band's bassist Wellman Braud had left Louisiana when Red was a young boy).

Although Luis Russell's Band never gained an enormous or durable following with the general public, in 1929 it was the sensation of New York among those musicians who placed excitement, bold improvisations, feeling and spirited rhythm above precision, smooth sounds and careful phrasing; ballroom dancers liked the band's swinging beat. Bassist Pops Foster summed it up when he said, 'Russell's Band was romping so good in '29, we had everything sewed up. We were playing the same style we played back in early New Orleans.'[13] Luis Russell, a small man, a little over five feet tall, was not an outstanding jazz pianist, but (like Fate Marable) he was a fine organizer and popular with everyone who ever worked for him. Unlike Marable he was very interested in jazz and encouraged his men to improvise whenever there was an opportunity. Russell, born in 1902 on a small reef island off Bocas del Toro Panama, was lucky enough to win $3000 in a lottery, enabling him to move, with his mother and sister, to New Orleans in 1919. During the early 1920s he played with various bands in New Orleans, then moved to Chicago in 1924 where he worked for King Oliver, later making the ill-fated 1927 trip to New York with him. When Oliver disbanded, Russell remained in New York and later that year joined a band led by drummer George Howe, which was resident at the Nest Club on West 133rd Street. Howe was a competent percussionist but he tended to sleep on the job – literally – causing a sudden and disastrous lurch in the music-making. The drummer was fired and Luis Russell was appointed bandleader in October 1927; he was far too easy-going to be truly successful, but nevertheless he always remained popular with his sidemen, and his tolerant attitude allowed his musicians to play an unconstrained style of music. Russell continued to lead his band (gradually augmenting it) at the Nest Club before moving on to richer pastures at ballrooms and bigger New York nightclubs. He preferred ballroom work himself: 'You played better because you could feel the dancers appreciated your music'.[14] One of the band's residencies was at the Roseland Ballroom, 1658 Broadway (at West 51st Street); it was there that Red Allen joined the band.

> That first week in New York was scary. Teddy Hill, who played tenor sax for Luis Russell, met me at the train and took me straight to the Roseland Ballroom where the band was playing. I was to learn it was the kind of band that hung out like a family. It had brotherly love going. It was also the most swinging band in New York. It put audiences in an uproar. Russell did most of the arrangements and whenever you took a solo there was a lot of fire up and down the band.[15]

Alto saxophonist Charlie Holmes commented, 'I don't think anybody in the band at the time was married, we were all young and wild, except Russell – he was married and separated'.[16] Unusually, the New Orleans members of the band did not form themselves into an exclusive clique. Holmes, who was from Boston, Massachusetts, felt totally at ease with his Louisiana colleagues. He told writer Stanley Dance about his stay with Luis Russell, citing the experience as 'the happiest days of my life'.

It was a different type of music to me altogether. They'd been playing that stuff for years, and it was born in them. We had a whole lot of head arrangements, but a good bit of the music was written out too. We'd get together, play it like it was written and then somebody would set a riff, change it halfway through the chorus, and before you knew it we had another tune.[17]

This flexible approach to creating jazz suited Red Allen perfectly, and he was instantly at ease, socially and musically. He soon found out that the Russell Band's rehearsals were almost as enjoyable as the gigs, with everyone blowing their utmost even when no audience was present. Pops Foster said, 'Some of the guys in New York used to call us "the rehearsal band" because we rehearsed a lot'.[18]

One of the first tasks that Red Allen wanted to fulfil, after he'd settled into the Russell Band, was to locate the bandleader, pianist and composer, Ferdinand 'Jelly Roll' Morton, and to pass on, as requested, good wishes from Fate Marable. During the late 1920s the daylight gathering place for black musicians who worked in New York City was on the corner of 132nd Street at 7th Avenue (close to the Rhythm Club and the Lafayette Theater). This was where Red found Morton, who was, as usual, putting the world right in a very loud voice. The irrepressible braggart was offering unsought advice to a small group of listeners, some of whom were there simply to tease him, and to induce him to exceed his previous boast. Red approached the flamboyant genius and introduced himself. 'Well, this is a real pleasure meeting you Allen. I knew your father,' said Morton. Then, turning his head, he shouted in the direction of some local New York musicians who were standing nearby, 'These guys can't play my stuff. Good news indeed to know that another fine musician from New Orleans has entered this city of musical incompetents.'[19] Red passed on Marable's greeting. Fate also told Red that Jelly Roll Morton had briefly played in Marable's Band, and to make conversation Red mentioned this. Morton's reaction was quite dramatic: 'He gave me a big, disbelieving stare and said nonchalantly, "Oh, that Fate Marable! He had this big old band that wasn't doing anything, so at one time I let him use my name to help out."'[20]

Absurd though he sometimes appeared, Morton, genius and hustler, always had his ear to the ground when it came to developments within the recording industry. On reflection Red felt sure that Morton had somehow found out about the offer he had received from the Victor Talking Machine Company, but he made no reference to it during their conversation. However, after saying farewell, Morton waited for Red to walk fifteen or so paces, then shouted out, so that everyone could hear, 'By the way, Allen, I'm going to see to it that you make some recordings for Victor with your own band.'[21]

This initial meeting sowed the seeds for the warm friendship that Red Allen and Jelly Roll Morton shared throughout the 1930s. Red never ceased praising Morton. When he got to know Morton he laughed at his extravagances, and was not averse to joining in when the teasing started, but he loved Jelly's sense of humour and beamed when he said, 'I had a real good time with him.'[22] Morton, for his part, always had great admiration for Red's playing and picked him as a member of his all-time trumpet section (alongside Muggsy Spanier and Russell Smith) in the February 1939 issue of *Down Beat* magazine. An interviewer once suggested to Red that Jelly Roll Morton's music didn't swing, and Red instantly remonstrated, 'All I know is that they're still using his numbers to swing by'.[23]

Red's musical apprenticeship in the competitive atmosphere of New Orleans served him in good stead in New York, which had become the gathering place for jazz musicians from all over the USA. Red said he suddenly felt his stomach churning with nervousness when he took part in his first New York after-hours jam session.

> I'd heard a lot about 'cutting' contests and I didn't know if I'd make out or not. I couldn't look to alcohol or tobacco for support. My father had never allowed me to drink or smoke and I'd obeyed him. I hadn't been in New York but a day or two when Alphonse Steele, who was a drummer, began taking me to the sessions at the Rhythm Club on 132nd Street. He was the Paul Revere, sending around the news of sessions and announcing a new man in town. They would have trumpet nights and trombone nights and saxophone nights at the Rhythm Club. The first session I went to, every trumpeter was there: Cootie Williams, Rex Stewart, Ward Pinkett, Freddie Jenkins, Sidney De Paris. Whoever was on piano decided on the key and set the tempo, and then everyone soloed. If you wanted extra choruses you stomped your foot.[24]

Red blew triumphantly at these after-hours basement combats and his confidence grew with each encounter. As a result he was feeling in good shape when the important day arrived for him to make his début as a recording bandleader in July 1929. The eight musicians he used in his group were all from Luis Russell's Band, including the formidable trombonist from Georgia, J.C. Higginbotham (who was the same age as Red). Jay Clarence Higginbotham, generally known as 'Higgy' (though Red usually referred to him as Jack), was as much the star of Russell's Band as Red Allen. Subsequently these two fine players worked together for many years in various line-ups. They had dissimilar temperaments, but their partnership initially ran smoothly on and off the bandstand. Where the two musicians differed so much was in the consumption of alcohol. Higgy always felt that he was a couple of drinks behind the rest of the world – he needed them under his belt to overcome a certain shyness – but once he was in orbit he needed constant refuelling and soon a devil-may-care attitude took over which sometimes got him into trouble. In contrast, Red never touched a drop of anything containing alcohol until long after his days with the Luis Russell Band were over. Red's wife, Pearly May, said, 'Higgy, well there was a nice guy. But you know, he was just a little bit wild. He drank, and well, he lived a different kind of life. Red never was one for that wild life. But he sure respected Higgy, I'll tell you that.'[25] Red and Higgy certainly played superbly well together, their brazen tones blended perfectly and their exciting ideas inspired each of them to top what he had just heard. Higgy, like Red, could be formidable in a 'cutting' contest, as rival trombonists found out. One of them, Floyd 'Stumpy' Brady, while playing in Cincinnati with Zach Whyte's Band, posted a challenge to Higgy, who remembered the details years later. 'He wrote me a letter. He said, "I'm going to come to New York and teach you how to play."'[26] But when the two trombonists met in musical combat at the Rhythm Club it was Floyd Brady who was taught a lesson and the expectant crowd that had gathered soon drifted away from what was a one-sided contest.

Red Allen could never establish who was actually responsible for getting him the contract to record for Victor. There was no doubt that Loren L. Watson had forwarded a recommendation, but Red felt that the original suggestion (which may have sparked Watson's interest) had come from King Oliver. It seems that Red's old friend, Walter 'Fats' Pichon, had also passed on an endorsement to Art Satherley, an Englishman then working for Victor. Red never had the chance to ask Loren L. Watson about the circumstances; they never met after their initial contact in Memphis, and Watson ceased to act for Victor after September 1929. Whatever the background, the first recordings by Henry Allen and his New York Orchestra were highly successful, so much so that each of the four tunes waxed was a triumph, full of panache, jazz feeling and a rhythmic drive that propelled the young soloists. This inspired band recorded a total of three versions of 'It Should Be You', 'Feeling Drowsy' and 'Swing Out', plus two of 'Biffly Blues', ensuring that the record company had a wealth of different 'takes' to choose. Each varying attempt is superb and reveals how much the musicians were improvising; Allen composed all four of the pieces (assisted by Higginbotham on 'Swing Out'). The faster tunes are full of swing and vitality and the slow pieces abound with genuine pathos and sombre magnificence.

On 'It should be you', Red uses the same opening break on each of the three 'takes', but this concession to repetition is a rarity on this session. The solo work, by Red, Higgy, Charlie Holmes and Albert Nicholas, is thrillingly different on each new attempt, with Red piling on the excitement throughout each successive effort. During the latter stages of the arrangement he retains an effective, elaborately syncopated figure for each version, but overall a marvellous, impromptu spirit is successfully conveyed to the listener – even the arrangement of 'It Should Be You' was changed after one take had been recorded.

'Biffly Blues', commemorating Red's early nickname, is a slow, stately composition, which allows Red to display his amazing assurance. There is nothing hurried about his timing as he blows a series of poignant phrases that utilize the fine sound of his full-toned low notes. The mood is aptly set by an introduction that features Paul Barbarin's vibraphone playing and the sound of Will Johnson's guitar, preparing the scene for the band to display a unity of expressiveness that is extraordinary. Pops Foster's bowed basswork sounds rich and sonorous, and although Will Johnson obviously felt safer in repeating the main outlines of his previously worked-out solo for each version (inspired, it sounds, by Eddie Lang's playing), what he plays does not imperil the elegiac mood of his colleagues.

The group's next effort, 'Feeling Drowsy', remains one of the greatest of all jazz recordings. All three of the band's versions are worthy of being marvelled at. Here Red pre-plans part of his solo, using the same framework (with slight variations) for each epic attempt; the culmination brings forth (on the third venture) one of the most eminent jazz solos on record. Again the vibraphone sets the mood. As the chiming effects fade away they are replaced by the sound of a clarinet trio; if there is a tiny flaw in this jewel it is in the performance of this section of the piece, which is purposeful rather than immaculate. However it is the jazz playing that makes 'Feeling Drowsy' so extraordinary, not the rendition of arranged passages. Though the contours of Red's efforts are similar on the three versions, something magical happens as he begins to play on the third take. One can sense bassist Pops Foster thinking to himself, 'This is the one', as he begins to pluck his strings a little more emphatically. Red, sounding as relaxed as he could be, glides up to a key phrase in his solo at the exact split second that Foster chooses to apply more power to his lines. The result is a sublime instant, an example of breathtaking musical accord. Trumpeter Humphrey Lyttelton described 'Feeling Drowsy' as 'Allen's masterpiece' and went on to say that Red's solo was 'a fine example of an "impressionist" approach, one which anticipates, by 30 years or so, the avant garde musicians who "painted pictures" in sound'.[27]

Following their colossal achievement in creating 'Feeling Drowsy', the band seem to treat the task of recording 'Swing Out' as something of a celebration. Certainly the brisk banjo and string bass introduction heralds a joyous performance. Even Teddy Hill's workmanlike tenor sax solo does not shatter the mood, which is fully revitalized by Higginbotham's bold trombone playing and topped up by the joyful solos of Holmes and Nicholas. Red Allen seems to be having slight lip problems during his upper register forays on the first two takes, but again the third attempt produces high phrases that catapult out of the bell of his trumpet. It is an indication of the band's determination, stamina and skill that their third endeavours on 'It Should Be You', 'Feeling Drowsy' and 'Swing Out' produced a superior version in each case.

Red explained to Swiss writer, Johnny Simmen, the reason for the high number of takes at this session, highlighting the difference between his approach to recording for the Victor company as opposed to that of his leader, Luis Russell, when the band recorded for Victor's arch rivals Okeh.

I wasn't thinking too much of what the others did. I was thinking of my own playing, and that's why there are several takes of quite a few of these numbers. These records were not only made under my name, but I also became leader for those dates. I was responsible for everything. My leader was the pianist, and I, his trumpet player, was the leader, if only for a few hours in a recording studio. Luis Russell was not such a stickler for perfection as I was. That's why I think that from a musical point of view the Victors are better than the Okehs. Luis was a quiet type of leader and only rarely did he insist on repeat takes.[28]

4

A MUSICAL FURNACE

Louis Metcalf, the previously featured trumpeter with Luis Russell's Band, departed in something of a huff when he heard that Red Allen was joining the band (Metcalf was replaced by trumpeter Bill Coleman). Coleman, an old friend of J.C. Higginbotham, was working in Pough-keepsie, New York, when he received a letter from Higgy informing him that there would soon be a vacancy in the Russell Band. Coleman joined in time to be part of recordings made by Luis Russell's Orchestra for Okeh in September 1929. Three impressive sides were made at this session: 'The New Call of the Freaks', on which Red Allen played superbly and also sang in a trio with Higginbotham and Louis Metcalf (specially imported for this vocal), 'Feelin' the Spirit', which had 16 fiery bars from Red and a brief solo from Bill Coleman (his first on record), and finally the ultra-lively 'Jersey Lightning' with another bold chorus from Red and fine contributions from Higginbotham, Nicholas and Holmes.

A week later the band was again in the recording studio, this time in a new guise. During the 1920s it was common practice for bands to record under pseudonyms (usually for contractual reasons); thus Luis Russell's Band were billed on two titles as Lou and his Ginger Snaps. On this occasion there was no danger of the band blowing the roof off the recording studio because their performances were commercially corseted for release on Banner, a bargain-price record label that was sold mostly in chain-stores. The arrangement of 'Broadway Rhythm' is both bitty and sedate; the main soloist, Charlie Holmes, acquits himself well, and young Bill Coleman in his eight-bar outing shows the beginnings of his future style, but the undistinguished material limits the overall per-formance. 'The Way He Loves Is Just Too Bad' is also harnessed rigidly to an indifferent arrangement, but nevertheless Red, Higgy and Holmes do their best to inject some excitement into the piece via their spirited solos (the two available versions reveal many variations). The recording microphone was often unkind towards Albert Nicholas's clarinet tone, as it is here, on both titles, making it sound more shrill and piercing than it ever was on live performances.

Bill Coleman did not expect to be heavily featured in Luis Russell's Band, but he soon became disheartened by the subsidiary role he was allocated. He explained his disappointment: 'Red played first trumpet on everything and took all the solos. Eventually I got a solo on a head arrangement of "Sweet Sue", but I never played a first part or had any other solo.'[1] After about six weeks with the Luis Russell Band, Coleman, a fine improviser in his own right, became increasingly disgruntled with the allocation of solos. He also disliked the management's rule that prevented the Russell musicians from mixing with the customers at the Roseland Ballroom. 'There was no such thing as socializing with the dancers or having a special booth inside the dance hall where we could play cards or drink as the white orchestra could do.'[2] All that was offered to the Russell Band (and other black units that played at the Roseland) was a basement locker room which adjoined the boiler house, so usually they spent their intervals sitting on the back staircase near the electricians' quarters, where they could talk or play cards out of sight of the public. The indignity of not having a dressing-room and a reserved table was made worse by the fact that the white band they were working opposite (Milt Shaw's Detroiters) were accorded these facilities. So Bill Coleman left Russell and rejoined his former leader Cecil Scott at the Savoy Ballroom (known to musicians as 'The Track') where, as Bill observed, 'I could socialize with the people'.[3]

Bill always admired Red Allen's playing, but I never got the impression that they were ever close friends. Bill summarized the situation: 'He never went out with the other musicians, not that I know of. He never went out with me at any time.'[4] Bill always remembered that Red had once reprimanded him for eating peanuts in public. There was a conservative side to Red's nature, and he actively discouraged any behaviour that he felt might be interpreted as not maintaining the dignity of the black race. In 1930, shortly after moving from New Orleans to New York, singer Blue Lu Barker (née Louise Dupont), the young wife of guitarist Danny Barker, was startled when Red advised her that it was undignified for her to hang her flannelette garments out to dry now that she had settled in New York.

A Musical Furnace

Red was certainly not a killjoy or a 'goody two shoes'. He enjoyed the band's jokes and contributed some of his own. In general his affable nature was well liked by his colleagues, but one can just sense a frisson of disapproval caused by his unwillingness to go out on the town with them after they had finished work. One member of Russell's Band interpreted Red's natural reserve as 'arrogance'.[5] His temperate drinking habits also made him something of an outsider: 'I used to hold the bottle in Luis Russell's Band, because I was the only one who didn't drink'.[6]

Red was certainly finding life hectic in New York. Besides his nightly employment with Luis Russell he was also on call for freelance recordings, one of which was with his old New Orleans buddy, the pianist and singer Walter 'Fats' Pichon, who had settled in New York. These two friends plus guitarist Teddy Bunn cut two attractive sides, 'Doggin' the Thing' and 'Yo-Yo'. Pichon's lighthearted singing is heavily featured but both Allen and Bunn make the most of their solos. This was one of the first occasions that the line-up of trumpet, piano and guitar had been recorded; even so the participants sound fully at ease in their pioneering roles, and the richness of Red Allen's tone is admirably captured. Red's next visit to a recording studio was with his own band, and the Luis Russell musicians he had used on his début date, but this time they were augmented by singer Victoria Spivey and a vocal group, the Four Wanderers. The singing group are featured effectively on 'Make a Country Bird Fly Wild', but the stand-out feature of this track is Red's trumpet work; he creates exploratory lines that coalesce brilliantly. The band accompany Victoria Spivey on two titles, 'Funny Feather's Blues' and 'How Do They Do It That Way?'. Despite being billed as a 'blues singer', Spivey often sang in a lilting, slightly vaudevillian manner, as she does here. Higginbotham's low-register, rugged trombone playing just has the edge over Red's fine efforts, which contain oblique references to Louis Armstrong's playing. Although Red had, by this stage, developed an individual style, again and again during these early years he reverts to phrases that stem from his mentor. On 'Funny Feather's Blues' the ploy is understandable – only two months earlier Louis had waxed the same number with the same singer. The session concluded with an instrumental 'Pleasin' Paul' (written by Allen and Barbarin). It is not an elaborate theme, more a launching pad for a series of solos. Higginbotham is sturdy, emphatic and wondrous, with Holmes providing a delicate but effective contrast. Luis Russell acquits himself satisfactorily during a 16-bar outing, but Red overshadows all, blowing perfectly placed phrases that meld an already formidable rhythm section into a glorious unity. His intrepid break on the first take is a sublime combination of skill and chance, but even his talents cannot reproduce the magic moment again on take two.

Two sides in a lively, racially-mixed, pick-up band organized by Fats Waller and featuring Red and Jack Teagarden provided Red with the chance to work with banjoist-guitarist Eddie Condon. Red recalled the session:

> The first time I met Eddie Condon was on a date with the Fats Waller Band on a number called 'Lookin' Good but Feelin' Bad'. Bessie Smith came to the rehearsal and Jack Teagarden happened to be playing trombone and the vibraphone, and in the rhythm section was Eddie Condon, Gene Krupa (on drums), Pops Foster (on bass) and quite naturally, Fats Waller.[7]

Apparently Fats Waller, as was his wont, had left the task of arranging the two numbers that were to be recorded (both his own compositions) until the last moment. All the same, the results are impressive, despite the hand-on-heart singing by the Four Wanderers, whose glee club efforts unfortunately form part of 'Lookin' Good but Feelin' Bad' and 'I Need Someone Like You'. Red is in torrid form on the first title, but the ensuing heat is maintained by trombonist Jack Teagarden's fiercely played eight bars; Krupa sounds enthusiastically industrious on drums. 'I Need Someone Like You', complete with an effective change of tempo, also shows the singeing side of Red's playing, but again he is matched by Teagarden's blowing. This date ended a month (September 1929) during which Red had played on five different recording sessions. Things were no less busy during the following two-month period. Another session with Victoria Spivey produced four sides, including the haunting 'Dirty T.B. Blues', which shows Spivey at her very best. Red emphasized the melancholic content of the song in his stately solo. Red also accompanied the eccentric musician (and contortionist) Wilton Crawley on two sides, and, as part of a quartet (Allen, Charlie Holmes, Luis Russell and Will Johnson), backed Victoria Spivey's sister, Addie 'Sweet Pea' Spivey, on four sides. Addie had little of her sister's élan or sense of melodic variation, but the timbre of her voice seems more apt for the blues. Allen and Holmes take turns to play fill-ins behind the singer, the only soloist being Will Johnson on 'Longin' for Home'.

Another session in late 1929 was with Jelly Roll Morton, when Morton used Red (and various other members of Luis Russell's Band) on four tunes recorded that November. As might be expected, the Allen/Higginbotham/Nicholas front-line sounds well integrated. Red's solo (except for an interlude on 'Mississippi Mildred') is restricted to leading the ensemble, which he does in a bold freewheeling fashion, punctuating his emphatic phrases with fierce lip trills. Higginbotham makes a full-blooded contribution to 'Sweet Peter', which also contains an attractive low-register clarinet solo from Nicholas. Morton utilizes an old New Orleans device in having the trombone and clarinet duet briefly on 'Jersey Joe', and the leader also allocates guitarist Will Johnson a 16-bar solo on this number. Second takes were made of each of these three bouncy tunes, but in each case it was the band's first efforts that were originally released. The fourth piece, 'Mint Julep' (also in a medium tempo), was captured in one take and shows Albert Nicholas in parti-cularly fine form. Morton solos in his inimitable way on each track, creating a fascinating mix of daintiness and strength. Drummer Paul Barbarin is mainly on brushes, and Pops Foster, whose bass playing dominates the first tune recorded, seems to have been moved further away from the microphone for the remainder of the session. If there is a weakness running through the four sides it is the lack of strong melodies from the composer. Red did not fail to observe that all four tunes were written by Morton, and commented,

> If Jelly recorded a hundred numbers, then at least 99 of them would be Jelly's. He was a real good musician. His piano playing was all right too. He played the right chords in all his numbers and that is the most I look for in any piano player. He put them in the right order and never waited for me, which was a good thing as I don't think I ever play right on the beat.[8]

Most of Red's freelance recordings in late 1929 produced admirable music, but their content was eclipsed by the New York sessions that Luis Russell's Orchestra shared with Louis Armstrong in December that year. Following his triumphs in Chicago with King Oliver's Creole Jazz Band, Louis had first played in New York in 1924, as a member of Fletcher Henderson's Orchestra. He returned to Chicago a year later and consoli-dated his previous achievements there by playing in clubs, theatres and on recordings. His next move was an attempt (one that proved success-ful) to take New York by storm as a soloist.

Louis had known Luis Russell in New Orleans and in Chicago, and had no hesitation in asking the pianist if he would be willing to provide an accompanying band for him when he reached New York. Russell immediately agreed and began writing arrangements that would feature Armstrong, including one on the trumpet player's celebrated composition 'Cornet Chop Suey' (unfortunately this version was never recorded). All this happened just before Red Allen joined Russell, but the success of Louis's initial collaborations with Russell's Band led to a further link-up which included live appearances and recordings (made in December 1929 and early 1930). Armstrong made no attempt to hog the recordings, and gave lots of solos to Higginbotham, and brief feature spots for Holmes, Nicholas and Russell. Louis also made sure that Red Allen wasn't kept in any sort of musical shackles. This produces some accomplished blowing by Red, who creates a series of phrases that are clearly inspired by Louis's genius. The move towards individualism is temporarily abandoned as the younger man eagerly shows the source of his inspiration just how diligently he had studied his playing. On this, their first recording session together, Red played so much like Louis that positive identification of each of the trumpet players' contributions threw record reviewers into confusion.

The two trumpeters were destined to spend a good deal of time working together on the same bandstand during the 1930s, and if anything this close contact increased Red's enormous appreciation of Louis's playing. In general conversation one could sense Red's deep admiration of Armstrong's talents, but it was also possible to observe that Red became irritable when a questioner only wanted to talk about Louis. Louis for his part was devoid of envy and apprehension and having received nothing but encouragement from his mentor, King Oliver, adopted a similar attitude when Red worked alongside him.

The 1990 discovery by Michael Brooks of alternate takes of 'I Ain't Got Nobody', 'Dallas Blues' and 'St Louis Blues' reveal how loosely arranged and informal the December 1929 sessions were. It was not uncommon during the 1920s and 1930s to follow up the recording of a vocal version of a tune with an instrumental take, for issue in territories where English was not the principal language. As a result of this practice we can hear markedly different versions of the three tunes recorded. On the first, 'I Ain't Got Nobody', Red and Louis share a brief passage, and no quarter is given or asked. On 'Dallas Blues', Red can be heard blowing lustily in the spirited ensembles and on 'St Louis Blues' he plays the melody in a way that suggested to some people that Armstrong's magic extended to his being able to sing and play the trumpet at the same time. The sessions ended with the original recording of a song that was subsequently much performed by Louis Armstrong, 'Rockin' Chair' (this version has the composer, Hoagy Carmichael, sharing the vocal duet with Louis). This sedate piece was not an appropriate vehicle for any shared fireworks between the trumpeters so the series ended on a mellow note. Red always smiled when he was asked about these particular recordings and I was present on one occasion when the sides were played to him for his comments. A look of what can only be described as glee entered his eyes as he said, 'My, my, those two trumpets do sound alike, don't they?'[9] But beyond that comment nothing further was added, and Red ending the discussion by shaking his finger in an unfathomable gesture.

A few days after the session with Louis Armstrong, the Luis Russell Band recorded 'Doctor Blues'. Red's playing here is noticeably less shaped by Armstrong's style, epitomizing, as it does, the exciting unpredictability with which he introduces startling notes and daring rhythms into his improvisations. The uncomplicated tune serves as the vehicle for an eventful drive through a standard chord sequence. Once the theme is out of the way the band get down to business. Higginbotham leads the way with a solo that bristles with ideas and exciting lip trills, then Holmes creates one of his finest solos before Red Allen stomps out a succession of thrillingly conceived phrases, reiterating, to great effect, a series of high 'stab' notes.

Armstrong and Russell's Band were soon back in the recording studio for further sessions together, but on these occasions the recording manager insisted on a more genteel outcome. As a result, 'Song of the Islands', 'Bessie Couldn't Help It' and 'Blue Turning Gray Over You' (two slow ballads and a medium tempo hit of the day) were recorded. None of them offered scope for trumpet battles, but Red had no complaints, he knew that the selections were made by the a-and-r man and not Louis. Red proudly remembered every detail of the recordings he shared with Armstrong, even when his role was only a subsidiary one. Discussing 'Song of the Islands', he made discographers aware that Louis's valet (known only by his nickname 'Tout Suite') played drums on this number while Paul Barbarin moved over to the vibraphone. Red also recalled that the three unknown violinists on this title were white musicians imported from a local theatre orchestra.

Louis Armstrong was in the studio to hear the Russell Band record 'Saratoga Shout', which immediately preceded the waxing of 'Song of the Islands'. Louis was visibly impressed by Red's startling 32-bar chorus on 'Saratoga Shout' and offered genuine congratulations, much to the young man's delight. One suspects that Louis, even then, knew that Red would never overtake him, but nevertheless Red, on top form, was a formidable rival. Interviewed by Robert Levin in 1957, Lillian Hardin Armstrong, Louis's ex-wife, remembered an occasion when Armstrong came home and discovered her playing a Red Allen record. 'He just stood there for a minute with an angry expression on his face, then, after a bit, he smiled and said "Yeah, he's blowing"'.[10] The collaboration between Armstrong and Russell's Band thrived both on record and live appearances. In January 1930 Louis guested with Russell's Band for a one-night stand in Baltimore and drew 1400 people to a midnight dance held at the New Albert Auditorium.[11]

'Saratoga Shout' was written to commemorate the Luis Russell Band's new residency at the Saratoga Club, a largish cabaret club, situated at 575 Lenox Avenue, between West 139th and 140th, New York (just across the street from the Savoy Ballroom). New publicity photographs were taken; captioned 'Luis Russell and his Saratoga Club Orchestra', they showed a ten-piece line-up consisting of Russell, Pops Foster, Paul Barbarin, Will Johnson, Charlie Holmes, Albert Nicholas, Teddy Hill, J.C. Higginbotham, new trumpeter Otis Johnson, and (tallest of all) Henry 'Red' Allen. Albert Nicholas recalled the band's long stay at this night spot:

> The Saratoga Club was our stomping ground for quite a while, it had mixed [black and white] audiences. Everybody came up to the club to hear us: Eddie Condon, Jack Teagarden, Gene Krupa and Jimmy Dorsey. We had three books of numbers – over 150 arrangements. I'll tell you the secret of that band – Luis Russell never wrote too much. He'd write enough to keep the backgrounds together, riffs and so on, and chords for the band. But you played what you felt. And every man in that band could blow, everyone was a soloist. Intermission at the club, and some of the band would go off, but not all. Russell stayed at the piano and the New Orleans guys would stay: Red Allen, Paul Barbarin, Pops Foster and me. We'd continue to play for 20 minutes, playing tunes like 'High Society', 'Clarinet Marmalade' and 'Bucket's Got a Hole in It'. Then we'd go off and Luis Russell would have Higgy double on drums, and with Charlie Holmes and those guys he'd play some pop tunes. Sometimes Benny Goodman or the Dorseys would sit in, and Gene Krupa. Paul Barbarin was a very good drummer, he knew everybody's style, played wonderful fill-ins.[12]

Luis Russell echoed Nicholas's words, saying 'Paul Barbarin was the greatest drummer around'.[13] Barbarin's colleague in the rhythm section, bassist Pops Foster, created a sensation with his playing when he arrived in New York. The work of various New Orleans bassists, including Wellman Braud, Al Morgan and the white player Steve Brown, had a dramatic effect in energizing the playing of their East Coast counterparts. It would not be an overstatement to say that the style of playing employed by the Louisiana string bassists virtually revolutionized the instrument's role in jazz. Early in 1929, not long before Red Allen joined the band, Russell, prompted by the New Orleans contingent in his outfit, sent for Foster to join the ensemble, displacing Bill 'Mule' Moore on tuba. Nicholas gave the background details: 'The tuba was going out and Russell wanted that string bass. Foster made the string bass popular.'[14] Foster arrived in New York and somehow skirted the Musicians' Union restrictions (imposed by Local 802) and began working immediately: 'I arrived on a Tuesday [probably 12 February 1929] and went to work on Friday. You were supposed to wait six months but they had to let me work because they didn't have no bass players who played my style in New York.'[15] On another occasion Foster said that he began working with Russell on the night he arrived in New York.[16]

Because of his ultra-tolerant attitude, Luis Russell was very popular with his sidemen. Charlie Holmes observed, 'Luis Russell was the nicest guy in the world, the kindest and very easy-going'.[17] But sometimes Russell's carefree attitude cost the band dearly. They lost a regular broadcasting contract when Russell missed a radio show because he and Louis Metcalf were (according to Russell) 'out romancing a couple of girls during our air-time'.[18] Holmes spoke of the band's early days at the Nest Club: 'Gangsters would come in at 3 o'clock in the morning and they'd hang there until 10 or 11 o'clock in the day… sitting there and requesting numbers and passing out the money', but, as he explained, the Saratoga Club was quite different from the Nest:

The gangsters didn't run that place. This was run by a numbers banker. The gangsters kidnapped him. They held him for a $50,000 ransom, and they got it too. Most of the time there wouldn't be anybody in the place and we'd be sitting around and talking, and he'd come in, he loved the band. This place was just a front for him. He'd get us all on the dance floor, pull our chairs out and sit around and he'd tell different stories and things. People would come into the club, and then the head waiter would say

'Mr Holstein, the customers would like to have some music' and he'd look and say, 'Well if the customers would like to have some music send 'em across the street to the Cotton Club'. He didn't care, and the customers would get up and leave. Then there were times when the place was absolutely jammed with people. That's when the band really used to romp.[19]

Trumpeter Bill Dillard filled in a little more detail about this extraordinary employer: 'The Saratoga was run by a black man, Casper Holstein. He was like a politician in Harlem in those days.'[20] When the Luis Russell sidemen looked back on this period their enthusiasm went beyond nostalgia. J.C. Higginbotham stressed, 'It was the swingingest band I ever played with'.[21] Red Allen said, 'I enjoyed playing in Russell's Band more than in any other I ever performed in. It was a real happy band. We didn't have any manager as other bands did. We just played and got the jobs as Luis Russell found them.'[22] Luis Russell himself liked every aspect of New York except for the weather. Having been born in a hot climate he found that even New Orleans was often too chilly for him. New York temperatures certainly did not suit him and except in heat waves, he usually wore an overcoat all year round.[23]

Every night various white musicians dropped into the Saratoga to listen to Luis Russell's Band and to marvel at the soloists and the powerful way the ensemble brought every number to a stirring climax. Many of the arrangements had 'open' final choruses to encourage the front-line players to improvise an exciting ending, each of their phrases being propulsed by the powerful rhythm section. The team spirit within the band was formidable and this encouraged Red Allen to experiment and to take daring chances during his solos. He had always been musically adventurous but now he began producing amazingly original legato phrases that were improvised in a way that crossed and re-crossed the bar-lines, without losing the original pulse. Most jazz soloists of that period (even those who created ingenious melodic patterns) delivered their improvisations within segments that were two or four bars long. Red's method was more abstract; he blew clusters of notes that seemed to hover over the metre, but these daring flights were often resolved with emphatic, contrasting on-the-beat figures, whose inclusion showed the listener that Red knew exactly where he was. It was as if he flew without a compass yet never got lost. His extraordinary sense of rhythm allowed him to take chances that could prove disastrous for lesser musicians, and he explored paths that other jazz soloists were to make into major routes years later.

Red was creating a revolutionary way of phrasing, but he was not a dedicated iconoclast. He was playing how he felt, creating bold new phrases that were couched in futuristic rhythmic patterns and packed with strange-sounding, unexpected notes that Red himself could far easier play than explain. Whitney Balliett pointed out that Red's style was noted for 'its agility and a startling tendency to use unprecedentedly long legato passages and strange notes and chords that jazz musicians hadn't, for the most part, had the technique or courage to use before'.[24] Trumpeter Humphrey Lyttelton wrote that Red was among those jazz musicians who had 'exploited "wrong" playing to convey their individual message'.[25] Red was not a naive man but he believed in simple explanations:

> The great thing we talked about in New Orleans was to be yourself musically. You didn't have to see which guy it was playing the trumpet solo, you knew who it was before the band came around the corner. So, naturally, I tried to make my playing different from the others, but there was no great plan, I just used to think ahead, so that my mind was always a few bars ahead of what I was playing.[26]

Red expressed similar thoughts to Val Wilmer when he said, 'I used to drift off a bit, but I didn't have any conscious thoughts in mind about modernizing anything.'[27] He made comparable comments to John Simmen: 'I'm doing the unexpected because that's what is in me, and I have to bring it out, not because I want to impress people. It's an extremely spontaneous thing.'[28]

Red's star was in the ascendancy by 1930, at a time when the reputation of another great New Orleans trumpeter, Joe 'King' Oliver, was definitely in decline. The musician who had given early opportunities to both Louis Armstrong and Red Allen was finding life difficult. His playing of the trumpet was hampered by gum and teeth problems, and every promising booking ended in disappointment. Albert Nicholas summed up Oliver's technical problems when he said, 'His lip petered out'.[29] However, Oliver still had a recording contract, and he returned to New York to make a series of discs using a pick-up band which was strengthened by having two top trumpeters, Red Allen and Bubber Miley, in the brass section. Oliver assembled a 12-piece band and chose to record two standard themes, 'St James Infirmary' and 'When You're Smiling'; both were adequately performed but neither displays the unique qualities that had distinguished so many of Oliver's early recordings. Red is given a brief solo, as is Miley, but Oliver himself keeps intentionally in the background.

By this time Red, through various sessions, was a regular visitor to the Victor studios. Good though his memory was, one date that he participated in remained a shadowy recollection. Such a lapse was very unusual. Discographers would fire complicated questions to him about his recordings and he instantly gave an answer that was full of detail, usually following up with his jocular aside, 'My, my, what a fertile brain'. But one session from this period of his life remains a mystery. The details that Red remembered were that after finishing a session at Victor in New York, he was asked to stay behind and play trumpet fill-ins on a gospel recording. He thought that the gospel group was headed either by the Reverend J.M. Gates or the Reverend McGee, and he seemed to recall that one of the titles was 'Dead Cat on the Line'. However, there is no trace of Red's presence on the Reverend Gates's version of that song, and the trumpeter on the Reverend McGee's recording of that piece sounds nothing like Red. Perhaps nerves played a part in depriving Red of his usual instrumental panache. He said he did his best to comply with the Reverend's instructions but did not feel at ease with the assignment. His discomfort was made more acute by the fact that one of the gospel singers brought her young baby into the studio and improvised a cot by pushing four wooden chairs together. Red had visions of the infant rolling out of this makeshift cradle on to the hard floor and as a result was unable to devote his thoughts to providing music appropriate for the occasion.

On another visit to the Victor studios his keen ear enabled him to link up with a fellow New Orleanian, white musician Monk Hazel, who was recording on mellophone with Jack Pettis. Hazel, who retained the vernacular of the 'Old South', recalled the occasion:

> So while we were making this date, who comes in the studio but Red Allen and a couple of other jigs. They were making a record with Ethel Waters [sic]. They came into the studio early and Red says, 'As soon as I heard the beat I knew it had to be somebody from down home'.[30]

A Musical Furnace

Another session with Fats Waller produced four good sides, including 'Lookin' for Another Sweetie', which has a melody identical to the big hit 'I'm Confessin'. Years later Red occasionally played this tune, always commenting on the marked similarity between the two themes, but he was never able to explain how a tune that he thought was written by the Washboard Rhythm Makers' pianist, Chick Smith, came to be published a year later as a composition by Ellis Reynolds and 'Doc' Daugherty. Freelance recordings came thick and fast at this period of Red's career including a further date with Wilton Crawley, which was tinted by acrimony. Due to a mix-up, two groups arrived to play on the same session. Crawley brought his own accompanists, unaware that the Victor officials had booked Jelly Roll Morton to organize a pick-up group to back him. Crawley's musicians were sent home, and eventually the session got underway. Red recalled the date:

> Crawley was more of an actor. He played all the top theatres, used to do a tramp act and as an encore he used the clarinet. Somehow or other he got a contract to record for Victor, and they used Jelly to get a group. I must have been a little favorite of Jelly's, so he used me. Crawley told Jelly he didn't like a certain riff Jelly was using. Jelly said 'Well man, you should like it because this riff is going to sell the record. Anyway you use my blues.' So Crawley says, 'Man, you'll never see Jelly Roll Morton strung across this record label. Blues don't belong to nobody. I'll call this the "Crawley Blues".'[31]

Despite the friction, some worthwhile music materialized, including the superb 'I'm Her Papa, She's My Mama', but Crawley's own clarinet playing remains very much an acquired taste.

King Oliver continued with his series of recordings for Victor, but there was no sign that his once formidable technique was returning. Accordingly he used Red Allen again (on his April 1930 session) alongside trumpeter Dave Nelson (related to Oliver by marriage), who was part-composer of three tunes recorded on the date: 'Edna', 'Boogie Woogie' and 'Mule Face Blues'. Record collectors used to assume that King Oliver had allocated most of the trumpet solos on the session to Nelson, but Oliver did not let nepotism sway his judgement. Red Allen explained, 'I don't want to sound like a "me". Dave Nelson was, of course, on the records, but I was the one who took all the solos.'[32]

Ride, Red, Ride

Up to this point, none of Red's contributions to the Oliver recordings could be compared to his best work. However, on a September 1930 date with Oliver he created one of his most impressive solos. On 'Stingaree Blues' Red is featured on the final two choruses and makes the most of the opportunity by producing a monumental solo. After a series of pleasant but undramatic 12-bar blues solos from Charles Frazier on tenor saxophone, Glyn Paque on alto sax and Jimmy Archey on trombone, King Oliver plays an unpretentious muted solo simplified, one suspects, because of his ailing physical condition, then Red Allen takes centre stage with a series of epic phrases. The intensity of the solo is breathtaking. After conceiving a magnificent opening chorus, Red increases the drama by moving to a higher register, blowing a series of climactic phrases that round off one of the finest jazz solos of the entire era. The eminent composer and musicologist, Gunther Schuller, in *The Swing Era*, urged his readers to 'hear Allen's wonderfully reasoned blues discourse… parsed into two quite distinctive and contrasting statements, the one solidly traditional, the other bursting with new-found invention'.[33] 'Shake It and Break It', the coupling for 'Stingaree', is lively, with a half-dozen brisk solos (including one from Red Allen) and a virile-sounding ensemble, but compared to 'Stingaree Blues' it is ordinary. Throughout his career Red Allen remained a formidable blues player. Decades later, in one of his last interviews, he told Whitney Balliett, 'The feeling of the beautiful things that happen to you is in the blues'.[34]

During the period of all these freelance dates Red was also fulfilling his own recording contract and being featured on sides made with Luis Russell's Band. In addition he played in J.C. Higginbotham's recording group, which produced two glorious sides for the Okeh company in 1930. On 'Give Me Your Telephone Number' the rhythmic thwacking of Pops Foster's rugged bass playing seems to be defying anyone in the group not to swing. Foster, like all of the great New Orleans bassists, was never content to chug along. Sometimes he played two beats in the bar, sometimes four, choosing opportune moments to unleash a series of counter-rhythms and syncopated thrusts. Holmes again provides elegant tracery in his alto sax solo, but Higginbotham, in keeping with the rough-hewn arrangement, blows with a combination of determination and artistry. Red Allen keeps up the impetus allowing Higgy to storm into the fiery cadenza that ends the record. The stirring sound of Pops Foster's bowed bass lays the carpet for 'Higginbotham Blues', which consists of an informal series of 12-bar blues choruses. Allen's contribution is a fine microcosm of his revolutionary art; his solo has the same sort of structuring that was perfected almost two decades later by saxophonist Charlie Parker. Higgy and Holmes duet affably, and when Will Johnson gets through his chorus without mishap the eponymous trombonist re-enters and, not to be outdone by Allen, shows that he too could construct a solo full of daringly timed motifs, delivered with bold virility. Higginbotham closes the piece with a little phrase that later turns up in the song 'Organ Grinder's Swing', but Red Allen has the final word by nonchalantly blowing a pungent flatted 5th as the concluding note, an ultra-bold move at that time.

Two weeks after that session, the participants (plus William Blue and Teddy Hill on reeds, and Paul Barbarin on drums) assembled in the Victor studio for another session under the banner of Henry Allen and his New York Orchestra. They began by recording a Charlie Holmes composition, 'Sugar Hill Function', which has some outstanding percussion work from Barbarin, who always managed to extract a vast array of tone colours from a standard drum kit. Red Allen's solo (in the minor-keyed section) encapsulates the consistency he achieved throughout this period, reflecting a maturity that had no traces of staidness. Later in the piece, his re-entry creates an effect that Roy Eldridge was later to develop whereby the trumpet phrases roam thrillingly above and between the accompanying band's written figures. The strategy is a transmutation of the counterpoints that Louis Armstrong devised when playing within a big band arrangement, but whereas Louis's supremely authoritative phrases immediately become the focal point, both Red's (and Roy's) efforts seem to be a stimulating part of the ensemble.

Red shares out the solos democratically on 'You Might Get Better' (ably sung by Will Johnson). Higginbotham opens and closes the proceedings, roaring out a series of exuberant phrases, proving that ingenuity need not be restrained and fey. Newcomer William Thornton Blue plays a nimble 16-bar clarinet solo, almost living up to his self-bestowed title 'The Reputed Blue', but Red Allen's heated middle-register improvisations prove that a jazz musician need not fly all over the instrument in order to gain a stellar reputation. Tenor saxophonist Teddy Hill makes the best of a rare opportunity for him to solo (on 'Everybody Shout') and here Blue's clarinet technique is effectively displayed; Red follows on with a series of dynamic phrases, very much in the Higginbotham manner. 'Dancing Dave' concluded a remarkably effective session. Red sounds totally relaxed despite the chugging banjo work by Will Johnson, and Blue's rendering of the melody shows him at his best, but Charlie Holmes demonstrates that the soprano saxophone is, by its very build, a more difficult instrument to master than the alto. Red plays an incisive muted solo, later reverting to open playing to create a fierce-sounding double-timed coda.

Red's next session as a leader took place in July 1930, almost a year to the day after the epoch-making début that produced 'It Should Be You'. A number of superb jazz performances were recorded by various artistes in 1929 and 1930, but as the first waves of the Depression washed away economic stability, the sales figures of these discs were often negligible. The Victor Recording Company made positive attempts to get Red to take a more commercial approach to his recordings, as shown by 'Roamin'' (written by Chick Smith), which also marks Red's recorded début as a solo vocalist. The track has some effective trumpet-playing by Red, but one is aware that the piece has been carefully arranged. The melody and the lyrics are a cut above a run-of-the-mill rating, and while Red's singing is distinctive, it sounds as though he is trying too hard to croon. The overall impression is that he is playing safe, both vocally and instrumentally, in creating a performance of controlled emotion. 'Singing Pretty Songs' is available in two versions nowadays but originally the first take was rejected, partly one suspects because, for one of the only times in his recorded career, Red hesitates before completing a trumpet phrase. Trombonist Jimmy Archey (a newcomer to Luis Russell's Band) is featured briefly and displays the reliability that marked all of his recorded work. Another newcomer, tenor saxist Greely Walton, is allocated a substantial solo, and shows, by playing differently in each of the takes, that he was an avid improviser.

The jewel of the session is Porter Grainger's sombre composition 'Patrol Wagon Blues', which Red sings with a great deal of feeling and considerable artistry. The lower frequencies of the band are enriched by the sonority of Ernest 'Bass' Hill's tuba playing. Paul Barbarin was making increased use of the vibraphone, and employs it here during the introduction, creating an atmosphere that Red's muted trumpet playing expands and develops. Will Johnson solos on guitar and Jimmy Archey (doffing his cap to J.C. Higginbotham) plays a telling solo before Red re-enters and eclipses all that has gone before. The final number of the four pieces recorded that day was 'I Fell in Love with You', which marks Red's début as a scat singer. Red later developed into a fine scat singer, but here his wordless vocal improvisations sound self-conscious, unlike that majestic stop-time chorus he takes on trumpet. Greely Walton again demonstrates his improvising ability, and though he was no jazz giant, he proves that he did not work out his solos in advance.

But all Victor's attempts to build up Red Allen's sales figures were ineffective. After a year on the market the 'Singing Pretty Songs'/'I Fell in Love with You' coupling had sold a mere 311 copies, and understandably it was deleted from the catalogue. Victor chose not to renew Red's recording contract.

5

STAR SOLOIST

The Luis Russell Band continued to engender excitement wherever they played, and besides their residency at the Saratoga Club the band also did theatre and ballroom dates. On one occasion, when the Russell Band had a week off from the Saratoga Club, Jelly Roll Morton approached the leader with an offer: 'Say, Russell, I want to use your band to make a little tour. I'm going to pay you to stay at home, I don't need you.'[1] Russell agreed to the deal and thus had a paid vacation while his sidemen did a brief but successful tour of Pennsylvania under Morton's leadership.

Regardless of venue or circumstances the Luis Russell Band always gave a swinging performance at this stage of their development. Besides the strength of the brass section the reed players' skills were also being continually lauded. Charlie Holmes blew beautifully shaped solos (similar in style to the work of his fellow Bostonian Johnny Hodges) and clarinettist Albert Nicholas added a delightful Creole flavour to the ensemble. The soloists revelled in the fortified support they received from the New Orleans-style rhythm section, underpinned by Pops Foster's powerful bass playing and kicked along by Paul Barbarin's vigorous but clever use of the entire drum kit. It was the jazz solos rather than the arrangements or the compositions (which, in truth, were not substantially melodic or ingenious) that elevated the unit above its rivals. Luis Russell himself played an unselfish background role on most numbers, but Will Johnson, playing banjo, guitar and singing, was often featured on live appearances, and the addition of Greely Walton (in place of Teddy Hill) definitely strengthened the personnel.

Teddy Hill was not in the same class as his front-line colleagues when it came to creating a jazz solo; as Paul Barbarin said, 'Teddy Hill wasn't much of a soloist but he was a good team man'.[2] Hill's administrative skills were thought of as being more substantial than his ability to play ad lib choruses, consequently he was often allocated non-musical tasks by Russell. Thus it was that Hill met Red Allen at Penn Station when Red arrived in New York. Hill was also in charge of the band's wardrobe, with the job of purchasing new uniforms which the musicians paid for out of their salaries. Hill took to this task with such zeal that he seemed to be continually buying new outfits for a band that already had several changes of stagewear. His eagerness caused a ripple of animosity within the usually placid band room. Charlie Holmes recalled the dissension: 'I got mad, you know, getting this small salary and Teddy was talking about buying yet another uniform. I said "Now look, I didn't come into this band to buy uniforms. I'd like to spend my own money the way I want to."'[3]

Fortunately none of this ill-will drifted into the recordings that Luis Russell's Band made between May 1930 and August 1931: during this period the band produced some vibrant recorded performances and one masterpiece, 'Panama'. Albert Nicholas was the least featured of Russell's stars, but he gets his opportunity to shine on 'Louisiana Swing', a neatly arranged piece, which also features Red Allen, who, on this occasion, uses the same framework to create his solos on the two issued takes. One can understand why he was keen to include the long turn-around phrase in bars 7 and 8 of his solo on both versions, because it so exemplifies his masterful rhythmic balance. He shifts a series of syncopated accents to create a prodigious example of musical tension. 'Poor Lil' Me' is a vocal feature for singing actor Jesse Cryor, who was imported for the session. Red again exudes a remarkable musical presence in his 32-bar solo, but Charlie Holmes resumes his battle with the soprano sax without achieving much glory. It has been said that Higginbotham's skills had their origins in the Baptist Church meetings he attended as a child in Georgia, which may account for his compelling performance on Andy Razaf's 'On Revival Day'. Although the piece is only a mock-gospel number it seems to stir something within Higginbotham. His playing was seldom restrained but here it is formidably galvanic as he creates a fine example of what he himself used to describe as 'shout trombone'.

Walton, Holmes and Higginbotham all solo expressively on 'Muggin' Lightly', but the most attractive offering on this number is the commendably 'springy' banjo playing of Will Johnson, his previous ponderous sounds being supplanted by buoyancy and crispness. If one listens to the Russell Band's recordings in sequence it becomes obvious that written arrangements were gradually taking the place of the freewheeling jazz ensembles. The dictates that had redirected the recording policy of Red Allen's Band were also having their effect on Luis Russell's output, but unfortunately the orchestrations that Russell featured rarely achieved any degree of brilliance. Excellent solos continued to burst forth but the momentum they created is often stifled by the succeeding arranged passage; however, there is no question of a musical straitjacket curtailing the exuberance of 'Panama', which typifies the exciting spontaneity of Luis Russell's Band at its best. The performance of the piece, taken at a fast clip, makes it easy to understand how the band was able to demolish its musical competitors. Higginbotham, Walton and Nicholas play sterling solos on a tune written by black composer William H. Tyers (and first published in 1911) but again Red Allen's achievements dwarf his colleagues' efforts. The theme had long been popular in New Orleans, and as a teenager Red had learnt it (and its celebrated trumpet figures) from his teacher Manuel Manetta (who is said to have written out the trumpet counter-melody originally for Emmett Hardy). In the intervening years Red developed technique, stamina and artistry, assets which all blend on 'Panama' as he blows in an electrifying parade style. It is as if all the inspiration that Red received from the various great New Orleans trumpeters he heard as a youngster had suddenly ignited the series of flaming phrases that burst into his mouthpiece and out through the bell of his horn. In his prime, Kid Rena (who made 'Panama' his speciality) could not have played the piece any better than Red Allen does here. Red's solo, as Gunther Schuller observed, is 'full of excellent phrases that Louis Armstrong would *not* have played'.[4] Even a piece as lively as 'High Tension', which ends the session, fails to maintain the excitement created by 'Panama'. Nevertheless it has its merits, one of which is a no-nonsense piano solo from Luis Russell (who rarely featured himself). Red sounds almost restrained on this track, but Nicholas and Holmes radiate the lively spirit of the reed section.

The Gershwins' composition 'I Got Rhythm' (from the 1930 show *Girl Crazy*) was destined to become one of the most recorded of all jazz standards; its chord sequence also became the basis of dozens of other themes. One of the earliest versions was by Luis Russell, and it sounds as though haste to get the piece recorded affected the finesse of the arrangement, which is the least adventurous the band ever recorded. The melody is pumped out almost without variation, scored in instrumental voicings that are poorly conceived, but at least Higginbotham takes a magnificently adventurous chorus; Red's contribution here is limited to eight bars. 'Saratoga Drag', a fast, pleasant tune, is arranged and performed much more ably. Red is in full command during his solo, nonchalantly leaping to and from his upper register, but the star of the piece is Pops Foster, who sounds even more energetic than usual. 'Ease On Down' (originally issued, via a misprint, as 'Case on Dawn') has a cohesive performance from the ensemble but Greely Walton's 32-bar solo overextends the resources of his musical imagination. Things pick up when Higginbotham begins his solo with a motif that employs a thrilling musical shake which launches a series of vehement but ingenious phrases. Whether Red Allen felt stimulated or challenged by his colleague's playing we shall never know, but he bursts into his solo as though he had just been untied. The excitement does not flag, eventually culminating as the band blow a series of call and response phrases. The session ended with a curio, namely a vocal feature for trombonist Vic Dickenson (who was not part of Luis Russell's Band). Dickenson told me that at this time he did not know any of Russell's musicians but had been brought to the recording studio by arranger-trumpeter John Nesbitt (of McKinney's Cotton Pickers fame). Nesbitt had written arrangements for the session and asked his friend, Vic Dickenson, to sing the vocal on 'Honey That Reminds Me'. He did so in competent fashion, but was not called on to play trombone.

Red did not realize it at the time, but his next recordings with Luis Russell were to be the last he made with that band. The session in August 1931 produced four sides, all of which bear out Russell's increasing use of formal arrangements. On 'You Rascal You', Red is (for the first time on a Russell recording) allocated a vocal; he responds by singing the song's lighthearted threats adroitly. By this time Dicky Wells had replaced Higginbotham on trombone. Wells was later to become one of the great individualists in jazz, but here he chooses to blow in the manner of his predecessor. Red produces one of his amazing siren-like entries and then proceeds to blow lustily over the arranged passages, but never sounding quite at his best. The band's brief on 'Goin' to Town' was to provide accompaniment for the ubiquitous singer Chick Bullock, a white vocalist who sang on hundreds of recordings during the 1930s. Chick turns in his usual affable and tuneful performance, and jazz contributions come from Dicky Wells's raucous but effective trombone solo, Albert Nicholas's agile clarinet work (unfortunately under-recorded) and Red Allen's late, fragmentary offering which provides a stirring conclusion. Bullock also sings a light, romantic vocal on 'Say the Word', and here the

Russell ensemble sounds very much like a dance band of the period though happily Red again provides a burst of ingenuity and excitement. Red does not solo on the final number of the date, 'Freakish Blues', an untuneful composition by Luis Russell and Paul Barbarin, which attempts to pay tribute to Duke Ellington but misses the target. Red's task is to blow some atmospheric growls while the main trumpet work is performed by Robert Cheek, who expressively interprets a solo that had been written out for him by Luis Russell. Pops Foster bows his part nobly, and altoist Henry 'Moon' Jones (taking Charlie Holmes's place) displays a rich, creamy tone in his solos, but overall the arrangement is more ponderous than poetic.

In 1930 Red Allen took leave from the Luis Russell Band's residency at the Saratoga Club to visit New Orleans, where he finalized plans for Pearly May to move to New York for their impending marriage ceremony. In an attempt to ensure as much continuity as possible Luis Russell sent for the Crescent City trumpeter Lee Collins to temporarily take Red's place (no recordings were made while Collins was in the band). Red enjoyed his Louisiana visit and was delighted to catch up with all the local news; he also found time to visit a musician with whom he had never played a note – Charles 'Buddy' Bolden, the most famous figure in early jazz history. At that time Bolden had been an inmate of the State Insane Asylum for almost 25 years. It was their first and only meeting, and years later Red recalled the details of this strange encounter:

> I never heard him. He blew his top just before I was born, according to my dad. I knew about him though, because he'd played with my father's brass band. I met him this once, at the Louisiana State Hospital where he was detained. I went into a kind of yard where there was a lot of people talking, or walking about, and asked someone for Charles Bolden. They said he was over there and I went up and spoke to him.[5]

Apparently Bolden couldn't comprehend who Red was and no worthwhile conversation ensued as Bolden simply shuffled to and fro.

Red and Pearly May journeyed to New York, were married, and then moved into a three-bedroom apartment on 136th Street which they shared with Mr and Mrs Paul Barbarin and with Paul's nephew, guitarist Danny Barker and his teenage wife, the singer Blue Lu Barker. The Saratoga Club was nearby so Red called in to see how things were going, and sat in alongside Lee Collins. Under such circumstances the competitive spirit inbred among New Orleans trumpet players was bound to surface. A no-holds-barred contest developed between the two musicians, from which Red emerged victorious. Looking back, Pops Foster recalled the battle in a conversation with British trumpeter Keith Smith, confirming that Red 'blew Collins away'. Tenor saxist Greely Walton also gave his verdict: 'Red blew Collins right back to New Orleans'.[6]

During 1931, Red and Pearly May became proud parents when their son Henry Paul Allen was born. Henry III took his middle name from his godfather, Paul Barbarin (his godmother was Blue Lu Barker). By this time the Saratoga Club residency was coming to an end, and to keep the band working Luis Russell took bookings at the Arcadia Ballroom and at various New York theatres such as the Alhambra and the Lafayette. But there were slack periods, and in one of these Red worked for about three weeks in a band that Fats Waller briefly led at Connie's Inn, New York, during the latter part of 1931.

The slow bite of the Depression caused a big drop in record sales, and as a result there were fewer freelance recording sessions. Red's income was considerably reduced so he was delighted to be offered the chance to play on a studio date in September 1931. On 'Shakin' the African' with Don Redman's Orchestra Red's torrid trumpet intro-duction provides the ignition for his fierce 16-bar solo, and Bob Carroll takes a brief tenor sax solo before Red bursts back into the limelight with eight bars of tigerish phrasing. The heat of the trumpet solo contrasts effectively with Don Redman's cool, recitative vocal – 'hip' before its time. Three weeks later the band again assembled to re-record the same arrangement, and again Red is a model of ardour, each trumpet phrase stoking up the excitement. Don Redman's eerie composition, 'Chant of the Weed' (for which agent Irving Mills took a half share), is tailormade for Red Allen's explorations, but even more fascinating is Red's playing on 'Trouble Why Pick on Me?'. After Lois Deppe's prim vocal Red creates a poetic, softly blown solo that is full of ingenious double-timed phrases, which are enhanced by his adroit use of alternate fingerings (creating an effect in which different valve combinations are used to impart a varying timbre to reiterations of the same note). Improvisations that initially imply jaggedness are smoothly resolved. The timing of the solo is courageous, but its exquisite form belies any hint of haphazardness. Red's efforts here augur developments in his style of playing that were to reach fruition many years later.

By early 1932 Luis Russell's engagement book had many blank pages. Red and the rest of the band filled in as best they could, deputizing in other bands and playing casual gigs. Gradually several of the old guard departed, including Higginbotham, Holmes and Nicholas; even Paul Barbarin wasn't always with the band when it reconvened. Red always gave first option on his services to Luis Russell and was by now the unchallenged star of the band. The *New York Age* of 28 May 1932 carried an advertisement for Luis Russell and his Roseland Ballroom Orchestra 'featuring Henry Allen Jr', with the added comment 'The boy that Louis Armstrong stated was his nearest rival as the World's Greatest Trumpet Player'. The departure of Russell's other key sidemen wasn't only caused by the lack of well-paid work; the musicians were also disheartened by the bandleader's gradual change of musical policy. Albert Nicholas explained:

> It was still a great band, and could keep swinging all evening, but Russell wanted to alter the style. We all told him, 'Luis, don't change our band's style'. But he was a hard-headed West Indian when he wanted to be, and when he got an idea nothing shook him off it.[7]

Pops Foster, who remained despite the change in musical policy, said 'Luis decided to change his style. We started fooling around with big arrangements, but when we started playing like all the other bands, finding work was rough.'[8]

One cannot lay too much blame on Luis Russell. It wasn't only record company executives who were urging a change of policy; so too were agents, club owners and ballroom operators. Russell was genuinely trying to keep the band working regularly, but he knew the public's taste was beginning to change, wanting their dance music soft and sweet, so Russell began using more orthodox arrangements, eliminating most of the numbers that ended in all-out improvisation. Gradually pieces connected with New Orleans, such as 'Panama', were eased out of the repertory; vocal features began to outnumber instrumentals. It wasn't only Russell's jazz-loving sidemen who tried to dissuade their leader from smoothing out a previously dynamic ensemble; Duke Ellington warned Russell, 'You must always keep that style',[9] knowing that Luis was in danger of surrendering a unique sound in order to gain what could well be transient commercial popularity.

A good deal of Luis Russell's work in 1932 was in theatres in and around New York, often playing between the showings of a recently released movie. This blending of stage and screen productions was increasingly becoming part of the American entertainment scene in an attempt to convince the public that they were being offered a bargain of two shows for the price of one. Although Duke Ellington's warning eventually proved prophetic, Russell's strategy temporarily kept the band working. The pattern that emerged from the Depression indicated that when the general public experienced economic hardships and despondency they wanted escapism not excitement, and consequently attendance figures at ballrooms favoured the smooth, sweet bands.

In July 1932, the Luis Russell Band (often mis-billed as the Louis Russell Band) played a week at the Lafayette Theatre, supporting the lively showman-singer Billy Banks (the movie attraction for that run featured Spencer Tracy in *Society Girl*). The tie-up with Banks was timely for Red Allen because he was in the middle of a series of freelance recordings (instigated by impresario Irving Mills) with the singer. The pick-up band was racially mixed and included white musicians: Charles 'Pee Wee' Russell on clarinet and tenor saxophone, Gene Krupa on drums, Joe Sullivan on piano, Jack Bland on guitar and Eddie Condon on banjo. Besides Allen and Banks the other black musicians were Al Morgan on string bass and Zutty Singleton on drums (he took Krupa's place on drums after the first session).

This group, later to be known as the Rhythmakers, produced music that was memorably fiery and totally devoid of any quaint Dixieland touches. It echoed a blend of skill and abandon that was the hallmark of the best of that era's jam sessions. As a reaction to the saccharine sounds that were playing an increasing part in their regular occupations, Allen and Russell create attractive, agitated jazz by rasping and growling their way through the ensembles, saving enough energy to catapult themselves into daring and imaginative solos. Both were fearless improvisers whose unique qualities come through in every solo. Even detractors who suggested that they were too idiosyncratic had to admit that in tandem Allen and Russell produced imperishable jazz. The writer and poet, Philip Larkin, had the highest regard for the Rhythmakers' recordings and said of the Allen-Russell collaborations, 'the filigree duets of their eccentric voices reveals instinctive kinship'.[10]

Unlike some veteran jazz musicians Red Allen was never averse to talking about recordings he made early in his career, but one sensed he was suppressing aggrieved feelings when the subject of Billy Banks's sides was raised. The reason was financial not musical. Apparently Banks never paid the sidemen for the first two sessions they did with him, though

Banks himself stoutly maintained that Irving Mills (the sponsor of the recordings) had never paid him. Banks got off on the wrong foot with the accompanying musicians by turning up late for the first date. While waiting for Banks to arrive the band went ahead and recorded two numbers, a vivacious 'Bugle-Call Rag' and a strident 'Oh! Peter', on which Red Allen sings and plays superbly. When Banks arrived the band set about the task of recording 'Margie' with a ferocity that provided an outlet for their annoyance. Banks, seemingly unaware of the cloud of animosity, sang the lyrics nonchalantly. A further session took place a month later (in May 1932) and this time Billy Banks recorded a vocal version of 'Oh! Peter', not managing to sing it quite as well as Red Allen had done. A 'Who's Sorry Now?', full of smouldering trumpet phrases and previously uncharted clarinet lines, is lifted by the uninhibited rhythm section. Banks sings this with skill and enthusiasm, occasionally breaking into a form of warbled scat singing that had recently been made popular by Bing Crosby (who in turn had adapted the effect from early Louis Armstrong recordings). Banks repeats the effect on 'Take It Slow and Easy', which is studded with perfectly delivered breaks from Russell and Allen, with Red imparting an aura of excitement to his low notes – a rare achievement for any jazz trumpeter. Although this session was under Banks's name he wisely lets the spotlight fall on his accompaniments and the resultant freedom allows the two front-line players to create some exhilarating interplay on 'Bald-headed Mama' and 'Spider Crawl'.

Another session, with a similar line-up, took place in July 1932, but the previous fees still had not reached the musicians. This time the band insisted that Banks was not designated the official leader, which meant that they could be paid direct. Jimmy Lord, a white clarinettist, was added, and Pops Foster replaced his fellow New Orleanian, Al Morgan, on string bass. The newcomer on piano was none other than Fats Waller and again Philip Larkin provides a pithy compliment by noting that the 'addition of Waller produced the power of a riverboat paddlewheel'.[11] The phrases that provide the main struts of Waller's solo on the first take of 'I Would Do Anything for You' turn up later in a Count Basie 1936 solo, and later on form the basis of his 1952 recording 'Basie Talks'. Although author Wilder Hobson cited 'Yellow Dog Blues' as a perfect example of collective improvisation, each of the four titles from this session is equally rich in spontaneous ideas. Banks sings on all four and on 'Mean Old Bed-bug Blues' indulges in the female vocal impersonations that were part of his stage act. Red solos superbly on 'Yes Suh!' and continually provides plus-perfect accompaniment to Banks's singing.

For the final session in this series Banks was absent and guitarist Jack Bland became the nominal leader. The nucleus of the previous group remained, but trombonist Tommy Dorsey was added for three sides. On 'Shine on Your Shoes' Dorsey plays the smoothest of solos, seemingly without effort – or emotion. Jimmy Lord is absent and Happy Cladwell joins on tenor saxophone airing sturdy, Coleman Hawkins-inspired phrases. Fats Waller's place at the piano was taken by the white New Orleanian, Frank Froeba, who plays particularly well on 'It's Gonna Be You' and 'Somebody Stole Gabriel's Horn'. Red Allen shares vocal duties (two songs apiece) with session singer Chick Bullock. The trumpeter was gaining confidence in his ability to sing and this adds a dash of exuberance and appealing humour to his vocals. On 'Who Stole the Lock?' his singing embodies the daring rhythmic approach that makes his trumpet-playing so appealing. On first hearing it seems that Red has not left himself time to fit the lyrics in with the backing chords, but, by deftly enunciating a rapid burst of syllables, he not only completes the stanzas in time but dovetails them artistically with the accompanying harmonies.

This proved to be the last of a four-part series of recordings that were issued and re-issued many times under various names, being ideal music for those who like their jazz to be ruggedly spontaneous. But, much to the chagrin of at least two of the participants, Red Allen and Pee Wee Russell, the recordings were often cited as prime examples of 'Chicago Jazz', though neither Allen nor Russell had any ties with Chicago whatsoever. Red had never even been to that city when he made the recordings and protested about the pigeon-holing, saying 'I never got to Chicago until 1933, when I went there with Fletcher Henderson's Orchestra'.[12] I was present when someone told Russell that he thought Pee Wee's work on the Rhythmakers' sides was 'typically Chicagoan'. Russell groaned, then fixed the man with an irritated stare and said, with clenched teeth, 'I never held a Chicago union card, and I never worked there regularly until I went there with Louis Prima in 1935'.[13]

Red Allen did all sorts of gigs in 1932 and 1933. In a New York report dated 8 September 1932 (published in *Melody Maker*), John Hammond wrote of a 'magnificent get-off band' that he had organized to broadcast on radio station WEVD. The unit was racially mixed, consisting of Art Tatum on piano, Red Allen on trumpet, Benny Carter on reeds and Artie Bernstein on string bass. It seems that this blending was too bold for the Claridge Hotel (where WEVD had its studio), who insisted that the musicians used the freight elevator. John Hammond and others picketed the hotel on the grounds of racial discrimination, but their protests were ignored.

To keep his 'chops' in good shape during bouts of unemployment Red usually found somewhere to sit in and blow. It was a good excuse for Red and other top trumpet players to check out and challenge any trumpeting newcomers that hit town (almost in the manner of gun-slingers in the Wild West). Taft Jordan recalled that Red and Rex Stewart came in together to listen to him soon after he first arrived in New York. Sometimes an unknown newcomer could provide unwelcome surprises. Bandleader Earle Howard cited one such example involving Billy Douglas and Red Allen.

> Billy then had a style that was more like a saxophone than a brass instrument, it was fantastic the way he got over his horn. I remember a night during the time I had the band in Rose Dance-land, on the corner of 125th Street. My two trumpeters were Eddie Allen, that sturdy old reliable first cornettist and Billy Douglas. About 10.30 p.m., in walked Red Allen, Ward Pinkett and Louis Metcalf. So without any fooling around, beyond the formalities of the good ole handshake and 'Hi Pops', we pushed the chairs back and made room for these cats. Billy was blowing when they came in, so Red paid him a compliment, 'Good going man!' Well for the next hour and a half it was trumpet, trumpet, trumpet. Red got to his current masterpiece, 'Stardust', well, Billy picked up the next chorus after Red and when he finished Red shook his head and said 'You're too much, ole man', and that was the end of the evening, the other two cats had long before given up![14]

Red spent most of late 1932 and early 1933 playing in Charlie Johnson's Band, whose home base was at Small's Paradise on 135th Street and Seventh Avenue. Unfortunately Red did not record with this group. The band's usual schedule at Small's was a two-show routine: one at 30 minutes past midnight, and another two hours later. Red usually got home around 5 a.m., but did not, as a rule, sleep much beyond noon. He was thus available for any freelance recordings or the occasional late afternoon gig. By this time Red and his family had moved to 48 St Nicholas Place in the Sugar Hill district of Harlem. While working at Small's Paradise, Red was heard by the composer Patrick 'Spike' Hughes (whose father was Irish and whose mother was English).

Hughes wrote a glowing account of the experience in the *Melody Maker* of April 1933:

> To Small's Paradise to hear Charlie Johnson's Band. The one and only Henry Allen (Junior) on trumpet and Chu Berry on tenor saxophone. Red is one of the very best trumpet players in the world. His star performances are 'Body and Soul', 'Ain't Misbehavin'' and a long series of breaks on Hoagy Carmichael's 'Thanksgivin''.

Hughes (who was the *Melody Maker's* critic 'Mike') had regularly praised Red's recorded work. While on a prolonged visit to New York in 1933 he organized a series of recording sessions; among the first musicians that he invited to play on these dates was Red Allen. The recordings featured a 15-piece band (originally listed on record labels as Spike Hughes and his Negro Orchestra), composed mainly of musicians who were part of Benny Carter's Band, fortified with stars such as Coleman Hawkins and Red Allen. Hughes arranged all of the numbers the band recorded, and also composed several of the themes used on the dates, including the haunting 'Donegal Cradle Song'.

In his autobiography *Second Movement*, Hughes writes extensively about his four-month stay in New York and goes into detail about hearing Red and Chu Berry at Small's, mentioning that after they had finished work 'both men would take their instruments off to spend the rest of the night until breakfast time playing for the sheer fun of it in somebody else's band in the most conveniently local gin-mill'. Red Allen chuckled when this summary of his nocturnal habits was read out to him during one of his visits to London during the 1960s: 'I may have done that occasionally, and maybe Spike saw me sitting in once or twice, but by that time of my life I was Mr Let's-get-home-and-go-to-bed.'[15]

Hughes's recordings took place in the Brunswick Studios, situated high up in a building at 1776 Broadway. Personnel changes occurred between one session and the next, and the band that had rehearsed the arrangements in the empty Savoy Ballroom was not exactly the same unit that made the recordings (Red had to miss the initial studio sessions because of other commitments); however, everything turned out satisfactorily, despite the unpunctuality of several of the participants. Hughes's arrangement for the full band are daring and non-formulaic; he was never given enough credit for their originality. The excellence of the writing was enhanced by the interludes that featured improvisations of the highest order from what was an all-star cast of New York's top jazz musicians.

Red Allen does not solo on 'Arabesque', which has admirable contributions from a dream pairing of the two tenor saxophonists Coleman Hawkins and Chu Berry, plus some intrepid solos from the highly explorative trombonist, Dicky Wells. Hughes recognized Wells's huge potential and featured him on virtually every track the band recorded. The trombonist responded by playing at the top of his form throughout the series, reaching heights of inspired creativity that he seldom recaptured. The same three soloists grace 'Fanfare' (a medium-paced 12-bar blues) but this time Red contributes two powerful choruses and Benny Carter plays clarinet effectively. The slow theme, 'Sweet Sorrow Blues', brings forth some profound solos. Here Red blows magnificently, creating a chorus that sounds related to his epic improvisations on King Oliver's recording of 'Stingaree'. He does not feature on the elegantly scored 'Music at Midnight', honours again going to Hawkins and Wells. The date ended with a jam-session version of 'Sweet Sue', featuring Red, Dicky Wells, Wayman Carver on flute, Benny Carter on alto sax, Hawkins and Berry on tenor saxes, Red Rodriguez on piano, Lawrence Lucie on guitar and Sid Catlett on drums. Spike Hughes made his own sturdy instrumental contribution by putting aside his baton and playing Ernest Hill's double bass. Red Allen is entrusted with the opening melody of 'Sweet Sue' and makes an ingenious job of re-allocating the tune's time values. Wayman Carver plays an attractive flute solo (in an era when jazz flautists were very rare). Hawkins is magnificently poised, Wells bold and imaginative, Benny Carter graceful and ingenious. Red Allen is particularly incisive during the final eight bars and blows, with great assurance, a daring concluding phrase.

The next day the band re-assembled and began by recording the lovely 'Air in D flat', which includes some delicate muted trumpet work (not by Red Allen) and a probing but fulfilling solo from Dicky Wells, which is full of boldly blown wide intervals. On performances like this Wells seems to echo Red Allen's approach to improvising. 'Donegal Cradle Song' (a deceptively simple composition by Hughes that reflects his Irish roots) is graced by one of Coleman Hawkins's most memorable solos, but Red Allen takes top honours on 'Firebird', blowing a thrilling 32-bar chorus that inspires a rather four-square rhythm section to unite into a swinging amalgam. Hughes broke with tradition and scored a soprano sax to lead the opening chorus, but then discovered that Benny Carter had pawned his soprano and could not remember where the holding shop was located. The instrument was eventually tracked down and the piece recorded. 'Music at Midnight' is a model of sumptuous scoring, with solo space illustriously shared by Hawkins and Wells. It concluded the full band's day, but, as before, a jam session provided the final recording. 'How Come You Do Me Like You Do, Do, Do' abounds with cogent solos. Red croons an effective vocal, then decides to resurrect some scat phrases that had originated in Louis Armstrong's throat. Pianist Rodriguez contributes an intricate solo (culled from many sources), then Red's trumpet leads a loping, relaxed and infectiously cheerful final chorus. Again Hughes plays string bass (for the last time in his career, as it transpired).

Hughes went on to write many books, notably on opera; he also created a series of guides, under the portmanteau title 'The Art of Coarse...', covering such diverse subjects as travel, gardening, bridge, cricket, etc. He continued to write for the *Melody Maker* throughout the 1930s but never again composed or arranged for jazz ensembles after he returned from New York in 1933, thus depriving Europe of one of its premier jazz orchestrators. Commenting on his American recordings, Hughes wrote, 'Red Allen I found particularly charming, and from what I can gather from his subsequent letters to me, he enjoyed playing at these sessions'.[16] Red summed up his feelings about working with Hughes: 'That was a most enjoyable date for me. I was very honored to be invited to that session, and what a happy one it was, right from the start. A wonderful date, very nice.'[17] Interestingly, when Red first visited Europe in 1959 the first album he bought was of his work with Spike Hughes. Hughes remained a long-time admirer of Red's playing, and six years after their recording together he wrote, 'Allen is greatly under-rated. The solitary true lyricist left in jazz.'[18]

6

THE BLUEPRINTS
OF SWING

Fletcher Henderson was certainly one of the leading black bandleaders
of the 1920s and 1930s. He had listened appreciatively to Red Allen's
playing on various occasions, and had employed him briefly as a deputy
for New York theatre engagements in April 1932.[1] After Red's stint ended
with Charlie Johnson he resumed gigging with Luis Russell's Band, but
was then invited to audition for Fletcher Henderson who was looking for
a replacement for Rex Stewart. The audition took place at the Rhythm
Club, where Henderson, on piano, tested Red by playing tunes in some
difficult and seldom encountered keys. Red's early training stood him in
good stead: 'When he hit those black keys I followed him'.[2] Henderson
hired Red there and then and the trumpeter agreed to join the band in
June 1933. The pay was $90 per week, more than he had been earning
with Luis Russell or Charlie Johnson. With Henderson there were ample
prospects for bettering oneself musically, Red said later:

> I got schooled a little more in that band. We had to play in what I
> would call awkward keys. Most bands played in simpler keys.
> Fletcher himself was very easy to get along with. As a leader he was
> not too strict, and of course his writing was very good.[3]

Red's full-time membership of Henderson's Orchestra began with a
six-week residency at the Hollywood Gardens, Pelham, New York (close
to the Bronx). There Allen acquired an additional nickname, 'Blondy',
and for the rest of their lives several of Henderson's musicians used that
sobriquet, much to the recipient's amusement. For a brief while Red
and J.C. Higginbotham were reunited in this band, but neither was the
musical star of the aggregation, for the band's undisputed champion

was tenor saxist Coleman Hawkins. Hawkins was delighted that Red had joined the band. He liked his daring approach to improvisations and appreciated his diligent and accurate work in the brass section. Red's predecessor, Rex Stewart, though never lacking in restraint when soloing, had in Hawkins's mind a slapdash approach to intonation, which resulted in his playing certain notes out of tune. Hawkins and Allen shared a way of using rubato phrasing in their solos, and this provided a pleasing continuity. The New England critic, George Frazier, heard the Henderson Band at the time and wrote, 'The presence of Henry Allen in Fletcher Henderson's trumpet section has helped it immensely. It is a genuine thrill to hear Henry take a solo, followed by the supreme Hawkins. Allen's marvellous work is acting as a fine stimulant to the best of the tenors.'[4]

Fletcher Henderson made no effort to curb Red Allen's musical explorations. There was no embargo on creativity within the band, even though Red sometimes introduced notes in his solos that did not seem to be part of the chords within Henderson's arrangements. Fletcher's brother, Horace Henderson, summed up this aspect of Red's work: 'He was one of the few trumpet players that I know who could run a diminished chord against a major and make it sound good. He'd invert it on the end and come back to the chord. But he didn't know what he was doing.'[5] The unorthodox aspect of Red's approach is demonstrated on his début recording with Henderson, 'Yeah Man'. The main trumpet solo on this track is a 32-bar chorus from Bobby Stark, a highly talented but non-revolutionary player. In contrast, Red seems determined to act the part of the musical anarchist, creating an acrid effect in a way that implies he is using dissonance for the sake of it. Given time to stretch out on 'King Porter Stomp' he is much more productive, underlining his choice of notes with greater finesse, but still throwing caution to the wind by superimposing phrases that defy the bar-lines, vying for top honours with Dicky Wells, whose individuality at this stage of his career was breathtaking. On 'Queer Notions' (a 'modernistic' composition by Coleman Hawkins) Red sounds to be in his element, weaving his way through the near-atonal theme by playing whole-tone runs and diminished arpeggios, his 'ear' taking him into what Gunther Schuller described as 'a harmonic no man's land'.[6] On the fast 'Can You Take It?' his role is restricted to that of a subsidiary soloist, as it is on Coleman Hawkins's feature, 'It's the Talk of the Town'; however, on this ballad Red creates a fleeting moment of musical magic by timing a slow-rising glissando to perfection, controlling its rise so that it hits the introductory note of a new phrase at the plus-perfect instant. Bobby Stark is the main trumpet soloist on the pot-boiler composition 'Night Life', and again Red uses shock tactics to stamp his own character on his 8-bar solo; it is as though he wanted listeners to realize how different from Stark he was, and accordingly exaggerates his own mannerisms. However on 'Nagasaki' Red thrives on being featured – as a trumpeter and as a singer. His voice takes on an attractive, husky timbre as he delivers the fast-flowing lyrics, demonstrating an amazing rhythmic aplomb, then going on to create a stunning 64-bar trumpet solo, pacing himself effectively by launching most of his phrases from the lower-middle register.

Red's stint with Fletcher Henderson coincided with a fertile period in that leader's arranging output. During the early 1920s Fletcher regularly arranged for his own band but then seems to have been overtaken by diffidence and chose to leave most of the writing to Don Redman. Even Redman's departure in 1927 (to join McKinney's Cotton Pickers) did not stir him into action and he continued to rely on others (including Benny Carter) for his band's arrangements. Then, after someone supposedly bet him $50 that he could not write a big band arrangement, he sat down and wrote an orchestration. Henderson was so pleased with the band's performance of this score that he again began to arrange regularly – with splendid results. He soon made up for lost time and produced a string of original orchestrations that prepared the way for the coming of the Swing Era. His scores were full of snappy rhythmic phrases, and he also granted ample space for improvised solos and created engaging riffs which allowed the band to back a soloist without drowning out his improvisations. Sometimes Henderson developed a simple riff into a counter-melody that co-existed alongside the main theme, allowing one section to blow against another in what became known as a 'call and response' routine.

Fletcher's brother, Horace, was also a pianist and arranger and in October 1933 he led the band for a Parlophone recording session that produced six sides, including 'Happy Feet', which contains a superb example of Red Allen effectively hitting a single note at a most unex-pected place, and, in an equally surprising way, releasing it several beats later. Horace Henderson ably demonstrates his own pianistic skills on this number. Red does not solo on 'I'm Rhythm Crazy Now' but plays effect-ively on 'Minnie the Moocher's Wedding Day' and 'Ain't Cha Glad'; however, his big feature is 'Ol' Man River', where his supple vocal swings effortlessly and his trumpet work creates a minor avalanche of new ideas. A less spectacular triumph occurs on Coleman Hawkins's ballad feature

'I've Got a Right to Sing a Torch Song', where Red's trumpet playing on the first bridge is a delightful combination of elegance and inspiration.

Several members of Fletcher Henderson's Band (including Coleman Hawkins) used to groan when asked to comment on the band's recordings, not because the performances were inept, but because the recording quality was usually poor. The band's in-person, full-sounding sonority was apparently rarely captured on wax. If one listens critically to the ensemble's 1933–4 output it often sounds to have been performed by a smaller unit than a 12-piece band. Rex Stewart (who worked in both line-ups) said that Henderson's Band in person could always outblow Duke Ellington's Orchestra, yet on record Duke's ensemble invariably created superior-sounding performances. Sound fidelity deficiencies are apparent on Henderson's March 1934 recordings. 'Hocus Pocus' has Buster Bailey producing cascades of busy phrasing, and a solo from Red Allen that suggests controlled flamboyancy. Red does not solo on 'Phantom Fantasie' and is only heard playing muted behind Charles Holland's vocal on 'Harlem Madness', which is virtually all Coleman Hawkins. Red is heard briefly on the dramatically swift 'Tidal Wave', but again the lion's share is taken by Hawkins. Red was quite aware that his arrival had not usurped Hawk's position as Henderson's premier soloist, and said, 'My, when that band took off you really heard some playing from Hawk. Everyone had to be on their toes to keep anywhere near him. When you heard that enormous sound coming out of his tenor sax you knew you had to blow too.'[7]

White big bands began incorporating Fletcher Henderson's ideas into their own arrangements. Later Benny Goodman, the so-called 'King of Swing', went one better by hiring Fletcher as his staff arranger, buying many of the orchestrations that had provided Henderson's Band with the fuel that fired its success. Henderson had a succession of high-profile jazz trumpeters throughout the 1920s, including Louis Armstrong, Joe Smith, Tommy Ladnier, Bobby Stark and Rex Stewart, each of whom in varying degrees influenced the course of jazz trumpet playing. But it is Red Allen's improvisations on Henderson's recordings that seem to have provided blueprints for Goodman's trumpet soloists, Harry James and Ziggy Elman. Their predecessor in Goodman's brass section, Bunny Berigan, had used Louis Armstrong as his main model, but though both James and Elman had the greatest admiration for Armstrong's work the contours of their solos on Goodman's versions of the Henderson arrangements owe much more to Red Allen than to Louis Armstrong. Many other swing stars echoed Red's phrases in their work. But it was not only white musicians who got inspiration from Red's playing; during the mid-1930s one can detect his influence in the solos of various black trumpeters including Shirley Clay, Ed Anderson, Walter Fuller, Harry Edison and Irving Randolph. However, just how big a part Red played in the evolution of jazz trumpet playing remains a controversial issue with jazz historians. The lineage that reads Buddy Bolden/King Oliver/ Louis Armstrong/Red Allen/Roy Eldridge/Dizzy Gillespie was emphatically challenged by Eldridge himself (who joined Fletcher Henderson in 1936). In an interview with Nat Hentoff, Roy made his views clear on the subject of whether or not he was influenced by Red's playing:

> I like Red – but oh God, no! When I first came to New York I used to wonder as people were saying he was playing wonderful chords. But I wasn't the type that would say a cat wasn't playing until I heard what he was doing and felt I understood. He used to come and sit in with Teddy Hill, and I felt something was wrong. I didn't know exactly what it was until I went with Fletcher and from the experience there I knew he had often been playing wrong notes.[8]

These two great jazz trumpeters not only had totally dissimilar personalities, but also had contrasting methods when it came to improvising. Roy's solos were based on a consummate knowledge of harmony and chordal substitutions whereas Red's improvisations relied mainly on his ear and his remarkable musical instinct. But both men were formidable innovators. There was no such thing as 'wrong notes' for Red. He'd insert any note into a solo if he felt it added passion or piquancy – regardless of whether or not it was part of the accompanying chord. Thus his use of non-chordal tones suggested all sorts of possibilities for future improvisers (on any instrument). As trumpeter-writer Richard Sudhalter pointed out, when discussing Red's playing, 'The "wrong" notes his colleagues sometimes derided had a way of turning up years or decades later, hailed as brilliant discoveries when someone else played them'.[9]

Speed, technique and range are the hallmarks of Roy Eldridge's early solos, but for Red Allen the task of creating and sustaining a mood within his solos was paramount. Nevertheless, Gunther Schuller felt that in the 1930s Eldridge was 'still very much listening to Allen, his denials thereof notwithstanding', and concluded that 'Eldridge was not entirely impervious to Allen's influences'.[10] I do not subscribe to the idea that Red's playing directly influenced Roy's work, though here and there we can hear Eldridge using the same concepts as the older man, but it must be borne in mind that in both men's formative years their styles were, in part, based on Louis Armstrong's achievements.

Despite the admiring interest of musicians and critics, Henderson's Band failed to get the prestigious, well-paid engagements they deserved. Hotel residencies were rarely offered to black bands during that era. On the repeal of Prohibition in 1933 various suburban and coastal-resort clubs opened, but many cabarets and speak-easies, which had relied on huge profits from the sale of illicit liquor to pay their musicians, cut down their wage bill drastically. Suddenly there was a glut of unemployed musicians on the market and ballroom operators found they could hire bands very cheaply. Trombonist Dicky Wells felt that the knock-on effect of these economic changes hampered the Henderson Band's prospects at a crucial time in that aggregation's development. Wells said that it was ironic that, despite the lack of recording opportunities (compared to the 1920s), many jazz musicians earned more during the Depression than they did in its aftermath.[11] Red's income was certainly affected, and Pearly May remembered Red solemnly pointing out in 1934 that they would have to tighten their belts.

But none of this gloom seeped into the Henderson Band's music-making, and in three sessions in September 1934 they produced 12 sides including one of their finest achievements, a swift version of 'Limehouse Blues', on which Walter Johnson's drumming is inspirational. Happily all of the soloists maintain the impetus created by Red's declamatory chorus, laying the groundwork for a worthy climax to a brilliant Benny Carter arrangement. By this time Ben Webster had taken over Coleman Hawkins's role on tenor saxophone, Hawkins having moved to Europe. Webster was to go on to greater things, but he plays satisfactorily here in filling what must have been a particularly demanding vacancy. With the departure of Hawkins, Red was now recognized as Henderson's premier soloist. Red's ideas on 'Shanghai Shuffle' sound slightly fragmentary, but he makes a surging, dramatic entry on 'Big John's Special', stimulated perhaps by the fine solo that had just been played by a new trumpeter in the band, Irving 'Mouse' Randolph. Whatever the reason, Red seems to burst into the arrangement, cutlass in hand.

Red also makes a stirring entry on 'Happy as the Day Is Long', and clearly delineates a path later taken by Harry James. Less hectic by far is his work on 'Down South Camp Meeting', where his relaxed, low-register solo is a model of thoughtful construction. This arrangement, and that of 'Wrappin' It Up', were destined to be heard in many ballrooms during the coming years, but few of the bands playing the note-for-note printed scores had anyone in their line-ups who could satisfactorily recreate the epic solos that Red Allen and his colleagues had spontaneously conceived. Red's anacrusis entry to his solo on 'Wrappin' It Up' is a microcosm of his art, and the eerie notes he plays during his final eight bars show that his restless artistry was still supremely active. He is both plaintive and fiery in different parts of 'Wild Party'. Honours here go to trombonist Claude Jones and to arranger Russ Morgan, whose admirable idea of using chromatic key changes during the final stages of the piece, and of allowing clarinettist Buster Bailey to play a loose counterpoint over these rising figures, creates a memorable climax. Red, using a cup mute, states the theme of 'Rug Cutter's Swing', Claude Jones and Ben Webster solo enthusiastically but throughout this period the alto saxophone solos (by Hilton Jefferson and Russell Procope) are usually weak and unambitious, though things are different when Benny Carter guests with the band. Red always maintained that he was the composer of 'Rug Cutter's Swing', and said he had written out the melody and passed it over to Horace Henderson so that he could make an arrangement of the tune for the full Henderson Band. To Red's surprise, when he saw the record label he realized that Horace had listed himself as the composer. Red clearly had a case for provenance of the tune because the label on his own small band recording, made in July 1934 (some two months before the Fletcher Henderson version), clearly cites Henry Allen as the composer. Red continued to work with Horace Henderson, and even used him on small band dates, but the incident slightly jaundiced their relationship.

On 'Liza', and on Fletcher Henderson's indifferent arrangement of 'Memphis Blues', the trumpet solos are by Irving Randolph (whose playing here clearly echoes certain Red Allen traits), but Red plays a full chorus on 'Hotter Than 'Ell'. This is not one of his best achievements, since he seems to be playing mainly for effect, splashing a series of dissonant phrases over the middle eight bars to no discernible purpose. Red's mind seems to be elsewhere and one can almost sense that he is gradually wearying of the Henderson Band's drifting prospects. One unusual aspect of this batch of 12 sides (recorded for Decca) is that there is not a single slow tune among the dozen. Other than the half-tempo introduction to 'Liza' nothing is slower than medium, and several of the pieces are markedly fast. It is as if the new recording company wanted to present Henderson's Orchestra as a hell-fire unit.

By now Red was being extensively featured by Fletcher Henderson, but he got no special billing in advertisements or on posters – the leader preferred to publicize his singers. Fletcher Henderson and Red got on well, and the leader never had cause to reprimand the trumpeter. This was not the case with J.C. Higginbotham, who was fired for unruly behaviour, having previously been fined $25 by Henderson for being drunk on the bandstand.[12] Henderson's decisive action was out of character. For years the bandleader was irked by Coleman Hawkins's unpunctuality, but, to the annoyance of some of his sidemen, he never expressed his vexation to Hawkins. J.C. Higginbotham looked back with some merriment at the dance that he and Hawkins led Fletcher Henderson: 'Nothing but plain fun. We didn't do nothing but have a ball. He'd say he wanted you there at 8 o'clock, you'd get there about 9.'[13] Red took no part in these shenanigans – he was always sober and on time. The nearest he ever got to wildness was on the rare occasions that he danced. Writer John Hammond evaluated Red's terpsichorean skills highly, and in 1934 wrote 'Henry Allen is one of the finest shim-sham dancers in existence'.[14]

Red told me that a destructive disappointment enveloped the Henderson Band when a proposed trip to the London Palladium was cancelled and the booking given to Cab Calloway's Band. Red heard a rumour on the musicians' grapevine that a compensatory fee was paid to Fletcher Henderson, none of which reached the musicians. Red found it difficult to criticize the various bandleaders he had worked for, but it was possible to sense that he, like other ex-Henderson sidemen, felt frustrated by Henderson's casual attitude to almost everything, and by his general lack of drive. Morale had begun to crumble when Coleman Hawkins abdicated his position as the band's premier soloist in March 1934 in order to work in England with Jack Hylton's Band. On Hawkins's recommendation Hylton cabled an offer to Red Allen also inviting him to join the band, but Red declined, feeling that the transatlantic upheaval would present too many difficulties for Pearly May and their three-year-old son, Henry. Henderson's Band carried on without Hawkins, first with a light-toned, highly individual tenor saxophonist who also answered to the nickname 'Red'. This was Lester Young (whose father Willis had played in the Allen Brass Band). Henderson and some of his band were disappointed that Young would not try to adjust his sound into something resembling Hawkins's huge booming tone, but the newcomer was intent on preserving his originality. Eventually, rather than change, Young left the band and was replaced by Ben Webster, a fervent disciple of Coleman Hawkins's style.

But Young had the last laugh. Within a few years he had established himself as the main rival to Coleman Hawkins, and eventually supplanted Hawk as a role model for young tenor saxists. One gets the feeling that it was not the innovative contours of Young's solos that upset the Henderson musicians; after all, they nurtured and enjoyed the proto-modernisms of Red Allen's playing. It was Young's sound they could not accept, because they felt it diminished the blend of rich tonal textures of the saxophone section when Coleman Hawkins was in the band. For all Red Allen's daring flights, his tone always matched well with his brass section colleagues. In England, Coleman Hawkins had not despaired of getting Red Allen to Europe and told the *Melody Maker*, 'I want to come back next year with some of the boys. You know, like Red Allen and Higgy.'[15]

Red's next move was engineered by the impresario and agent Irving Mills, who controlled a number of important black orchestras, including those led by Duke Ellington and Cab Calloway (Mills was also a music publisher and record company executive). One of his musical aggregations, the Mills Blue Rhythm Band, worked steadily throughout the 1930s, often deputizing for other, better-known, bands from Mills's 'stable', as well as doing extensive touring. Often the band was sent to far-flung engagements that had been declined by Ellington and Calloway, but by 1934 Irving Mills was planning a strategy that kept the Rhythm Band working mainly at various East Coast venues. This factor helped Red to make up his mind about joining the band. He did not fancy extensive touring that would separate him from his wife and child, who by then had moved into a first-floor apartment on St Nicholas Place (near 152nd Street) in Harlem's Sugar Hill section. But Irving Mills was not one to turn down lucrative offers, and before Red's first year was out the Mills Blue Rhythm Band did a gruelling tour of the South.

The standard of musicianship in the Mills Blue Rhythm Band was satisfactory, but Irving Mills felt that the unit needed some 'star' players in its line-up in order to catch the public's attention. Accordingly he persuaded Red Allen, J.C. Higginbotham, Buster Bailey and guitarist Lawrence Lucie to fortify the band. Lucie gave the background to the move:

Red Allen and I were offered more money to go with the Blue Rhythm Band. We were with Fletcher Henderson in Cleveland at the time and the future was pretty uncertain. We told Henderson how we enjoyed the band, but here was a chance to make some money.

Fletcher thought it was all right for us to go, so we left and went to the Cotton Club as members of the Mills Blue Rhythm Band.[16]

Although the Cotton Club was a leading centre of entertainment in New York City, and famed for its presentation of black artistes, it operated a firm 'whites only' admission policy. Black performers had to enter and leave by the back door, but musicians who had worked at the Roseland Ballroom (and many other segregated places of entertainment in New York) were used to the procedure.

When Red Allen joined the Mills Blue Rhythm Band in October 1934 Irving Mills suggested that he became leader. Red declined the offer and said later, 'The last thing I needed was to have all the worries that go with leading a big band. I just wanted to go on the gig and think about playing the trumpet.'[17] The band had originally been fronted by violinist Carroll Dickerson, then drummer Willie Lynch became leader before compère Jimmy Ferguson (who was billed as 'Baron Lee') took over the task. He in turn was replaced by an even more dynamic showman, Lucius 'Lucky' Millinder; though not a musician, Millinder was an adept conductor. Red Allen said that Millinder, despite never having learnt to read music, could conduct the most complex arrangement faultlessly after only two hearings.[18] Millinder's sunny personality pleased audiences and his musicians, and Red had nothing but happy memories of their association. But Red never forgot the initial air of tension that greeted the musicians who had been transplanted into an already established band; he later commented:

I guess the reaction was natural, we joined what had previously been a 'family band', full of guys who had worked together for a long time. Higginbotham, Buster and yours truly were sort of intruders, but the guys relaxed when Irving Mills spelt it out that the move was for the good of the band. We really got to know the guys when we worked a residency at the Cotton Club. We played there often. The resident band was either Duke Ellington or Cab Calloway, and we used to replace either when they were away. Throughout all this action I continued to make small band recordings under my own name, most were for the record company that Irving Mills ran, and I guess it is well known that his name found its way on to many records (by many bands) as a co-composer. A guy would record his own tune, then, when the record came out he'd look at the label and find out that he had a co-composer, maybe even two, who hadn't added or altered a single note, yet they took even shares. It was all part of the music business in that era. One day I happened to see Irving Mills when I was visiting his office, he passed me in a hurry and said 'Allen, I'm glad you're keeping up our standards' – that was just about the sum total of his collaboration! But I have to agree that it was Irving Mills who set up the recording deals, he was in control of that situation. He'd send me a letter confirming that a record date had been set and enclosed a list of possible tunes to be recorded. I'd read down the list and if I'd never heard of the tune I'd think 'That looks a nice title'. I'd let the office know which songs looked likely and they'd get the publishers to send the song copies. The material on offer was usually stuff that all the big-selling stars had rejected. Sometimes I'd already heard a tune on the radio that was on the list, and that was a big help in judging whether it was right for our recordings.[19]

Irving Mills, a short dapper man with a slightly combative look, had entered the music business as a singer and song-plugger, then, gradually, with his elder brother Jack he built up a successful agency. In the 1930s Irving was a force to be reckoned with, particularly because of his partnership with Duke Ellington. He was a tough man to deal with, but Red Allen was well aware that there were many more ruthless entrepreneurs in the New York entertainment world. John Hammond, who worked briefly for Irving Mills, summarized his achievements: 'He was a man who saved black talent in the 1930s when there was no one else who cared whether it worked or not'.[20]

Before his recordings for Mills, Red had, of course, been featured on his own New Yorker sides. He had also recorded as co-leader with Coleman Hawkins. Their first joint efforts were initially rejected and remained unissued for years, probably because of a poor recording balance that makes Red's muted chorus on 'Someday Sweetheart' difficult to hear; also Dicky Wells, on trombone, is out of tune. 'I Wish I Could Shimmy Like My Sister Kate' is admirably spirited, with Hawkins in robust and inventive form; however, in those days of 78 r.p.m. couplings, having only one good side to issue was like having one good shoe. Four subsequent sides made in July 1933 by the Allen-Hawkins line-up were eminently satisfactory, even though the session was made under duress, according to John Hammond, who wrote in the *Melody Maker*, 'The Brunswick moguls have recorded Hawkins and Allen for their cheap label, with dire results, since they insisted on the use of banjo and tuba.'[21] In hindsight, John Hammond seems to have been unduly harsh about this session, perhaps because he was intent on recording Hawk and Red for the British Parlophone label, so he was not likely to heap praise on this endeavour. In fact, the results are pleasing, being prototypes of a whole series of recordings that Red made under his own name from 1934 to 1937.

Red's vocal on 'The River's Taking Care of Me' is particularly interesting, it being very similar to the non-growl singing that Louis Armstrong had recently recorded (the effect becomes even more obvious when the track is slowed down). This was the first side recorded that day and it is as if Red, hearing the playback, realized that he sounded too much like an imitation of Armstrong. He does not repeat the tactic on subsequent recordings; instead he establishes his own vocal personality by projecting a soft, throaty crooning style, imbued with the same rhythmic sureness that graces his trumpet-work. The numbers are loosely arranged, with scored modulations and brief solos from the front-line (Dicky Wells being outstanding on 'Ain't Cha Got Music'). The arrangement of 'Shadows on the Swanee' is distinctly commercial – other than brief solos from Hawkins and Allen the whole thing is scored – nevertheless, Red's 8-bar vignette is perfect and shows how tenderly he could play when the occasion demanded. Red also demonstrates this aspect of his skills on the September 1933 recordings made under Coleman Hawkins's name. John Hammond's Parlophone plans had achieved fruition, but as Hawkins was better known in Europe than Red Allen, it was Hawk who became leader of the octet. Everyone is in top form throughout and Hawkins performs one of his most ravishing recorded solos on 'The Day You Came Along'. Here Red again shows how skilfully he could glide up to the first note of a solo. By using a superb lip control and a remarkable rhythmic balance his glissando reaches the beginning of the phrase at the most effective split second possible.

A follow-up session by the Allen-Hawkins Orchestra had a change in personnel that introduced the spiky but appealing clarinet sounds of Edward Inge and the smooth-toned playing of trombonist Benny Morton. All four sides, 'Hush My Mouth', 'You're Gonna Lose Your Gal', 'Dark Clouds' and 'My Galveston Gal' have vocals by Red that range in mood from brooding intensity to the lighthearted. Red plays an admirably poised cadenza on 'Dark Clouds', and Hawkins gives his usual magnificent performance, but here the recording balance is genuinely disappointing with Bernard Addison's guitar-playing blocking out the sound created by his colleagues in the rhythm section.

Roles were reversed when Benny Morton used Red as a sideman for his own recordings in February 1934. The rest of the band comprised musicians with whom Morton worked in Don Redman's Band, including bold Edward Inge, whose clarinet phrasing here sounds as though it were modelled on Red Allen's methods. Red is allocated the bulk of the solos, and sounds extremely relaxed throughout the session, effortlessly delivering complicated ideas on 'Get Goin'', 'Fare Thee Well to Harlem' and 'Taylor Made'. The bonus on 'The Gold Digger's Song' is Red's jubilant vocal – years later in recalling his financial circumstances at the time of the recording he said that the line 'We're in the money' was the most inappropriate lyric he ever sang. Despite this Red sings cheerfully and follows up by creating a clarion-like modulation that heralds a final chorus full of powerful, inspired trumpet-playing.

When Red began his 1934–7 series of sessions for the American Record Company, Irving Mills pointed out that they were to be aimed at the general public (rather than at jazz fans), but Red's innate, irrepressible jazz sense imbued the straightest of songs with a satisfying glow and turned ordinary pop compositions into evergreen musical treasures. There were no royalties for Red from these sessions; no matter how many records were sold he still only received a basic fee of $100 per session. Red sang on most of the sides, his vocals enriching some songs with an appropriate warm romanticism, delivering others with a rhythmic sureness that was attractive and infectious. In January 1935, at the suggestion of a-and-r man Harry Gray, the white trumpeter Pee Wee Erwin was added to the session that produced 'Believe It, Beloved' (two versions) and 'It's Written All Over Your Face'. Erwin's task on these tracks was to play the melody in the manner of Paul Whiteman's star trumpeter, Henry Busse. Erwin, on the threshold of an illustrious career, dutifully turned up at the Brunswick Studios and performed his task convincingly, delighted to be playing alongside someone he described as 'my favourite trumpet player'.[22] The two trumpeters became good friends and years later Erwin said, 'He was one of the easiest people to get along with that I've ever met'.[23]

Throughout the series Red's trumpet-playing covers the whole gamut of jazz expressiveness, creating many examples of superb small-band jazz. None of the 72 sides are less than good and many are superfine. Despite the various changes of personnel that took place over the three-year period, the recordings present an impressive level of consistency and feeling. Every fan of Red's playing and singing has their own particular favourites, and no-one can deny the magnificence of 'Rosetta', 'Body and

Soul', 'It's Written All Over Your Face', 'There's a House in Harlem for Sale', 'Every Minute of the Hour', 'Algiers Stomp' and 'Can I Forget You?' Some of these tunes found a permanent place in Red's repertoire, but others were only ever performed by Red on the day he recorded them. The same situation applied to many of Billie Holiday's most esteemed recorded performances, but neither Red nor Billie had any idea that their recordings from the 1930s would be treasured over 60 years later.

The period 1935 to 1938 marked a plateau in Red's stylistic development, and one cannot play the sides he made with his own small bands during this period and detect any episodic developments in his playing. He said that he had no great plan to develop a revolutionary trumpet style and he lived up to this creed. If the harmonic or melodic twists of a particular piece stimulated his imagination then a startling new idea would burst out, but the playing can easily be recognized as being by the same musician whose daring ideas enriched the Luis Russell sides. Technically he continued to blossom throughout this whole series of recordings, playing with greater facility in the upper register and fingering difficult runs with increased speed. There is an uneasy period in 1936 when his intonation (never his strongest point) creates some slightly out-of-tune ending notes, but they are not disfiguring.

The music on the early titles in this series is not greatly elevated by the trombone solos of Keg Johnson and George Washington. Neither is in the same class as Higginbotham, who is featured on five sessions in the 1935–6 period including 'Roll Along Prairie Moon' (which contains some of his finest playing). The seeds of the tavern-style jazz that Red and Higgy featured in the 1940s make their first appearance on this title, with Red shouting encouragement as a responsive Higginbotham blows a tempestuous solo. The trombone was soon dispensed with on the recordings, at the behest of the 'front office' who wanted the discs to feature smoother ensemble sounds. Accordingly Red used a trio of reed players but unfortunately the feeble quality of the arranging does not allow the three saxophones to produce a robust, attractive sound. The charm of Red's singing adds to the appeal of most of the recordings but his voice takes on a slightly uncomfortable edge as he tackles songs as poor as 'Darling Not Without You' and 'Lost in My Dreams'. The format adopted usually allowed Red (on trumpet) to skilfully re-interpret the first chorus of the melody, often enhancing the composer's original lines. His laid-back timing on 'You' and 'I Found a Dream' are perfect examples of a great jazz melodist at work. But Red's daring spirit is never far away and surfaces during his unaccompanied introduction to

'On Treasure Island' – trumpeter Cootie Williams was so impressed by this burst of brilliance that he made it the basis for his introduction to 'Chasin' Chippies' recorded three years later.

The most important endeavour for Red throughout most of the period covered by these recordings was in earning a living with the Mills Blue Rhythm Band. Despite the injection of top-class musicians, the band was never able to command the fees or the public acclaim enjoyed by orchestras led by Duke Ellington, Cab Calloway and Chick Webb, and even the earnings of these successful units were dwarfed by the incomes of the leading white bands. The problem was that the band never gained its own identity – it continued to deputize for Ellington and Calloway, but never built up its own following, and consequently there were gaps in their list of bookings. Red compensated by playing on as many freelance recordings as possible.

In December 1934 Red's sidekick, Buster Bailey, led his own 8-piece recording band and naturally invited Red to be part of it. The presence of these two plus J.C. Higginbotham and Benny Carter meant the octet had a front-line comprising ex-Fletcher Henderson sidemen, and this link was strengthened by the fact that Henderson did the arrangements for the two tunes recorded, 'Call of the Delta' and 'Shanghai Shuffle'. Bailey creates an evocative mood as he wistfully renders the melody of 'Call of the Delta', but Red, relaxed and inventive, is the star. The general pattern of Red's solos on the two issued takes is similar, but a succession of variations show that he was improvising throughout. One take has a middle register turnaround phrase (in the 7th and 8th bars) that is positively ingenious, but even masterful ideas were 'easy-come-easy-go' for Red and he discards the pattern on the next take and follows a totally different plan, this time using a forceful high-note fill-in. He is not as illustrious on 'Shanghai Shuffle', where he tends to rely on stock phrases, perhaps because his inspiration had been blunted by having to play this number hundreds of times with the full Fletcher Henderson Band.

In the late summer of 1935, during a Mills Blue Rhythm Band 'rest' period, Red and Buster Bailey accepted an offer from the white musician, Adrian Rollini, to play at a club he had opened in the basement of the President Hotel in Manhattan. This cellar venue was called Adrian's Tap Room, and although Rollini occasionally played a number or two on the vibraphone (or on bass saxophone) he was there principally to act as 'mine host'. Red and Buster were part of a quartet, along with Pops Foster on string bass and Bernard Addison on guitar – for Red and Buster the booking only lasted for one night. By 1935 Red Allen was a well-known figure to New York jazz aficionados and writers, several of whom visited the club for the quartet's opening. Critic Leonard Feather was part of a group that included musician Red Norvo, his then-wife, singer Mildred Bailey and writers Marshall Stearns, John Hammond and Felix King. Feather had good reason to recall the occasion: 'The evening at the Tap Room ended abruptly when Rollini objected to Red Allen sitting with the customers. Allen and Bailey immediately quit the job and the rest of us walked out in anger and sorrow.'[24] Red was sure that the reprimand was racially motivated, and in this he was supported by Buster Bailey. They both resolved never to return to the club and sent substitutes (Freddie Jenkins on trumpet and Cecil Scott on clarinet) to play the remainder of the booking.

Red did not allow the incident to embitter him and during another period of Mills Blue Rhythm Band inactivity (in July 1936) he played at the Hickory House (144 West 52nd Street) in a quintet alongside four white musicians: Eddie Condon on guitar, Mort Stuhlmaker on string bass, Joe Bushkin on piano and the group's leader, Joe Marsala, on clarinet. Mixed bands featuring white and black players had occasionally recorded together since the 1920s, but despite pioneering efforts by Benny Goodman, Charlie Barnet (and others) in ballrooms and hotels, the blending was still a rarity on the club scene, even in New York City. Joe Marsala recalled, 'We didn't ask the bosses. We just brought Red in.'[25] Happily there were no unpleasant incidents at the Hickory House; when Red was unavailable his deputy was another black trumpeter, Otis Johnson. The group might have stayed together longer but Condon and Marsala had already accepted work aboard a cruise liner and Red had to return to the Mills Blue Rhythm Band.

Red's international reputation was regularly being boosted by the critics. In the September 1936 issue of the British magazine *Rhythm*, the American writer George T. Simon described Red as 'the most brilliant and least inhibited of all the coloured trumpeters. He possesses his own distinctive knock-out attack, which is just as brilliant as it was ten years ago. A very easy-going chap, tall and lanky.' Red's talents were also being lauded in his homeland. In the July 1936 issue of *Down Beat*, John Hammond commented on the trumpeter's work with Condon and Marsala, 'Red is a bit inclined to rhapsodize, but his attack and warmth more than makes up for any excesses'. On another occasion Hammond said of Allen, 'He had this wonderful kind of self-assurance'.[26] This poise was never more obvious than in November 1936 when Red guested on the popular radio show *Saturday Night Swing Club*. At the behest of

Bunny Berigan, who led the house band, Red brought along to the studio a contingent from the Mills Blue Rhythm Band to play a few numbers including a magnificent version of 'Body and Soul'. The main structure of Red's trumpet and vocal work is based on his April 1935 recording, but here his phrasing is more majestic and more relaxed than on the original version.

During his tenure with the Mills Blue Rhythm Band, Red began a series of recordings with Putney Dandridge (several of the sides included Joe Marsala and Eddie Condon). Dandridge played piano enthusiastically, but on most of his recordings the keyboard duties were entrusted to players who were more adept (artists such as Teddy Wilson, Jimmy Sherman and Clyde Hart). Fats Waller's considerable success on recordings had stimulated every record company to try and tap this market by having cheerful vocalists irreverently performing popular songs of the day (accompanied by a small jazz group consisting of trumpet, reeds and rhythm, but no trombone). Some engaging music was put on to wax by Putney Dandridge and others (notably Bob Howard) but the vocal charm of these performers was not durable and as time has passed it is the work of the accompanying musicians that provides lasting pleasure. Red took part in four sessions with Dandridge, whose voice has a good, lively quality. The object of the exercise was to make recordings for people who liked to hear the latest songs, brightly presented. The strategy worked well on 'I'm in the Mood for Love', where Red gently presents the melody, shading the composer's creation with subtle variations, but on 'Isn't It a Lovely Day' Red blows an exploratory introduction that is full of eerie blue notes. It makes wonderful jazz, but the phrases must have bewildered those who had bought the record to sing along with. Red, as ever, was the irrepressible artist who played as the mood took him.

Red's ingenious solo on Dandridge's version of 'Shine' is shaped quite differently from Louis Armstrong's epic 1931 recording, but in bars 5 and 6, with what can only be described as a musical wink, Red inserts a brief quote from Armstrong's version; Teddy Wilson's piano solo on this track is also superb. The quality of the compositions recorded by Dandridge was variable, but Red manages to cloak each piece with artistry, even 'Mary Had a Little Lamb', one of the silliest ditties to emerge from an era when fatuous novelty songs abounded; anyone doubting Eddie Condon's effectiveness as a guitarist should listen to this track. On 'A High Hat, a Piccolo and a Cane', Red shows how skilfully he could bend notes, and on 'Here Comes Your Pappy' he stays in the middle register, punching out 'jump' phrases that create a prodigious swing, well supported by Wilson Myers's powerful string-bass playing. On the slow 'If We Never Meet Again', Dandridge drops his usual falsetto and sings a low-register ballad; the effect is not unpleasant, but the singer's wide vibrato prevents it being totally satisfactory. Here Red's solo is distinctly futuristic: his low-register double-timed embellishments suddenly spiral upwards, his phrasing hovers over the metre before swooping down to re-establish the beat. It is a reappearance of the approach he used on the 1931 'Trouble Why Pick on Me?', one that he was later to develop to great effect. Most of Dandridge's recordings make pleasant listening, but one has to forgive him for his occasional, ludicrous attempts at English and Irish accents; there is consolation in Joe Marsala's work on clarinet and alto saxophone and, of course, in Red Allen's playing. Red is not at his very best, but his performances show that his musical imagination was always active, whatever the circumstances.

Early in 1937, as part of Teddy Wilson's Orchestra, Red did his only 78 r.p.m. recording session with Billie Holiday. He plays poignantly on 'My Last Affair', making effective use of smooth glissandi. Though not heavily featured, he is effectively emotive on 'Sentimental and Melancholy' and spectacularly bold on 'You Showed Me the Way' and 'The Mood That I'm in'. Red and Billie enjoyed an affable relationship that was never particularly close; he enjoyed her singing, and her company, but was appalled by her unpunctuality. Red had worked with Billie's father, guitarist Clarence Holiday, in Fletcher Henderson's Band. The small number of recordings shared with Billie may have had something to do with Teddy Wilson (then a sort of unofficial musical director for Billie). Wilson, one of the finest of all jazz pianists, was generally predisposed towards musicians who displayed an urbane style (as he himself did) and I once heard him describe Red, and Dicky Wells, as 'untidy players'.

7

THE GREAT UNDERSTUDY

Although Red Allen was regarded as the star of the Mills Blue Rhythm Band he fared no better in the band's press and poster advertising than he had done during his stay with Fletcher Henderson's Orchestra. Usually the only people mentioned, apart from Lucky Millinder, were pianist Edgar Hayes (who went on to lead his own big band) and vocalist Chuck Richards. The situation did not change throughout the two and a half years (October 1934 to February 1937) that Red spent in the band. Buster Bailey, Red's close friend, left in October 1935 to return to Fletcher Henderson. J.C. Higginbotham remained with the band until 1936, then he too made his way back to Fletcher Henderson. Red could have made the same return move, but he was happy to remain where he was, playing in affable surroundings for a hundred dollars a week. He did not care about not being featured in the publicity. The main problem was that the wages were based on a 'no play, no pay' structure, so a gap in bookings resulted in no income.

The audiences liked Lucky Millinder's bravado, but he never attracted the instant acclaim of Cab Calloway. Unfortunately the band never got any nearer to establishing its own identity. One moment it sounded like a copy of Fletcher Henderson's band, and next it produced a pastiche of Duke Ellington's style before moving through a series of imitations including one of a big commercial white dance band (with Edgar Hayes playing an Eddie Duchin-like role at the keyboard). Many of the arrangements were well written, but few of the band's recordings achieved big sales figures, though the coupling of 'Ride, Red, Ride' (a feature for Allen) and 'Congo Caravan' came closest to being a hit. The story might have been different had more been made of Red Allen's musical abilities, but he was not one to push himself forward. He rarely

90

complained and summed up his attitude by saying later, 'I was satisfied to be where I was'.[1]

Red was featured on the very first number he recorded with the band, 'Swinging in E flat'. Here he takes a flamboyant solo that includes brief excursions up above top C. Red's range, though ample, was never exceptional; he said, simply, 'I get whatever I go for'. His venturing into the top register may have been a case of showing his new colleagues what he could do. However the prominence accorded him on Mills Blue Rhythm Band recordings was not permanent, and on several subsequent dates his solo outings were restricted to eight bars ('Solitude', 'Let's Have a Jubilee', 'Like a Bolt from the Blue'). Sometimes his allocation was increased to 16-bar segments, as in 'Back Beats', 'Spitfire' and 'A Rainbow Filled with Music' – which was recorded under singer Chuck Richards's name). Higginbotham was even more poorly served, and Buster Bailey had to wait a long time before he was accorded a solo, on 'Dancing Dogs'. Several of the band, including Red Allen, were seen on screen in the short film *Symphony in Black* (made in New York in March 1935). They were not heard on the soundtrack but were 'on camera' to augment Duke Ellington's Orchestra.

Red's big feature with the band was a spectacular workout (on the harmonies of 'Tiger Rag') entitled 'Ride, Red, Ride', which seesawed between a very fast tempo and a gentle lope. It was composed by Lucky Millinder and (in absentia) Irving Mills; guitarist Lawrence Lucie originally transcribed it for the band. Millinder himself took the engaging vocal, but it is Red's trumpet-playing that is so memorable, utilizing, with great potency, the various changes in tempo. He begins by punching out an incisive muted solo, then, dispensing with the mute, he roars into two choruses of tumultuous, open trumpet-playing. His fierce blowing climaxes with a grandstand finish that is fuelled by Millinder's encouraging shouts: step by step, Red climbs to a thrilling final high note. Long after Red had left the band Lucky Millinder continued to receive requests for this number, and effected a satisfactory compromise by featuring an arrangement (by trombonist George Washington) in which the whole trumpet section played Red's original solo in harmony – an early use of this arranging device. Red spoke about the initial recording of 'Ride, Red, Ride':

In those days one always recorded in even numbers. Never three or five titles, always in evens, for two sides of the record. Well, we recorded 'Ride, Red, Ride', but when they played it back we got a 'no' on it. So Lucky recorded three numbers only that day, so that we should have to come back again to fill in the odd side. But to save expense they decided to use 'Ride, Red, Ride' after all, so as not to have to bring us back for another date. As it happened it became a big seller.[2]

After 'Ride, Red, Ride' the band recorded 'Harlem Heat', on which Red moves down a gear to create a 16-bar burst of skilful nonchalance. Buster Bailey is at his most twittering here, but the final choruses (built on the last strain of 'Weary Blues') achieve a rare feeling of spirited abandon in the band. 'Congo Caravan', with atmospheric tom-tom effects, and a Red Allen solo that doodles through some whole-tone scales, never gets to its destination, but the next piece recorded, 'There's Rhythm in Harlem', brought composer Joe Garland a fortune when it was revamped by Glenn Miller and issued as 'In the Mood'. The medium-fast 'Tallahassee' ended the session and allowed Red to create a brilliant 8-bar vignette, blowing a pert descending figure, then shaping a clever variation in a higher register – a case of artistry thriving under cramped conditions.

On the next session Red was featured as a vocalist on 'Truckin'', the only time he sang with the band on record. The opening chorus is cleverly scored but things sag a bit during Edgar Hayes's rhapsodic interlude. Red sings well enough here, but nothing like as pleasingly as he does on sides he made under his own name. His trumpet solo is good and lively, and Higgy sounds bright in his eight bars; Lucky Millinder's voice provides the spoken coda. The band's regular singer, Chuck Richards, gives his usual smooth and skilful performance on 'Dinah Lou', then Red's positive phrasing effects a startling modulation which leads into a half chorus in which he stresses the melody, without sounding quite in tune. Red seems happy and relaxed on 'Cotton' (another Richards vocal) but the most vigorous contribution to this piece comes from Joe Garland, here playing tenor saxophone.

The band's next effort, 'E flat Stride', was rejected by the recording company but surfaced years later. The original decision is easily understood: the composition is dissonant and unmemorable. Red takes a medium-register solo that is not among his more enterprising efforts, but the track allows us to appreciate the power and energy of Elmer James's string bass playing. On 'Yes, Yes' Lucky Millinder sings about the saga of Jivin' Sam, and is answered by the band's vocal responses. Edgar Hayes, who arranged many of the band's numbers, sounds unusually trenchant at the keyboard, but, despite the merits of the performance, the piece, like so many of the band's other offerings, only merited one 78 r.p.m. issue. 'Shoe Shine Boy' (a hit song of the day) is charmingly sung by Chuck Richards; Red blows emotively for 16 bars and caps his efforts with a powerful ending. Higginbotham gets a chance to shine on an uneventful arrangement of 'Midnight Ramble'. His unaccompanied introduction promises much, but although his tone sounds satisfyingly robust, the zip seems to have temporarily gone out of his solo playing. Red again creates an exhilarating miniature in his 8-bar solo.

Almost six months passed before the Mills Blue Rhythm Band re-entered the recording studio, to create a follow-up to 'Ride, Red, Ride'. Red Allen composed a fast riff number entitled 'Red Rhythm'. Higgy takes a whole chorus, then Lucky Millinder introduces Red Allen by shouting 'Here comes old Red riding on Red Rhythm'. The alliteration launches a fine solo from Red which flows easily into an ingeniously scored final chorus, but the infectious rapport that enriched 'Ride, Red, Ride' is missing. The bonus of the track is that it allows us to marvel at the superlative brush work from drummer O'Neill Spencer. Buddy Rich (and others) cited Spencer as one of the finest ever exponents of brush playing, and listening to 'Red Rhythm' one can understand why. 'Jes' Natch'ully Lazy' is mainly notable for the playing of the band's new alto saxophonist Talmadge 'Tab' Smith, whose technique and flowing phrases definitely strengthened the band. Smith was part-composer of 'St Louis Wiggle Rhythm', a fast number on which Red demonstrates that his fingers were as nimble as ever during a crisply played first chorus.

Red had little to do, solowise, on the band's next visit to the recording studio. The growling work on a version of Duke Ellington's 'Merry-Go-Round' is entrusted to a colleague in the trumpet section. Red solos briefly on 'Until the Real Thing Comes Along', and not at all on 'In a Sentimental Mood', but he acquits himself well in playing the muted melody of 'Carry Me Back to Green Pastures' (a quasi-spiritual written by Harry S. Pepper). An upheaval in the band's personnel brought in the superior pianist Billy Kyle and a new bassist, John Kirby. By then the band policy was beginning to change, as it veered to meet the demands of the Swing Era audiences. 'Balloonacy', a typical riff number of the period, reflects the development, but Red seems undeterred and constructs an engaging middle-register 32-bar chorus. His work on 'Barrel House' is less satisfying; here his cup-muted solo sounds overfull of his own stock phrases. The highlight of the track is Joe Garland's vigorous stop-time bass saxophone solo. Higgy marks time in his half chorus, but Tab Smith gracefully puts together a series of fine ideas in a smoothly presented solo. The oddity about this composition is that it utilizes the same melody as 'Jive at Five' (recorded by Count Basie over two years later, in February 1939), even the middle section is identical. 'Barrel House' is credited to Tab Smith, but Harry Edison is listed as the composer of 'Jive at Five'. Smith and Edison had worked together in Eddie Johnson's Crackerjacks during the early 1930s.

Red was not featured on Fletcher Henderson's composition 'Big John's Special' (perhaps because he had soloed on Henderson's own recording). The simple, repetitive melody of 'Mr Ghost Goes to Town' exemplifies the band's 'switch to Swing'; Lawrence Lucie plays one of his rare Mills Blue Rhythm Band solos. Red's chorus begins in a whisper and he increases the volume subtly, then cleverly enhances the contours of the solo by dropping down to the trumpet's lowest notes, emphasizing both his use of dynamics and his sense of musical form. His solo on 'Callin' Your Bluff' is perhaps a little too orderly; it again covers 32 bars, but gives the indication that Red is playing well within himself. There is a flare-up during the final bars of his solo but the overall feel, unusual in Red's work, is of pre-planned symmetry. Red's final recording with the Mills Blue Rhythm Band was his own composition, 'Algiers Stomp', another salute to his home town. The theme itself (plunger-muted trumpet instigating a call-and-answer routine with the saxophone section) is simple, with uncomplicated harmonies. Red's farewell is, by his standards, an ordinary solo, bedecked with blue notes that sound as though they were included as some sort of obligation. While he did not consciously shirk his musical duties on this session, he gives an indication that he was tiring of this particular musical environment.

It seems that every musician who worked with Lucky Millinder became restless after a year or two, usually with the realization that the band would never reach the top bracket, either in performances or in earnings. Red Allen used to joke about how Millinder went about replacing a departing trumpeter: the leader would make a list of every possible candidate and attach it to the back of a door, and would then aim a dart at the roster. The person whose name was spiked was asked to join the band. Red decided to move on. He parted on good terms with Millinder, showing no signs of being disgruntled. This was typical of the man. Lawrence Lucie, his long-time colleague in the band, said, 'I can't ever recall seeing him get angry'.[3] Red seriously considered an offer to become part of the big band led by white saxophonist Charlie Barnet, along with the black Washington drummer Tommy Myles. But even though *Down Beat* magazine announced that both men were due to join Barnet, the move never took place. According to Red's friend, guitarist Danny Barker, in previous years two white big bands, one led by Isham Jones and the other the Casa Loma Band, had both considered signing Red as a permanent guest star, but the racial climate of the early 1930s wasn't ready for such an epoch-making move. Earlier, in 1930, trumpeter Bubber Miley had left Duke Ellington and was briefly featured with a white orchestra led by Leo Reisman in New York, but Miley suffered the indignity of being made to play behind a screen.

Word of Red's availability soon reached the powerful agent, Joe Glaser, who immediately invited him to join Louis Armstrong's Orchestra (which was in effect Luis Russell's Band fronted by Louis Armstrong). Glaser was probably well aware of a recent report in the *New York Age* that placed Red Allen second only to Louis Armstrong among jazz trumpeters.[4] Armstrong, having returned to the USA after a long sojourn in Europe, began touring with a rather hit-and-miss band formed in Chicago. Results were variable and the presentation was not helped by the fact that Louis was suffering from a painfully overworked lip. In the late summer of 1935, after some unspectacular touring, Louis was persuaded by Joe Glaser to change his accompanying unit.

Louis had first met Glaser in Chicago during the mid-1920s. At that time Glaser was one of the forces behind the Sunset Café, where Louis worked. Glaser's family owned a good deal of valuable property in Chicago, and it was long rumoured that Joe himself had direct connections with Al Capone and other noted gangsters. Glaser had various brushes with the law, but somehow sidestepped charges of counterfeiting postage stamps and assault. Armstrong was aware of this but agreed to the suggestion that Glaser become his agent and manager. Joseph C. Glaser was an enigmatic character and a ruthless negotiator who was regarded with abhorrence by those who saw his relationship with Armstrong as styled on that of a master and his bondservant. However, I have read various letters that Armstrong wrote to Glaser over the years and there is no trace of subservience there. The Glaser-Armstrong association continued until the agent predeceased Louis in 1969. As if to underline the equitable nature of their partnership, Glaser, in his will, left a fortune to Armstrong in the shape of vast shareholdings.

In 1935, at Louis's instigation, Glaser asked Luis Russell to provide the personnel for a permanent backing band for Armstrong. This move allowed Armstrong to establish what proved to be a lifelong trait of leaving all the musical organization of his bands to a 'straw boss', a position that Luis Russell gladly accepted. He became the musical director for Armstrong, but the power behind the throne was Joe Glaser. Trombonist Jimmy Archey, a long-time member of Luis Russell's Band, observed the changeover at first hand: 'Joe Glaser did everything. He did the hiring, the firing, the booking and he was Louis's personal manager. Louis just played the horn.'[5]

In signing Red Allen (in March 1937) Joe Glaser had no plans to feature Louis and Red in a series of trumpet battles, either on stage or in the recording studio. He was shrewd enough to know that if Louis continued to spend hours each night blowing powerful high notes he might well inflict permanent damage on his lips. Audiences were bitterly disappointed when Armstrong was forced to curtail his blowing schedule, and to forestall any further problems Glaser decided to import a stand-in that he (and many of the world's jazz critics) thought was the next best thing to Louis Armstrong, namely Henry 'Red' Allen. Red's entry into the fold immediately lightened Louis's work load.

Glaser's strategy in signing Red was very canny. Firstly he had someone on hand who could play magnificently should Louis ever be temporarily incapacitated; secondly, Red's talents allowed him to play trumpet features that kept up the crowd's interest before Louis came on stage; thirdly, Glaser was able to control the destiny of someone who was increasingly being described as Armstrong's nearest rival. Later, Joe Glaser, in his capacity as an agent, pursued this last policy further by signing up two other great jazz trumpeters, Roy Eldridge and Hot Lips Page. Red was not duped by false promises; he knew that he would not be featured on record with Louis Armstrong's Orchestra, but he was assured (correctly as it transpired) that he could play feature numbers before Louis made his appearance and was even given the go-ahead to use special arrangements that showcased his trumpet talents. When asked about the lack of solo space on recordings, Red replied, 'It was no fault of Louis's, and I played plenty on the stand'.[6] Though it was not part of the deal, Red's name was often given special billing on posters and in advertisements. In one publicity handout Red is actually described as 'Louis Armstrong's understudy'.[7] Everyone in the band was always on first-name terms, which was slightly confusing to outsiders since all the New Orleans men in the line-up pronounced both Luis and Louis as Lewis. Years later, when Red talked about the two men he always added the relevant surname: Lewis Russell or Lewis Armstrong, just to make things clear. It might have given the impression that a formality existed within the band, when, in truth, it certainly did not.

The Great Understudy

Familiarity breeds contempt among jazz musicians. A player can be hailed by critics as an improvising genius, but those who work with him regularly know that most of the elaborate phrases are laboriously conceived in practice sessions. However, in Louis Armstrong's case it was quite different. His biggest admirers were those who worked alongside him for years. Charlie Holmes was typical:

Whatever the arrangement Louis Armstrong just came out and played it. He was a great one. We were blowing on a broadcast and somebody walked by and requested a number, and Louis turned to the band and was gonna start straight into it. Well, you just don't do that on a broadcast. He didn't care. He loved to blow. He's the greatest. He didn't bother with business. He didn't know where he was playing the next night – he didn't care![8]

Albert Nicholas added his praises:

On one of the numbers the trumpets ended on a G in unison. Now those guys could all blow, all loud, and they hit that note and Louis would come and hit that note, but an octave above them, and Louis would hit that note as big as a house every performance, afterwards 'Scad' Hemphill (who played trumpet in the section) would say, 'Goddam, how does he do it?'[9]

Red, who rarely spoke about his stay in Louis's band, opened up on one occasion:

It was a happy feeling. I don't care whose band it was, I'd have been happy about it if Louis was there, because I enjoy being in his company so much, on and off the bandstand.[10]

Despite Louis's enormous reputation as a trumpeter and singer, his big band never built up a huge following, and though the band earned good money when it worked, it too had a 'no play, no pay' deal, which meant the musicians had some lean spells when bookings were scarce or when Armstrong was away filming or doing radio shows as a soloist. Red summarized the situation: 'At times things got a little rough, you see we had no big-selling records and that meant a lot in the Swing Era. My landlord used to look in *Down Beat* magazine and when he saw that Louis's band was listed simply as being "on tour" he knew that we weren't working so he'd come straight around for the rent.'[11]

It was as difficult to get Louis Armstrong talking about Red Allen as it was to get Red discussing Louis. They shared a friendly and respectful relationship but any lack of cherished closeness was probably caused more by the two men's disparate upbringings than by any musical rivalry. Most of Red's comments about Louis had a set-piece sound: 'He always featured me with his big band, I've got no complaints', 'Louis is great', 'We New Orleans boys must stick together', 'Louis and I paid a lot of our dues together', etc. Even in relaxed after-hours conversations Red rarely went any further. This was a great pity, because Red, having worked alongside Louis for so long, could have given the jazz world a unique insight into Armstrong's genius. A case of the main contender talking about the champion, or as Robert Goffin wrote, 'The Prince of Algiers speaking of the King of New Orleans'. For his part, Louis, often very expansive about musicians he had worked with, was equally reticent to talk about Red, though I did see him smile when he described how diligently Red had handled the task of looking after the band's spending-money kitty:

Anyone who needed a loan when we were on tour had to go to Red. Trouble was he was a hard man to get the better of, because he was always sober and had such a good memory. A guy would borrow money when he was drunk and he'd soon forget that he'd borrowed it, but Red, who always kept a clear head, soon put him right.[12]

But there is no doubt that the New Orleans bonding played its part in Red and Louis's relationship. This was borne out in a November 1937 letter that Louis (then in Los Angeles) wrote to the Waifs' Home teacher, Captain Joseph Jones, in New Orleans:

I am sure you've heard of some of these boys that's from the almighty New Orleans. First I will start out by calling Henry Allen Jr. He's the featured trumpet man in my band and he can really blow that thing in fine fashion. Red Allen as we calls him is from Algiers, Louisiana. His daddy is the brass band leader from there, who used to play for the Oddfellows and the Goblins' Parade, remember?

The Great Understudy

The only anecdote that I ever heard Red tell about his years with Louis concerned an incident that occurred in Beaver Dam, Wisconsin, when the band were on tour. The band bus stopped at a roadside diner. No sooner had the musicians alighted than they were approached by a tall, well-built middle-aged white man who strode up to Red and said, 'Okay, where are the boxers?' Red asked apprehensively what the man meant. The stranger pointed to the Louis Armstrong lettering on the side of the bus and said, 'I'm a fan of the fight game and I see you're advertising Joe Louis and Henry Armstrong. I want to meet them.' Red, sensing trouble, tried to placate the man, 'No, I'm sorry but you've got that wrong. We're a travelling band, the leader is Louis Armstrong.' 'Do you mean I'm not going to get a chance to shake hands with the boxers?' the man said angrily. Red nodded, and the man said, 'So what might your name be?' Red told him quietly but firmly as the rest of the band moved closer to support their colleague. 'Oh, I see, Henry Allen,' said the stranger, 'I guess that must be Henry "Red" Allen.' Red looked at the man in astonishment. 'I've heard of you, and come to think of it I've also heard of Louis Armstrong.' With that the man rattled off the titles of dozens of records that Louis and Red had made. The entire band listened in utter disbelief. The stranger then burst into hearty laughter and said, 'Hello, Red. I'm Bunny Berigan's father.' Louis and the rest of the band all shook hands with William 'Cap' Berigan and everyone joined in the near hysterical laughter.[13] Not long after this event Louis's and Red's names were linked with that of Bunny Berigan – the three of them were chosen by Harry James as being his three favourite trumpet players.[14]

Red accepted his role as Louis's stand-in with equanimity. On the forty or so titles that Red recorded as a member of Louis Armstrong's Orchestra (covering the period from March 1937 to September 1940) he is not granted an improvised solo. One can occasionally hear Red's singing voice in the band's vocal answers but his trumpet-playing is never highlighted due to the managerial decision by Joe Glaser. Pops Foster in his autobiography suggested that Louis was jealous of anyone attracting the limelight and this played a part in his dealings with Red Allen. Foster made this comment at a time when his feelings toward Louis had soured. Foster did not like the fact that Louis had, on more than one occasion, sternly contradicted Foster's account of early musical life in New Orleans. Although Louis often used the expression 'Pops', sometimes to complete strangers, in later years he pointedly called Foster by his first name, George, and not by the familiar nickname. This may seem a very small point but it was one that irked Pops. Red felt no grudge whatsoever towards Louis. Long after Red died, his widow Pearly May talked to Richard Sudhalter about her late husband and said, 'He idolized Louis.'[15]

Louis Armstrong's Orchestra continued to have some lean spells in the late 1930s, and because the band was not popular enough to pick and choose its engagements the working itinerary sometimes involved travelling awesome distances. Drummer Paul Barbarin gave details of one trek: 'We left New York and went to Old Orchard, Maine, from there we went down to Miami, Florida to play a dance then back again to Old Orchard, Maine'.[16] To keep the band working Glaser sent them out on a long succession of one-night stands, and Pearly May and her young son saw little of Red for weeks on end. Henry III recalled, 'The thing I remember most was he was always gone or going. When he played with Louis I remember the buses pulling up in front of the house and all the musicians going out to get on it and going on tour.'[17] Louis Armstrong could probably have done much better financially by working as a solo artiste, but he was determined to keep the orchestra going. Occasionally when he took leave to appear in a Hollywood movie the band went out as Luis Russell's Orchestra, but Joe Glaser had difficulty in selling a name that the public had virtually forgotten. But even in difficult times Louis's sidemen were better off than the ex-bandleader King Oliver, for whom several of them had worked in earlier days. Oliver's plight was brought home to Armstrong's musicians when they played a gig in Savannah, Georgia, and found the former star selling fruit from a stall in the market. They invited him to their venue that night, and he duly appeared, wearing what they took to be his only suit. Louis started off a collection for him and all the musicians contributed towards it; but Oliver was in poor health and died less than a year later.

After returning to New York, Louis Armstrong and his musicians enjoyed a happier reunion. While playing at the Palais Royal on 45th and Broadway they were visited by another ex-employer, Captain Joseph Streckfus, the President of the Steamship Company. Several of the band had worked on the Streckfus riverboats, but any memories of excess discipline were forgotten as the musicians warmly greeted the visitor.[18]

Red's contract to record with his own band ended soon after he joined Louis Armstrong, so a small but regular income disappeared. Happily, during the years 1937 to 1939, Red was booked on a whole series of freelance dates on which he accompanied singers for Decca recordings (the results were issued on what they still called their 'Race

Series'). Decca, rightly sensing an awakening of the public's interest in the blues, began bringing various singers to their New York studios, situated at 50 West 57th Street. The record company were also aware that small 'jump' bands, like the Harlem Hamfats, were achieving healthy sales, and some of the singers that Decca signed, like Frankie 'Half Pint' Jaxon, Blue Lu Barker and Rosetta Howard, could cover both fields (blues and jump music) satisfactorily. Red does not feature strongly on the sides he made with Rosetta Howard, and the bulk of the solos were played by Duke Ellington's star clarinettist, Barney Bigard, who performs wondrously, despite a woefully stodgy rhythm section. The trumpeter is given the chance to blow several fine solos during a series of dates with Jaxon, his muted middle-register improvisations on 'Turn Over' achieve an infectious swing, as does his work on 'Be Your Natural Self'. Red airs his top notes on 'Let Me Ride Your Train' and plays a poignant blues chorus on 'Take Off Those Hips'. Unfortunately he does not solo on a song that Bessie Smith made famous, 'Gimme a Pigfoot', which Jaxon performs with zest – and new lyrics. Usually Red's recordings were enthusiastically (even ecstatically) received by the critics, but it seems that not everyone was delighted with his work here. In a contemporary review, published in *Jazz Information*, the view was expressed that Red played 'appropriate blues trumpet in the backgrounds; his solos are unfortunate'.[19]

Blue Lu Barker could sing the blues effectively, but she was better known for her cabaret songs, such as the slightly risqué 'Don't You Make Me High'. Red backs this singer attentively, and on 'He's So Good' unleashes a trumpet introduction that shows his embouchure was in good shape, the bright high D contrasting effectively with the dark low notes that garland his 12-bar solo. Red's fill-ins enhance 'Never Brag About Your Man', and he is imaginatively supportive on 'Handy Andy'. One of the best moments in Red's recordings with Blue Lu occurs when he suddenly doubles up the tempo on 'Jitterbug Blues', and then masterfully restores the piece to its original speed. Blue Lu Barker's artistry is a thousand leagues above another singer that Red backed, as part of his Decca deal. The unfortunate Helen Proctor gave her accompanists some anxious moments during her October 1939 recordings. This young woman from Louisville, Kentucky, was a discovery and a close friend of J. Mayo Williams, a black veteran of the recording industry, described at this time as 'a talent impresario for Decca's race records'. Two of the songs that Helen Proctor chose to record were her own compositions, 'Let's Call It a Day' and 'Take Me Along with You'.

It soon became clear that the singer did not have the confidence or vocal technique to follow her own melody, leaving the band to guess at the intended goal; as a result, the accompanying harmonies buckle on both songs. Red attempts a display of fortitude in his accompaniments, and on 'Let's Call It a Day' does his best to instil confidence in his colleagues by playing a bold and complex 16-bar solo, a worthy attempt to solve the mystery of the accompanying changes, but one that does not quite succeed. The band must have found the title of this song all too apt, and after the session the singer and her accompanists took separate paths that never again entwined.

Lee Brown was something quite different, an authentic blues singer. His 'Mississippi Water Blues' obviously stimulated Red, who plays a profound 12-bar muted solo and continues to feed the singer sympathetic backing phrases throughout. The main trouble with the Lee Brown sessions was that all of his compositions sounded markedly similar, he changed the lyrics but not the tune, steadfastly reiterating the same melody over and over again, often in the same key. After encountering Brown's theme several times Red seems to have nowhere to go and he too became repetitive, but in the midst of blowing some perfunctory doodlings he suddenly produced a magic phrase on 'Rolling Stone'.

Generally the organization of these blues sessions was slipshod, with the musicians often hastily working out head arrangements for singers, some of whom were not used to working with bands. There is a feeling that some of the takes that were accepted and issued might not have passed muster under closer scrutiny, but the Decca blues project was not allocated a large budget and studio time was at a premium. The result is a mixed bunch, few of which show Red Allen at his best. His playing on the series is never less than accomplished, but he would not have liked his reputation to be judged solely on these efforts. Things were organized better on the sides Red made with Johnny Temple, a blues artiste who sings well. Temple benefits from a Red Allen-Buster Bailey pairing in which the two friends took the trouble to work out backing figures and cohesive endings. On a side with Trixie Smith, 'No Good Man', Red shares duties with Barney Bigard, and they both sound comfortable performing with a very experienced singer.

Recording sessions with a band led by pianist James P. Johnson (in 1939) highlighted some accomplished performances, particularly 'Harlem Woogie', featuring singer Anna Robinson, a model of vocal vitality. Red is in a daring mood throughout his 24-bar solo, but he is positively intrepid on both takes of 'Memories of You', dancing fearlessly along a musical tightrope as he creates a flow of superimposed timings. The sides on which the band accompanied Bessie Smith's niece, Ruby Smith, are less successful; here a growling singer strains out her notes in a vain attempt to pay tribute to her famous relative. Red's work on the James P. Johnson sides show that he was still playing very well, and from this point on his reputation (which had been under wraps for almost three years) began to re-germinate; in the July 1939 issue of *Down Beat* he was described as 'America's most under-rated trumpeter'. Despite being still submerged in Louis Armstrong's Orchestra for most of his time, Red proved on a session with Lionel Hampton (in October 1939) that he had not lost the knack of small band playing. He sounds a bit cavalier on 'The Heebie Jeebies Are Rockin' the Town Tonight', but he is back to his very best on 'I'm on My Way from You' in a performance that underlines his durability. Over the years I have heard various trumpeters attempting to recreate the way that Red phrases this melody, but none comes close to capturing the exquisite nuances of the original. What Red plays on this recording is not technically awesome, but the artistry he gives to the performance is beyond imitation.

Soon afterwards (in early 1940) Red created another exceptional display of jazz talent on 'Sweet Substitute', recorded at a Jelly Roll Morton session. Morton, in the throes of making a comeback after years of semi-obscurity, had moved back to New York where he led his own small pick-up bands for studio dates. His first choice trumpeter was Red Allen, who was delighted to be reunited with the veteran pianist. Other than the old New Orleans favourite 'Panama', all the compositions were by Morton (some are his adaptations of traditional themes). Unfortunately not all of the musicians on the dates were accustomed to playing New Orleans music. The band is under-rehearsed and several of the arrangements meander. On 'Panama' (one of Red's earlier triumphs) the trumpeter's surefootedness temporarily deserts him and he loses a bar at the end of the second theme, but on 'Swinging the Elks' Red's lead playing is fierce and exciting, exemplifying New Orleans trumpet playing at its very best; his muted solo on this number is positively incandescent. 'Sweet Substitute' stands out as the pick of the 12 titles recorded, but 'Good Old New York' and 'My Home is in a Southern Town' embody Morton's panache, and, like 'Sweet Substitute', highlight his nonpareil singing. Red Allen later introduced 'Sweet Substitute' into his own repertoire and performed it regularly during his later years, describing it as 'the most beautiful number ever to have been written'.[20] Red's admiration for Morton's work and his personality never dwindled:

'He was a real good musician, you know. He was a boastful guy, but he could prove his boasts, and one can't say anything bad about a guy who can do that.'[21] While the two men were sharing some goodnatured banter at the January 1940 recording session Morton decided to call the piece they were working on 'Big Lip Blues', telling Red that he was naming the song after him – much to the trumpeter's amusement. But despite this lightheartedness from Morton, in a letter (dated 6 January 1940) to publisher-pianist Roy Carew he revealed the administrative headaches he had encountered in organizing the sessions:

> I had to make the recordings under difficult conditions. The men would not rehearse, the union demands pay for rehearsal, and the [recording] company was not willing to pay for it, so there will be bad spots, BUT there are much worse recordings.

Some days later, on 18 January, in another letter to Carew, Morton again revealed that he could be modest: 'I just wrote "Big Lip Blues" in the studio and it don't amount to much'.

Jelly Roll Morton's re-emergence was one of several signs that New Orleans jazz, and Dixieland, were undergoing a revival of interest. The discovery of veteran trumpeter Bunk Johnson in New Iberia, Louisiana, was another stimulus to those who were keen to be part of a return to the older styles of jazz. The movement was seen as a reaction to the so-called commercial approach latterly taken by the big swing bands who were increasingly relying on vocal recordings and gimmicky instrumentals to gain success in that era's equivalent of the Hit Parade. Collective improvisation had become a rarity.

8

BOLD BANDLEADER

During the late 1930s a small but dedicated clique of writers began a propaganda campaign to resurrect the instrumentation and the repertoire of early jazz bands. They felt that a trumpet, trombone and clarinet line-up would successfully reintroduce collective improvisation and thus ward off the public's interest in the smooth sounds of the highly organized commercial big bands: a noble art would replace the manipulations of the music business entrepreneurs.

New Orleans musicians, who had been earning their livings in big bands for a decade, were urged to recapture a golden past by playing in small, so-called traditional line-ups, even though some of them had hardly ever worked in bands with a trumpet, trombone, clarinet front line. People who had hitherto been unaware of where New Orleans was on a map began devoting much of their time to learning its geography, street names and legends. Soon the seeds of the revival movement had spread to many parts of the world.

No city in the USA evokes more civic pride among its inhabitants and its wandering sons than New Orleans, so musicians who had long since left the city were delighted that its part in the birth of jazz was being exalted. The demand was for authenticity, so naturally players like Red Allen, Sidney Bechet, Edmond Hall, Pops Foster and Zutty Singleton were offered roles in what turned out to be a longrunning production. Certainly whenever Red was in New York in 1939 and 1940 he was happy to renew his ties with small band playing and took part in jam sessions regularly organized by Milt Gabler or by Harry Lim. A typical line-up for one such gathering featured a band consisting of Red, Higgy, Bechet, Pee Wee Russell, Zutty Singleton, bassist Wilson Myers and pianist Joe Bushkin.[1] These sessions gave many people their first opportunity to sample live a jazz band's collective improvisations; some found the spirited skills and enthusiasm of the musicians very appealing, and they became fans. Some listeners even felt that by supporting this type of music they were helping in a struggle against mammon.

Record companies observed the growing number of followers that 'hot jazz' was gaining and decided to offer more examples of the style in their catalogues (both re-issued material and bands freshly recorded). Lil Armstrong was a musical adviser to Decca at this time; she played piano on, and suggested personnel for that company's blues and jump band sessions. By virtue of the many recordings she had made with New Orleanians in Chicago during the 1920s she was also, quite rightly, considered to be an expert on early jazz. At her instigation an all-star pick-up ensemble recorded in May 1940 two titles under Red Allen's name, and two as Zutty Singleton's group. The band consisted of Red Allen, Ed Hall on clarinet, Pops Foster and Zutty Singleton (all from Louisiana) plus Lil Armstrong on piano, Bernard Addison on guitar and Benny Morton on trombone. The four pieces they recorded were all themes of yesteryear: 'Down in Jungle Town', 'Canal Street Blues', 'King Porter Stomp' and 'Shim-me-sha-wabble'. 'Down in Jungle Town' had been a popular song when all the musicians involved were young-sters. The mood at the beginning of this version is akin to the sound of a marching ensemble, a feeling fortified by Zutty Singleton's crisp snare drumming. Red's phrases have a clipped, emphatic ring and Ed Hall provides a lively counterpoint to the trumpet lead, but trombonist Benny Morton's phrasing is endowed with a smoothness that suits his soloing more than it does his ensemble playing. Morton and Hall (sounding husky and lively) take 32 bars apiece, then Red Allen re-enters to lead the line into a hectic finale, during which his trumpet playing fills in most of the available space, to the cost of a unified overall sound.

The septet combine well on the early stages of 'Canal Street Blues', with Red again firmly laying down the melody. Clarinet, piano, trombone and guitar are all featured in satisfactory solos but again the final ensemble seems too busy by far, the consolation being Singleton's energetic and pulsating offbeat cymbal playing. Singleton is featured on the early stages of 'King Porter Stomp', where he blends rim-shots, cymbal work and press rolls in a spectacular display of New Orleans drumming. A rather ragged ensemble follows, then Ed Hall zestfully plays the tune's second theme. The three front-line players solo, and Red makes it obvious that he has no intention of attempting to play as he might have done 20 years earlier. A drum solo that combines gusto and grandeur heralds in a final ensemble that sounds perilously close to a free-for-all. The session concluded with a tidy version of 'Shim-me-sha-wabble', taken at the perfect tempo. Ed Hall delightfully weaves over and under the stark opening melody, then Red creates a brooding solo that is graced by some wonderful drumming. Ed Hall again improvises effortlessly before Red re-enters to play a speculative solo again supported by Singleton's emphatic offbeat figures. Benny Morton plays a mellow trombone solo before a cohesive ensemble ends the session neatly.

These recordings mark an important crossroad in Red Allen's career. No-one was more passionate about New Orleans than Red; no matter how busy he was he made regular pilgrimages back to Louisiana throughout the 1930s and 1940s. He loved talking about the 'old days' in the Crescent City, but this dedication to his roots did not mean that he felt duty bound to continue playing in the way he had done as a young man. Red knew all about playing lead in a New Orleans band, having served an apprenticeship listening and playing alongside the masters of that difficult art, but by 1940 he was developing a way of playing that belonged to no particular jazz style. Years later this was summed up by someone who said of Allen's later work, 'Red played traditional, modern and mainstream all in the same solo'.[2] On the 1940 sessions Red could have reverted to an orthodox lead, but by then he was not excited by the prospect of fulfilling the set trumpet role that most of the followers of early jazz (by now mockingly referred to as 'mouldy figs' by those who liked only contemporary jazz) felt to be an essential part of the small band style. Red continued to follow his own inclinations during many subsequent recordings, but he would occasionally play a sparser, 'authentic' lead just to cock a snook at his detractors. Martin Williams summed up the situation aptly when he wrote, 'Allen has often been associated with contemporary quasi-Dixieland playing. Good New Orleans-Dixieland is primarily an ensemble style and Red Allen is not an ensemble player. Allen's best melodic lines are perhaps too active and exploratory to be lead parts in an ensemble.'[3]

During the period covered by the various 1940 freelance recordings Red was still a member of Louis Armstrong's Orchestra, but he was restless, and he was made more so in July 1940 when the band temporarily settled in New York for a series of rehearsals (at the Bronze Studio on Lenox Avenue) prior to playing a residency at the Paramount Theatre. The appeal of going home every night after finishing work, instead of facing a long late-night journey to the next gig, unsettled Red (and several others in the band). By then some of the 'old guard' had already left. Albert Nicholas was one of the first to go, explaining 'I got tired of travelling and pulled out'.[4] The only long-term member who was fired was drummer Paul Barbarin, who had always prided himself on his reliability, punctuality and personal neatness. He accepted, with equanimity, that he was to be replaced by the hugely talented Sid Catlett and recalled saying to Louis's agent and manager, 'Well Mr Glaser, it's my privilege to quit and it's your privilege to fire me, so there's no hard feelings'.[5] However Barbarin later brooded on the dismissal when he heard that he was sacked because he complained of being homesick, which he strongly denied. Louis Armstrong continued to allocate instrumental features to Red on live dates, and up to late August 1940 Red was being billed in the band's newspaper advertisements, but by then he wanted no more of the ups and downs of the touring life; he handed in his notice and played his final job with the band at the Regal, Chicago. His long-time colleague Charlie Holmes left at the same time; he too had had enough touring, and said, 'Hitting the road, you start coming back with 2 dollars and fifty cents after being out there for five weeks'.[6]

Red's decision to leave Armstrong was hastened by news passed to him by record producer and writer John Hammond, who told him that Barney Josephson (a night-club owner) was interested in the idea of having Red bring a small band into his Café Society Downtown (situated at 2 Sheridan Square in Greenwich Village). Hammond, who had been dedicated to jazz since his early teens, was from an immensely wealthy background. He wrote candidly about jazz for various European publications during the 1930s and often praised Red Allen's work, particularly when the trumpeter was with Luis Russell and Fletcher Henderson. Among the many historic recording sessions that Hammond instigated were Bessie Smith's final date, Billie Holiday's first, Lester Young's first and many by Fletcher Henderson, Coleman Hawkins, Red Allen, etc. He continued to be a force in the recording industry through the 1970s. Hammond's interest in Red Allen's career was purely philanthropic; he obtained bookings for many jazz musicians without seeking any sort of commission or payment. The main snag that these players encountered in their dealings with John was in coping with the proprietorial attitude he frequently adopted.

Barney Josephson, an ex-shoe salesman, was also a key figure in New York jazz circles. For many years he ran two highly successful venues: Café Society Downtown which opened in December 1938 (capacity 220 customers) and Café Society Uptown (at East 58th Street) which held 300 and was opened in November 1940. Both featured small band jazz, solo pianists and top class singers (Billie Holiday sang the première of her celebrated version of 'Strange Fruit' at Café Society Downtown). For all his involvement in the music business Barney never really became an expert on jazz. When reminiscing about the various artistes who had worked for him over the years he tended to remember their personalities more than he did their musical abilities. He certainly had not selected Red Allen as a possible bandleader for his club, but John Hammond had. Hammond and Josephson shared an affable relationship; both were interested in leftwing politics, and in breaking down the colour bar. Josephson welcomed white and black customers at a time when racially mixed audiences were still a rarity on the New York club scene. There was no cover charge at Café Society Downtown, but on weekends the usual minimum cost per person was raised from one dollar 50 cents to two dollars. The club's advertising slogan 'The wrong place for the RIGHT people' was Josephson's 'dig' at those whose political views were opposite to his own.

Josephson took advice from John Hammond, but chose to do his own negotiating. Hammond had no trouble in convincing Red Allen that it was a propitious time to start a small band, and followed up by suggesting which musicians Red should employ. Hammond was not trying to create a revival of traditional jazz – he had nothing against the movement but his jazz tastes were too broad to be pigeonholed. The use of a clarinet (as opposed to a saxophone) was not for stylistic reasons; it happened because Ed Hall was a friend of Barney Josephson. It was as though Hall (a very talented musician) was part of the Café Society Downtown fixtures, and while bandleaders came and went Hall remained and simply joined the incoming personnel. Hall, besides being an outstanding clarinet player, was also that rare creature, a jazz musician who was deeply interested in politics; he and Josephson shared similar views. From late 1939 Hall became what he described as 'a regular house man' at Café Society Downtown. He told writer Max Jones, 'I was there a long while. Any band that came in, I was in it. Barney Josephson, the owner, made that clear.'[7]

Red Allen toyed with the idea of employing trombonist Benny Morton in the group. Red was quite aware that J.C. Higginbotham was a superior jazz musician, but Benny Morton was an affable, totally reliable, non-drinking sideman. Higgy was a popular man in the music profession who enjoyed drinking and carousing more than was good for him, but, whether he was drunk or sober, he usually played magnificently. John Hammond pointed out the musical benefits that Higgy would bring to the new band, and stressed that jazz fans automatically paired Red with Higgy because of the years they had spent together in various bands. Higginbotham was still in Louis Armstrong's Orchestra in late 1940, but he was unsettled, and it was mooted in *Down Beat* that he was about to join either Count Basie or Benny Goodman. Red's offer of $150 a week (which was apparently what Red himself was getting) soon made up Higgy's mind that it was time to hand in his notice to Joe Garland, who was by then the 'straw boss' of Armstrong's Band (later at Café Society, Higgy's salary was increased to $200 a week). Higgy gave in his notice while Armstrong's Band was in Louisiana, and spent time working it out on a tour of the South before flying from Memphis, Tennessee, to New York to join Red's new group. Higgy recollected, 'John Hammond sent me a plane ticket and 50 dollars'.[8] Apparently boarding that flight in what was then a very race-conscious locale presented problems for Higginbotham, but John Hammond wielded behind-the-scenes power by threatening to sue, and Higgy, after a long wait, was allowed through. Not long after Higgy arrived in New York, Armstrong's manager Joe Glaser issued a statement that was published in *Down Beat*, which said that Higginbotham had been fired because he was 'hard to get along with and was always griping about salary money'.[9] Higgy was very hurt by the inference that he had been sacked, and in January 1941 took a letter that Joe Garland had given to him in Memphis on 2 December 1940 to the offices of the *New York Amsterdam News*. In the letter, which the newspaper published on 18 January 1941, Garland said:

> You're going on your own volition and to something that we both hope is better. I know I voice the sentiments of the entire organization when I say I'm sorry, very sorry to lose you, not only because you're a marvellous musician and trombone player – second to none – but also because as a regular fellow you have few equals... if you ever want to come back we will welcome you with open arms.

This letter did not alter the fact that Louis Armstrong himself was disappointed that Higgy chose to leave the band in the middle of a tour. The two men had a brief feud that was soon resolved, with Higgy describing Louis as 'one of my best buddies'.[10] Louis showed no signs of anger when Red Allen quit the band, but some months later, in an interview published in the May 1941 issue of *Swing* magazine, he sounded slightly aggrieved about Red's departure:

> We're still on good terms. I'm always glad to see a man better himself. Of course he doesn't know all the worries of having a band these days, but it won't hurt him none to try. He won't be bettering himself financially. My boys are the best paid of all the colored bands, that goes for Duke or anybody.

Fortunately for the Allen-Armstrong relationship, Red's original plan to entice drummer Sid Catlett away from Louis did not materialize, and bad feeling was averted when Carlett decided to stay where he was. John Hammond and Red agreed that there was no question of using an 'old time' rhythm section in a sophisticated night club where the musicians were also required to accompany visiting cabaret artistes. Drummer Jimmy Hoskins had played well at the initial band rehearsals so he was given the job permanently. Billy Taylor, bassist and arranger, had, like Ed Hall, worked often at Café Society Downtown, so there was no dispute about his joining the ensemble. The pianist chosen for the band, by mutual consent, was the brilliant young musician Kenny Kersey. Red's band completed a successful audition for Barney Josephson before Higginbotham had returned to New York (using Claude Jones on trombone). Josephson arranged for the new band to begin a long residency later in the year. This suited Red, who was happy in the knowledge that he had no immediate commitments and could therefore pay a visit to his folks in Louisiana:

> After leaving Louis Armstrong's Band I thought I'd take a little vacation back home to see Father and Mother and the family and the old gang I used to play around with.[11]

On his second day in New Orleans Red visited the Musicians' Union, A.F. of M. Local 496, where he met up with Sidney Desvigne, Papa Celestin, Peter Bocage, Manuel Manetta, Leonard Bocage, Willie Humphrey and the two Barbarin brothers, Paul and Louis. Red spent a good deal of that vacation listening to various old friends and made special mention of Paul Barbarin's Band, who were appearing at Vinette's Night Club in St Rose. When he returned to New York Red said, 'I really hated to come back, but wanting to work around New York City I decided to return after a week's fun'.[12] On the journey back Red's Buick was loaded down with red beans, pickled hot peppers and sundry Louisiana delicacies. Bringing back the raw materials for Pearly May's fine Creole cooking was a procedure he adopted on all his trips back home. Red, who preferred to eat after he'd finished work, always disliked the touring routine that meant rushing meals in order to catch up with an ill-planned schedule.

In late October 1940, soon after Red had returned to New York, he did a series of dates with Benny Goodman. After rehearsing in New York, Red temporarily joined the clarinettist's band and did his first date with them at Lehigh University in Bethlehem, Pennsylvania. Goodman was apparently well satisfied with Red's playing, but the trumpeter's imminent début at Café Society Downtown precluded any long-term association. Henry 'Red' Allen's Café Society Orchestra, as the group was billed, began its three-shows-a-night residency at the club on 26 November 1940 (their stay there was to last nine months). Because of the commitments to Louis Armstrong, Higginbotham missed the first part of the residency, during which time Claude Jones and Gene Simons took it in turns to deputize. Red's group usually shared billing with various star pianists (including Art Tatum and Meade Lux Lewis) and a featured singer – Billie Holiday was there prior to Red's initial dates but her place was filled by Ida Cox; later Lena Horne took the featured spot.

It was with Ida Cox that Red's new band made its recording début, waxing four sides for the Okeh company. Other than a brief spell of open blowing on 'Last Mile Blues', Red's role is mostly restricted to cup-muted playing. Higginbotham's burnished tone is also masked by a mute. Red, Higgy and Ed Hall shared the obbligati behind the singer but there is little opportunity for the instrumentalists to shine as the four numbers recorded are all heavily arranged; even the background figures were written out. As a result, Ida Cox's rich voice is predominant; Red's most worthwhile solo (muted) occurs on an unissued take of 'I Can't Quit That Man'. The pianist on this session is Cliff Jackson, who had been accompanying Ida Cox on her New York dates. The sextet achieve an admirable cohesion in their phrasing of the arrangements, and display an effective use of dynamics, showing that, even under wraps, they had considerable potential. They were gaining a following at Café Society Downtown, where Red and Barney Josephson enjoyed a happy relationship. Forty years on, the club owner spoke of Red: 'He was one of the nicest guys, clean cut, wonderful temperament. Always a smile, never got angry, an ideal person, and he could play like hell – but he didn't have the slightest conceit about himself.'[13]

The band was soon involved in a busy schedule, not only playing the Downtown residency but also doing NBC radio broadcasts and taking part in a series of Sunday sessions. Red and Higgy also continued to be featured at the Sunday afternoon jam sessions that were organized by Milt Gabler at Jimmy Ryan's Club. Soon Sunday afternoon jam sessions were being held at Café Society Downtown, where, for one dollar, jazz fans could sit from 4 p.m. to 7 p.m. enjoying the improvisations of everchanging all-star line-ups. On March 1941 the gathering included Red, Higgy, Kenny Kersey, Jimmy Hoskins, Woody Herman and his trombonist Neil Reid, plus Muggsy Spanier and his tenor saxist, Nick Ciazza. Red also found time to sit in at various clubs and took part in a jam session at Minton's Playhouse, 210 West 118th Street (soon to be the cradle of the new 'bebop' style). Red's visit there was a favour to his old Luis Russell Band colleague, tenor saxophonist Teddy Hill, who took over duties as manager of Minton's in early 1941. In this same period Red also played at a benefit dance held in the Renaissance Casino in aid of his former bandleader, Fate Marable, who was in poor health. By this time, Red and his wife and son had moved to a fifth floor apartment at 1351 Prospect Avenue in the Bronx (this was to remain Red's home for the rest of his life). It was a walk-up apartment and Red always maintained that climbing the flights of stairs kept him fit; as a joke he'd tell first-time visitors to keep on walking up until they came to the elevator.

In 1941 J.C. Higginbotham recorded as part of the Metronome All Stars, a unit made up of musicians who had achieved high placings in the annual poll organized by *Metronome* magazine. Over the years Higgy enjoyed numerous successes in polls run by *Metronome* and by *Down Beat*, winning first place on several occasions. Red never fared well in these polls. In the *Metronome* 1942 poll (won by Ziggy Elman with 870 votes) Red got 3 votes, which was 3 more than he received in the 1941 contest. Years later Higgy somewhat touchingly commented on his many poll victories, 'I wasn't trying to win, I was just playing'.[14] Both Red and Higgy took part in some 1941 recordings with the great soprano-sax player and clarinettist, Sidney Bechet. Bechet, one of the doyens of New Orleans jazz, was receiving a good deal of publicity in various jazz magazines, and through the efforts of his friend and unofficial manager, John Reid, secured a favourable contract to record for the Victor company. On one of the early sessions in this series Bechet booked Red and Higgy as his front-line partners. The veteran New Orleans bassist, Wellman Braud, anchored a rhythm section that included two young musicians, pianist James Tolliver and drummer J.C. Heard.

At the time of these recordings Bechet was playing an out-of-town residency in Fonda, New York. To save Bechet coming into Manhattan to rehearse, pianist James Tolliver sketched out some trumpet and trombone parts for three of the numbers, including 'Coal Black Shine', which was a feature for Bechet's clarinet-playing. In this piece, which seesaws between major and minor themes, Bechet's highly emotional playing, full of exciting, rasping phrases, creates some triumphant music. Red, as a teenager, had listened in awe as senior musicians in New Orleans talked of Bechet's adventures in Europe. By the time Red recorded with him, Bechet was regarded as one of the great veterans of the music. Red observed a tradition of being respectful towards his elders that was instilled in him during childhood, but on this session there is a slight feeling that Red was intimidated by the fierce old genius. Higginbotham blows boldly on 'Coal Black Shine' but Red's solo is quite disjointed. The trumpeter sounds no more at ease on 'Slippin' and Slidin''; admittedly his tone in the low register creates a satisfying timbre but again his phrasing sounds stiff. The high spot of the session is 'Egyptian Fantasy' on which Red's role is to play the arrangement of a highly evocative composition. Bechet is again on clarinet and uses it to produce some wonderful, bloodcurdling effects; Red cited this as one of his own favourite recordings. The fourth title of the date was an unusually brisk version of 'Baby, Won't You Please Come Home?', featuring Bechet on soprano saxophone. Higgy is granted two choruses and revels in the extended space. Red never sounds likely to cut loose in his solo but airs some balanced ideas before Bechet swoops in and showers the group with inspiration, lifting them for a spirited ending. For most of the session the rhythm section display a crisp unity, but on this track the piano is virtually inaudible.

In April 1941 Red's group made its first instrumental recordings (for the Okeh label). Their first priority was to produce a version of the band's most popular number, 'K.K. Boogie', a piano feature, composed by Kenny Kersey. Here the band engenders a powerful swing, with Red's solo topping excellent work by Hall and Higginbotham. Kersey then reprises the boogie-woogie feel with the band supplying riff-like figures that create a stirring climax. The next most requested number in the band's repertory was their unusual version of Vincent Youman's 'Sometimes I'm Happy'. The band shortened their arrangement for the recording, but even a truncated version remained a long routine. Trumpet, trombone, clarinet, piano and string bass are all allocated 32-bar solos, then Ed Hall returns for an extra helping. The arrangement continued to exceed the time limit for a 78 r.p.m. ten inch record (usually a little over 3 minutes), but Red managed to persuade the recording company to adopt an occasional procedure whereby a double-sided disc was issued, necessitating turning the record over to hear the conclusion. The band made a couple of satisfactory attempts to record the piece but unfortunately the Okeh executives were not impressed enough to issue the results. Parts one and two remained on the company's shelves for 40 years until they were issued on collectors' labels.

The rejection by Okeh of this number was a disappointment to Red, and in terms of the band's long-term reputation a huge pity, because the presentation of the piece is virtually a blueprint for what was to be called 'mainstream' jazz, some 10 years later. The band sounds ahead of its time, not by the inclusion of ostentatious substitute harmonies or 'bomb-dropping' by the drummer but by the phrasing of the sparse arrangement, by the roles adopted within the unified rhythm section and by the way the solos are structured – there are no attempts to force the pace by including stock 'killer-diller' phrases popular in the Swing Era. Higginbotham begins his solo with a restrained motif and builds thematically; Hall is a model of straight-ahead improvising and Red's flamboyant reshaping of the theme is spectacularly inventive, both rhythmically and harmonically, indicating that his restless musical ingenuity was as active as ever. Had the Okeh recording company been a quarter as daring as Red, the opus would have been issued within a month.

In performing 'Ol' Man River' Red was reviving a number he had recorded with Fletcher Henderson, but his own band's version is built on boogie-woogie foundations. After a couple of false starts the band created an exhilarating performance of the song, complete with a wonderfully expressive vocal from Red. Unfortunately this was not the version that was originally issued; the recording manager chose a later attempt, which he thought had superior solos, and on subsequent takes Red never recaptured the brilliance of his initial vocal. 'K.K. Boogie' and 'Ol' Man River' made up the coupling that was released some weeks after the April 1941 session. The critics were not greatly impressed by the issue, particularly Dave Dexter Jr of *Down Beat* who wrote, 'Red's trumpeting is out of tune and poorly recorded. Higgy blows like hell but never quite gets there, Kenneth Kersey pounds a cargo of boogie piano.'

Dexter castigated the 'screwed-up, discordant ensembles' but praised Ed Hall's clarinet-playing, which he described as 'the saving grace of the whole shebang'.[15] A review published in *Metronome*[16] also praised Ed Hall's clarinet-playing, citing him as the most impressive soloist, but concluding that Allen and Higginbotham were 'trying a little too hard for comfort'.

At a follow-up session in July 1941 the band recorded 'A Sheridan Square', an unelaborate blues composed by Red Allen as a tribute to a section of Greenwich Village. Improvised 12-bar solos are interspersed between replays of the simple theme, but the hypnotic momentum that musical repetition can sometimes develop fails to occur and one is left with the feeling that this untaxing number was used in order to allow the band to settle into the session smoothly. It certainly fared better than the more complicated Allen composition 'Siesta at the Fiesta' which the band recorded next. This catchy theme gives way to a rather perfunctory solo from Red. Ed Hall is his consistent self but Higginbotham, perhaps attempting to provide some contrast to the somewhat dainty proceedings, blows with a near brutal directness. All these efforts were in vain: Okeh felt that the record was not suitable for release. The saving grace for Red as a composer was that 'Siesta at the Fiesta' had already been recorded by Jimmie Lunceford's Orchestra, so at least he would earn royalties from the tune. The band went on to record a head arrangement of the old favourite 'Indiana' with Red playing a solo that is full of ideas, but perhaps overbrimming with vigour. A second take shows how much everyone in the band was improvising, but these skills did not help the final number of the day: both attempts to record 'Jack the Bellboy' (a feature for drummer Jimmy Hoskins) proved abortive.

Dave Dexter certainly had no vendetta towards Red and the band but he was no more kind about the second release: '"A Sheridan Square" is a little on the square side from a compositional standpoint and "Indiana" is hurt by a bad intro and astonishingly poorly integrated ensemble passages.'[17] Besides being disappointed by the reviews Red could look back ruefully on the fact that two full recording sessions had only produced four issuable titles. In truth he does not seem to have chosen numbers that were ideal for the market that Okeh was aiming at. For all Red's skills as a trumpeter he was new to full-time bandleading and was probably misled by the reactions of a live audience to certain numbers his band played. Customers might cheer the club rendering of a tune to the echoes, but in the cold air of a recording studio the magical stimulus created by that sort of rapport is impossible to recapture. When Red led his recording bands from 1934 to 1937 he did not have to face the decision of selection – that was virtually made for him by his agent and various music publishers.

These 1941 recordings received a mixed reaction from Red's fans. Many of those who cherished his work on the Luis Russell, Fletcher Henderson and Mills Blue Rhythm Band sides were mystified and disappointed by what they thought of as Red's harsh, strident blowing and brash phrasing on these new releases. Even one of Red's most ardent admirers, writer Albert McCarthy, commented that in this period of Red's career, 'Exuberance was replaced by vulgarity and a frenetic quality'.[18] But Red had not suddenly become haphazard. The 1941 recordings link with the May 1940 Lil Armstrong sides in revealing that Red was deliberately adopting a style that could not possibly be mistaken for that of Louis Armstrong. He had just spent three solid years acting as a stand-in for his early hero, but he had no wish to be thought of in those terms for the rest of his life. Red was determined that his own music-making must take a new direction, even if it meant that during the initial search he had to blast a way through to reach it.

9

SUPER SHOWMAN

In July 1941 Red and Higgy took part in a prestigious, but not very demanding, recording session, forming part of a large, string-laden orchestra that bandleader and clarinettist Artie Shaw had assembled. The overall sound produced was that of a jazz octet playing in front of violins, violas and cellos, the arrangements leaving brief interludes for improvisation. Shaw himself introduces the melody of 'I'm Confessin'', then, after a modulation by the strings, Higginbotham and Benny Carter (superb on alto saxophone) play alternating 2-bar phrases. Red flirts with the melody of the middle eight, playing a cup-muted solo that is full of bite. All the horns gather to play an elegantly voiced finale. Red has no solo duties on 'Love Me a Little', sung with extra precise phrasing by a young Lena Horne, and neither does he solo on 'Beyond the Blue Horizon', on which Higgy takes 16 bars. Red, again cup-muted, simply states the opening eight bars of 'Don't Take Your Love from Me', then moves into the background while Lena Horne sings. Though Shaw had enjoyed a number of big-selling records by this time, nothing from this session dented the hit parade.

Red's band continued to play a series of residencies at both Café Society clubs through 1941, but they also began to take work at other New York clubs, including six weeks at Kelly's Stables (137 West 52nd Street), two weeks at the Village Vanguard (on 7th Avenue) and a brief stay at the 181 Club on Second Avenue, which ended when the venue burnt down. Fortunately none of the musicians were in the club at the time, but Higginbotham's trombone was destroyed in the blaze; within a week the band had taken up a residency at the Famous Door on West 52nd Street.

The series of residencies at the Café Society venues ceased when Joe Glaser took over the exclusive booking rights for Red's band. Glaser, by now head of the Associated Booking Corporation, was playing an increasingly powerful role as an agent. After moving from Chicago to New York in the late 1930s he began to build what was virtually an empire of black musical talent, including Lionel Hampton's Band and Billie Holiday, but he was also the agent for various white aggregations, notably Les Brown's Band. Red's signing with Glaser meant that he had few further business dealings with John Hammond. Red never developed the sort of close relationship that Louis Armstrong and Joe Glaser shared. Despite years of association Red always regarded Glaser warily, being well aware of the agent's abrasive manner, but almost every artiste who signed for Glaser obtained better bookings, at more money, than they had previously, enjoyed. The financial gains had to be weighed against the problems of dealing with Glaser's dictatorial attitude and his sudden bursts of antagonism. Red knew all about these aspects of Glaser's personality having seen him often making Luis Russell's life a misery. Charlie Holmes gave his recollections: 'Joe Glaser was a funny person. He was shell shocked in the first war. He'd get to hollering and screaming at Luis Russell, you could hear him all over the theater, but next day he'd go out and buy Luis Russell a great big fancy wardroom trunk, something expensive.'[1] Apparently Glaser's main gripe against Luis Russell was his failure to discipline the musicians. Eventually Russell had had enough of Glaser's outbursts and handed over the leadership of Louis Armstrong's backing band to saxophonist Joe Garland.

A big change occurred in Red Allen's band when Ed Hall decided to leave in order to join Teddy Wilson's Sextet. Hall had experienced a good deal of touring during his long stay in Claude Hopkins's Orchestra. He did not want to repeat the ordeal, and, as Red's band seemed about to be taking on more widespread itineraries, he felt he would be happier working closer to his home in the Bronx. Franz Jackson was Hall's initial replacement, then Eddie Williams took Jackson's place. At the time of Pearl Harbor, pianist Kenny Kersey realized that he was soon to be drafted into the services and decided to spend his waiting months working in New York-based units led by Cootie Williams and Andy Kirk. Being a married man with a child, Red Allen was initially deferred; later, when he went before the draft board he was graded 4 F, and so he remained a civilian.[2]

The early 1940s marked a boom time for those New Yorkers who liked to hear their jazz performed in concert halls. Jazz concerts had been occasionally held during the 1930s, but by 1942 they were a regular part of the Manhattan calendar. Events where as many as 30 jazz musicians gathered on stage for a jam session finale (after being featured in small groups) were commonplace. Barney Josephson sponsored his own Café Society Concerts at Carnegie Hall and at the New York Town Hall. One such bill at Carnegie Hall featured Red's Band, the John Kirby Sextet, the Eddie South ensemble, the Golden Gate Quartet, Art Tatum, Hazel Scott, Pete Johnson, Meade Lux Lewis and Albert Ammons. Immediately before the obligatory massed finale Red was featured singing and playing his tour de force 'Ride, Red, Ride'. In 1942, Eddie Condon and publicist Ernie Anderson observed the successful trend and began a longrunning series of Saturday early evening concerts at the New York Town Hall. Red played on a few of these, as did Higginbotham, but by then their out-of-town commitments precluded their becoming regular participants. Their travels took them on a theatre tour, but when they returned to New York various promises of employment failed to materialize and there was no immediate work for the group. *Down Beat* announced that Red had broken up his band, and Higginbotham's action, in going off to play in a pick-up group organized by pianist Edgar Hayes, seemed to confirm this. Fortunately the tide soon changed and Red was able to reassemble his musicians for various bookings, including a week at the Apollo Theater (as part of a 'Salute to Negro Troops' presentation), and a six-day residency at the Gaiety Vaudeville Theater in New York. These dates were followed, from 18 May 1942, by the first of a series of residencies at the Ken Club in Boston, Massachusetts. There the band enjoyed a coalescent partnership with the great Sidney Bechet, who appeared with them as a special guest.

But the success that Red enjoyed at this first Boston booking was tempered by a visit he made to see his old friend, trumpeter Bunny Berigan, who was playing locally at the Tic Toc Club. Berigan, devastated by alcoholism, had only just got out of hospital. He was in such poor shape that he had to sit down to play his solos. Red, who had always regarded Bunny as a master trumpeter, was genuinely aggrieved to see him like this and urged Berigan to return to New York for treatment rather than journeying on to distant Norfolk, Virginia, to play the next gig. Berigan failed to heed Red's advice, and sadly died two weeks later.[3]

Red's initial bookings in Boston helped him to establish a reputation that made him a popular visitor with New England jazz fans for the next 20 years, but the city where Red really triumphed in the early 1940s was Chicago. On 15 August 1942 Red's band began a residency in the Downbeat Room, part of the Garrick Lounge, situated in Chicago's

'Biffly Bam'   The Young Professional

Henry 'Red' Allen with his wife, Pearly May Allen

The Star of the Show. Henry 'Red' Allen fronting Luis Russell's Orchestra. Left to Right: Jimmy Archey, Bill Coleman, Luis Russell, Bill Dillard, Will Johnson, Henry 'Red' Allen, Paul Barbarin, Albert Nicholas, 'Pops' Foster, Henry 'Moon' Jones and Greely Walton

Mills Blue Rhythm Band on tour, *c.* 1935. Henry Allen Sr with Henry 'Red' Allen, Edgar Hayes, J.C. Higginbotham, Lawrence Lucie and friends

'Three Buddies' *c.* 1936, William 'Buster' Bailey, Henry 'Red' Allen and J.C. Higginbotham

Irving Mills

Henry 'Red' Allen with
Baron Timme Rosenkrantz,
New York, late 1930s

Henry 'Red' Allen with Gene Krupa

Joe Glaser

Henry 'Red' Allen with his father and his son

Henry 'Red' Allen and his Orchestra, 1946 Left to Right: Eddie Bourne,
J.C. Higginbotham, Bill Thompson, Henry 'Red' Allen, Clarence 'Benny' Moten
and Don Stovall

Recording with
George Lewis,
New Orleans, 1951

Freddie Moore,
'Sonny' Greer, Louis
Armstrong and Henry
'Red' Allen

The Kid Ory Band in Europe, 1959. Left to Right: Cedric Haywood, Henry 'Red' Allen,
Bob McCracken, Kid Ory and Alton Redd

Henry 'Red' Allen with the author, 1964

Louis Armstrong and Henry 'Red' Allen 1963

Henry 'Red' Allen with the author, 1967 (the last photograph ever taken of Red)

Loop district; there they shared the billing with Billie Holiday. The band opened to a full house, and continued to play for capacity crowds throughout a stay that lasted four months. It transpired that this was the beginning of a long association with the venue. In a lengthy review that covered one of their early nights at the Garrick, *Down Beat* critic Dixon Gayer wrote:

Red Allen is stellar on trumpet. His ideas are superb and casual. There is no great fuss over his work, only cleanness, ideas and piercing tone. J.C. Higginbotham plays trombone. That is an understatement in itself, because if Jay merely plays trombone we have to think up a name for what the rest of the country's trombonists do. Jay is head and shoulders above come one, come all. With apparently no mouthpiece pressure Jay achieves power or delicacy, blast or bluff. His blues are excellent. His ideas on all things are wonderful.[4]

Gayer went on to praise alto saxophonist Don Stovall, who had recently joined Red's band after working with Cootie Williams. He too had once been part of Fate Marable's Band. The review also mentioned the other relatively new members of Red's group: bassist Clarence 'Benny' Moten, pianist General Morgan and drummer Kenny Clarke (who was soon to become one of the central figures in the emerging 'bebop' style). Dixon Gayer ended with a plea, 'All in all, this is a top-notch crew. Please let them stay that way. No commerciality.'

Kenny Clarke left the band shortly after that review appeared and was soon drafted into the US Army; his place was taken by Red's close friend and ex-Luis Russell colleague, Paul Barbarin. 'Benny' Moten (no relation to the bandleader of that name) was a New York born bassist, then in his mid-20s and single. General Morgan (apparently his real name) was from Savannah, Georgia. Though not quite 30 years old he was married with four children, and had a Grade 3 draft rating, making it unlikely that he would ever be called into the services. Don Stovall was also married. He was a competent vocalist, whose shyness made him reluctant to sing in public. With Red's encouragement Stovall joined his two front-line colleagues in a jovial vocal routine on 'They All Ask for You', and later graduated to a solo vocal feature on Duke Ellington's wartime advice against careless talk, 'The Slip of a Lip Might Sink a Ship'. Good though his performances were, Stovall's full talent on alto saxophone was never really captured on record. His playing on various 'air-shots' (particularly an up-tempo version of 'Body and Soul') reveals that he was an even greater player than his achievements on disc indicate.

Red's individual brand of showmanship, plus the sextet's musical expertise, won over the Garrick's clientele. Most of the customers were not jazz experts, but Red managed to turn them into jazz enthusiasts. The owner of the club was an ex-boxer named Joe Sherman. He knew very little about jazz but loved to see his customers happy. Billie Holiday had a few run-ins with Sherman, most of them about her lack of punctuality, but observing her popularity with the audiences, he learnt to accept her foibles about getting to work on time. Red Allen was delighted with the receptions and the reviews. One of the only bleak occasions during his Chicago stay occurred when Red attended the funeral there of one of his father's close friends, George Sims, the former baritone-horn player in the Allen Brass Band. But it was often like 'old home' times at the Garrick because lots of the New Orleans musicians who were working in Chicago dropped in to see Red. One visitor was trumpeter Punch Miller, who had given the young Red technical advice. Red told his band this, but they teasingly said that this seemed difficult to believe as Punch looked younger than Red. Punch had to settle the rising irritation by saying 'Red is a young fellow. He came up way under me.'[5] Bassist Percy Gabriel, another New Orleanian, worked for a time in Stanley Williams's Band, which played opposite Red's group at the Garrick. During a brief period when Buster Moten was off sick Gabriel helped Red out by playing with both groups. Red and Higgy's appetite for playing was insatiable: on a night off from the Garrick they guested with Bud Freeman's Band at the Panther Room of Chicago's Hotel Sherman.

The boom in business at the Garrick Lounge meant that the famous Louisiana-born clarinet player, Jimmie Noone, was booked with his trio to play in the upstairs section of the club, which catered for the overflow of customers. This booking was to have dramatic reper-cussions. Joe Sherman had an argument with Noone's drummer, Mel Draper, and told him 'If you don't like that way I treat you, you can get out'.[6] When the drummer took Sherman at his word and began carrying his drum kit out of the premises the club owner's anger overflowed and he punched Draper, knocking him out. As a result, Harry Gray, the President of Musicians' Union Local 208 (then designated 'a Negro local') called all the members out of the club. Billie Holiday, though not under the jurisdiction of the Union, walked out of the booking in sympathy. Sherman temporarily left Chicago and his brother attempted to hire white musicians for the club, without success. Joe Sherman decided to return to Chicago, but he was made to pay full wages to Jimmie Noone's Trio in lieu of dismissal, plus damages of $700 to Mel Draper.

Red Allen and Billie Holiday resumed their residency at the Garrick. One of the visitors to the club was a young singer (and pianist), Ruth Jones, who was immediately enamoured by Billie's stage performance. She had doted on Billie's recordings for some while, but had never seen her perform live. Ruth was so impressed that she went against the wishes of her recently acquired husband, John Young, and (according to Red Allen) took a job looking after the ladies' cloakroom at the Garrick so that she could observe Billie at close hand, and learn as much as she could about her style of presentation. When Ruth got the chance she sat in with the various groups that played upstairs, and that was where Red first heard her sing. He advised Joe Sherman that it would be worthwhile signing her up as a featured vocalist – Red gave the girl the nickname 'Dynamite'. Sherman agreed to let her sing in the downstairs section of the club on Sundays (as part of a gospel session) and whenever Billie Holiday was late showing up, but he hesitated about offering her a contract. Before Sherman had made up his mind Lionel Hampton and Joe Glaser entered the picture and within days the vocalist, by now renamed Dinah Washington, was singing with Hampton's Band as a prelude to becoming an international star. Hampton himself confirmed Red's story about 'Dinah' working as an attendant in the ladies' cloakroom.[7]

Joe Glaser was happy with the reports he received on the successes of the Allen-Holiday pairing and early in 1943 he got the team a booking at Kelly's Stables in New York where they played to good business for a month (sharing the billing with Coleman Hawkins). Red Allen's departure from the Garrick Showbar (as the room was now called) meant a return booking for Louis Jordan's up-and-coming small band, which had previously played a long residency there. Red said later that when he was in Chicago he bought some of Jordan's recordings, to check on the formula he used, and soon found himself enjoying the music.[8] Jordan's fame was growing rapidly and when Joe Sherman was unable to fulfil a clause in Jordan's contract that stipulated that the club was to guarantee live radio transmissions by the band, Jordan pulled out of the booking. Sherman had hoped to recall Red's band back to Chicago but by then they were in California, where on 1 March 1943, they began a two-month residency at Herb Rose's 331 Club in Hollywood (replacing Nat 'King' Cole's Trio). The band's stay on the West Coast coincided with drummer Zutty Singleton settling in California and a visit by Louis Armstrong's Orchestra, so Red, Zutty and Louis were able to enjoy a happy reunion one afternoon. Red's band left California to play for a week in Salt Lake City, Utah.

Joe Sherman had replaced Louis Jordan's group with a sextet led by trumpeter Hot Lips Page. He summarized his views on the incoming group by saying 'It isn't Red Allen and J.C. Higginbotham, but it is a nice band'.[9] A few weeks passed and Sherman began praising Page's Band, but this was only the preliminary to another fracas in which Page was hit in the mouth. He never returned to the Garrick, and again the Union placed an embargo on the club, this time for five days. Hot Lips Page returned to New York to play at the Famous Door, and Red Allen's Band went back to the Garrick where they opened on 21 May 1943, initially working alongside singer Alberta Hunter. Don Stovall dropped out briefly and his place was taken temporarily by altoist Earl Bostic. Unlike Hot Lips Page, Red Allen never encountered any hostility from Joe Sherman and the band settled down to begin what turned out to be a long and successful residency. In August 1943 when Paul Barbarin decided to leave to form his own Illinois-based small band (which soon played residencies in Springfield and in Peoria), his place on drums was taken by Alvin Burroughs. Some months later General Morgan left to work as a solo pianist and was replaced by 23-year-old Alfred 'Al' Williams (born in Memphis, Tennessee, but raised in Chicago). Violinist Stuff Smith's Trio shared the Garrick booking with Red's band for ten months, during which time radio shows were being broadcast from the club on station WBBM. This radio exposure was welcome but not vital for Red's band. Their fame was being spread mainly by word of mouth from those many people who enjoyed listening to the music and being entertained by affable showmanship. Unlike a number of other small groups of that era, Red's band did not depend on big record sales, so the 1942–3 American Federation of Musicians' ban, which virtually brought a complete stop to the making of recordings, did not affect Red's progress whereas it caused a number of bands to drift out of popularity.

The Garrick residency saved Red from facing the problems that travelling bands were experiencing through the wartime shortages of gasoline and replacement tyres. His long stay in Chicago allowed him to invite Pearly May and Henry III (during his son's school vacations) to move temporarily there. Red's wife joined him at the Du Sable Hotel, and their son went off to stay nearby with his Aunt Sylvia. The long stay also allowed J.C. Higginbotham to make a temporary home in Chicago for his wife Bea. The two musicians did not spend much time socializing with each other but both visited the Preview Club (on Randolph Street) to hear Roy Eldridge playing at the top of his form. Red and Roy exchanged guarded greetings, but did not, on this occasion, get involved in musical combat. After Stuff Smith's Trio left the Garrick the club booked a series of guest stars to appear with Red's band, including alto saxophonist Pete Brown and the ex-Duke Ellington tenor saxist Ben Webster, who became something of a fixture at the Garrick. For a brief while at the Garrick Red rekindled his youthful habit of playing the drums and worked up a shared percussion feature with Alvin Burroughs. An eminent visitor to the club in late 1944 was Louis Armstrong, who had his photograph taken with Red, Higgy, Ben Webster and Don Stovall. Higgy took brief leave from Red's band to appear with Louis Armstrong at a New Orleans jazz concert sponsored by *Esquire* magazine. While there Higgy learnt that he had again won first place in the popularity poll organized by *Down Beat* magazine. If Red was upset by the contrast between the low number of poll votes he received and Higgy's continual successes, he never said so. As a bandleader he realized that the trombonist's triumphs were a selling-point for the group and this probably subdued any disappointment he may have felt. It must also be borne in mind that while Red was only making records with his own band throughout most of the 1940s, Higgy became a candidate for popularity by being featured on freelance dates under his own name and as part of various all-star groups.

In 1944 the band did a series of recordings for the World E.T. radio transcription service (a subsidiary of Decca), which were later released on the Brunswick label. The results were not entirely satisfactory and the band sounds positively fidgety on a fast version of 'Ride, Red, Ride' (newly arranged by Al Williams). Higginbotham punches out a solo (backed by a Latin-American rhythm) before Stovall enters, sounding less inspired than usual, then, in answer to the band's vocal exhortations, Red blows with more spirit than direction. It is a poor offering. 'Dark Eyes' (also arranged by Williams) is an improvement. Red's fiercely blown out-of-tempo cadenzas create a dramatic introduction, which features his ability to glissando down to his lowest register. Another inappropriate Latin-American interlude intrudes, then Red skilfully imparts just the right degree of humour into some revised lyrics before soaring into an up-tempo trumpet feature that is studded with adept trilling. 'Dear Old Southland' is a feature for Higginbotham's formidable playing in which he loosely follows an arrangement originally recorded by Louis Armstrong. The bonus here is the attractive sound of the bowed string-bass and the panache with which Higgy plays the four-in-a-bar section. 'Red Jump' is a succession of quirky riffs; the piano-playing sounds indeterminate but Stovall here makes the most of his brief solos. Compared to the confident musical poise that graced all of the sides that Red made with his own bands in the 1930s, these recordings have an unattractive, ruffled feeling.

During the late stages of World War II the US government issued an edict that enforced a temporary curfew on night clubs remaining open after midnight. As a result Joe Sherman decided to change the Garrick's schedule by opening for business at 5.15 p.m. – previously the club had opened at 8 p.m., with Red's band doing their first set at 10 p.m. Sherman's ploy had an adverse effect on business, and though Red's band continued to be billed as 'perennial favorites', Allen himself saw the writing on the wall and in August 1945 accepted a lucrative offer to take his band back to California, this time to play at the Club Savoy in San Francisco. There were no hard feelings between Red and Joe Sherman as the band concluded their two-and-a-half-year stay in Chicago.

San Francisco was one of the focal points in the revival of old style jazz, with the twin trumpet team of Lu Watters and Bob Scobey enjoying success in their attempts to recreate the music of King Oliver and other wonderful innovators. Good Time Jazz (as this Californian creation was often labelled) was performed in various clubs dotted around the Bay area. There most of the bands shared a rugged approach that was anchored to stolid rhythm sections (usually complete with a tuba and a banjo). They gave a good deal of pleasure and introduced many listeners to vintage jazz but few of these new fans were interested in the more up-to-date approach that Red Allen's Band adopted. The veteran trombonist Kid Ory, who had recently come out of retirement, effectively won over young jazz zealots on the West Coast by basing most of his repertoire on tunes linked with the early days of New Orleans jazz. In San Francisco, Red experienced a situation that recurred over the coming years whereby earnest followers of the jazz revival solemnly (and sometimes abrasively) advised him about the work of King Oliver and Jelly Roll Morton, suggesting that their tunes should form the basis of his performances, seemingly unaware that Red had recorded with both these giants. Red gave himself amusement by saying that he had heard these names but was unsure as to what sort of jazz they had played. He then sat back and smiled benevolently as the fans poured out what was usually a wildly inaccurate history of early jazz. But, no matter how broadly Red smiled on these occasions, he did not approve of people pigeonholing jazz stylists and expressed himself forcefully on the subject, 'I don't go for the classification idea. It's not musicians who make the classifications.'[10]

Red's band played for almost two months in San Francisco, then moved back home to the East Coast in time to open at the Onyx Club on West 52nd Street in November 1945. That same month Red's band played for a week at the renowned Apollo Theater in Harlem. Despite the fact that the popularity of modern jazz, or bebop as it was also called, was growing steadily, Red's band did good business at the Onyx. Red and Higgy had their own following in New York and many wellwishers went to that club to welcome them back to the Big Apple. Red's band retained its Chicago personnel throughout their stay on the West Coast, but drummer Alvin Burroughs left in New York, during the spring of 1946, to form his own sextet; his place was taken by Eddie 'Mole' Bourne.

Musically Red's band was midway between the boppers on one side and the revivalists on the other. It seemed de rigeur that if you liked one style you hated the other. Dizzy Gillespie, then the leading exponent of modern jazz trumpet playing, said:

The squabble between the boppers and the 'moldy figs', who played or listened exclusively to Dixieland jazz, arose because the older musicians insisted on attacking our music and putting it down. They really did, but then you noticed some of the older guys started playing our riffs, a few of them, like Henry 'Red' Allen. The others remained hostile to it.[11]

In those days any horn player, eager to keep his 'chops' in good working order, could find any number of venues where jam sessions were regularly held. One such place was Clark Monroe's Uptown House (then on 52nd Street). Red and Buck Clayton, sharing a casual, unpaid blow there, were approached by a teenaged trumpeter who asked if he could join in. Red said 'No kid. We don't want you up here', but after Buck Clayton had said 'Let him play', the young Miles Davis was allowed on to the bandstand.[12] Miles never held the snub against Red, for whom the action was out of character – he enjoyed a reputation for helping young musicians whenever he could. Years later, in a 1963 interview with Nat Hentoff, Red said:

One of the critics wrote that I sounded as if I'd been listening to Miles Davis. The fact is that Miles used to come around to hear me during his first years in New York. I like Miles's work very much, but I'd been playing the way I did on the record for a long time before I ever heard Miles.[13]

Red, who had been considered to be 'modern' during his younger days, could appreciate the problems that some of the emergent musicians were having. He summarized his attitude in an interview with Val Wilmer:

I don't go for putting people in different categories like Dixieland, Chicago, West Coast and so on. You don't have time to analyse those things, else you turn out to be a frustrated musician. As long as anyone is playing music, that's alright with me because I love it. I listen to everybody, you know. Bop didn't bother me. This was just another style. It's all kinds of new chords, but all of them wind up with the same spark plug. I had no squawk when bop came in. I had no days off unless I wanted them.[14]

The only aspect of the modernists' efforts that baffled Red was their deliberate avoidance of showmanship:

All the early musicians had it, you had to, but the ones who came on the scene later had nothing. To each his own, but the funny thing is that Dizzy Gillespie has that personality and most of them copied from him, so why didn't they find out about showmanship?[15]

Bunk Johnson, by now settled in New York, was playing to the faithful at the Stuyvesant Casino on the East Side, but as the publicity about Johnson dwindled so too did his audiences and in May 1946 the residency ended (though Johnson briefly played there again in 1947). Red paid a social visit there, climbing the one flight of stairs to say hallo to old friends from Louisiana. Out of courtesy, Johnson then went to hear Red and Higgy in New York – and promptly fell asleep. Pianist Art Hodes, who witnessed the scene, was flabbergasted that anyone could doze off two rows away from the sounds of two such powerful brass players. In January 1946 Red's band was on the same bill as Bunk's group. They both were part of 'The Roots of Jazz', a presentation narrated by Orson Welles at the New York Town Hall. But big concerts featuring 'hot jazz' were gradually being replaced by a longrunning series of shows featuring non-traditional jazz, organized by promoter Norman Granz and billed as 'Jazz at the Philharmonic'. Red was not booked to appear in any of these concerts but he and his band got top billing at a 'Jazz Cavalcade' held in February 1946 at the New York Town Hall. The show also featured Sidney Bechet, Sid Catlett, Wellman Braud, George Brunis, Art Hodes, Wild Bill Davison and others, but the attendance figures were disappointing and, according to a *Down Beat* interview, it was Red's two sets that saved the day. Not long afterwards Eddie Condon ended his longrunning series of New York Town Hall concerts, several of which, over the years, had featured Red Allen. Red always held Condon in high esteem, and described him as 'one of my ace boys – a great leader. He knows how to get guys together. He knows how to get a great feeling out of them.'[16]

Red's stay at the Onyx Club lasted for six months, but as the jazz 'war' over stylistic differences erupted, his band was in danger of being stranded in a 'no man's land'. Business at the Onyx gradually decreased and the manager, Mike Westerman, told Red that the club was about to close temporarily. In May 1946, customers turning up at the club found a sign reading 'Closed For Alterations' placed on a locked door. Red and his band were described in a contemporary report as being 'at liberty'.[17] Fortunately Red was able to bolster up his income in late 1945 and 1946 by playing bookings at a series of Sunday matinee jam sessions at the 845 Club on his home patch, Prospect Avenue in the Bronx. There a local entrepreneur, Johnny Jackson, engineered a series of musical duels between celebrated jazzmen, including a memorable 'Battle of the Alto Sax', which matched Earl Bostic and Don Stovall. In January 1946 Red and Higgy were involved in one of the most spectacular jam sessions of that decade. To celebrate the sixth anniversary of recording 'Flying Home', Lionel Hampton threw a backstage party at New York's Strand Theater. A jam session developed that included Louis Armstrong and Red Allen on trumpets, Higgy on trombone, Jimmy Dorsey on reeds and three exceptional drummers, Sid Catlett, Cozy Cole and Buddy Rich.[18]

Thanks to Joe Glaser's efforts the brief period of unemployment for Red's band ended on 21 June 1946 when they began work at the reopened Kelly's Stables (on 52nd Street) sharing top billing with Stuff Smith's Trio, pianist Garland Wilson and singer Thelma Carpenter. The club's co-owner, former saxophonist Ralph Watkins, had earlier that year tried to perk up business by devising (with his business partner George

Lynch) a new policy of soft music and scantily clad singers. When that failed they closed the premises for a while before announcing they intended to 'return the Stables to Swing' by booking Red Allen's band. The opening night was wild, with Stuff Smith joining Red's band for some inspired jamming. Business picked up at the club and continued to hold steady when Stuff Smith's Trio moved on to be replaced by Mary Osborne's Trio. After a few months at Kelly's Stables Red's band left town to play a lucrative booking at the Brown Derby in Washington, DC. When they returned to play further engagements at Kelly's they discovered that in their absence the number of customers had dropped drastically so they were soon on the move again, this time to the nearby Spotlite Club, run by Harry Holland, who, like almost every club owner on 52nd Street, was uncertain as to what sort of music he should feature. His pairing of Red's band and pianist Lennie Tristano's Trio showed that he was intent on using a spray-shot policy. Within weeks that club had closed, and any thoughts of Red's band returning to Kelly's Stables went up in the smoke caused by the late-night blaze that destroyed what was mercifully an empty club.

By this time the recordings that drummer Alvin Burroughs had made before he left had been released. These four sides also featured the band's new pianist, Bill Thompson. The recordings give a clear indication of the band's style, which was based mainly on the playing of riff-like themes (usually up tempo). 'The Crawl' (a number jointly composed by Red and Don Stovall) is typical. Each of the band take 32-bar solos, with Red giving a friendly nod to the beboppers in his chorus. Stovall was a fine alto sax player whose style owes a little to Willie Smith, Pete Brown and Johnny Hodges, but he was a consistent improviser who built up his solos logically and never seemed at a loss for ideas. 'Buzz Me' is a vocal feature for Red based on the harmonies of a 12-bar blues. Red sings and plays impressively here, and introduces one of his pet bandstand comments by shouting 'Carry on! Carry on!' as an encouragement to a fellow soloist. Benny Moten's bass playing is strong and accurate and Bill Thompson's presence has a unifying effect of the rhythm section. 'Drink Hearty' is, as the title suggests, a tavern song, one that is enthusiastically sung by the entire ensemble. Saxophone and trombone have brief solos before Red creates some skilful solo vocalizing. Red's exuberant voice is also well to the fore on his own song 'Get the Mop', a fast riff that sounds to be closely related to 'Red Jump'. A couple of these numbers ('Drink Hearty' and 'Get the Mop') were also featured in a soundie (a brief film that was made for coin-operated visual jukeboxes). It allowed

Red's fans to see that as he was entering his forties he no longer had a thin, lanky look. Instead he was thickset and hefty which, with his height of 6 feet, made him a very imposing figure.

Some months after 'The Crawl' session the band returned to the recording studio, this time with Eddie Bourne on drums. The main fare was again riff numbers, with 'Count Me Out' featuring some nicely conceived alto sax playing from Stovall. 'Check Up' is in a similar mould, but here Red struggles to get going in his solo. Happily pianist Thompson makes up for his leader's temporary aberration. The band then showed its versatility by recording two mellow ballads, both with appealing vocals by Red. Red uses the rich sound of his trumpet low notes to interpret the melody of 'If It's Love You Want', a thoughtfully structured opus that inspires Red to sing well. His vocal on 'Let Me Miss You' (a blues which he co-wrote with his old bandleader Luis Russell) is even better, and again the trumpet work is atmospherically couched in the lower register. Higginbotham, playing at his smoothest, fortifies the tender mood, and makes it clear that his admiration for Lawrence Brown's trombone-playing was consciously, or subconsciously, influencing his interpretation of ballads. On both the 1946 Victor recording sessions Red introduces numbers by shouting 'Wamp! Wamp!' in place of a 1–2–3–4 count-in, recreating his bandstand habit of alerting musicians (and audiences) that a tune was about to begin. The strategy was effective (if a little wearying) and later Red wisely rationed his wamps.

Nothing from these recording sessions achieved the big record sales (and subsequent airplays) that could have caused a surge of national interest in the band. Louis Jordan, whose Tympany Five had played a similar club circuit to Red Allen's band in the early 1940s, was, by this time, thanks to a series of successful recordings, offered more engage-ments than he had time to fill, including work on the big ballroom circuits where lucrative deals involving 60 per cent of the door-take were offered. With work scarce in New York it seemed a good move for Red's band to return to Chicago, but club business there was also in the doldrums, partly because of a worsening in race relations sparked by the Chicago Housing Authority's decision to move black families into hitherto whites-only areas. Nevertheless, in late April 1947 Red's band were booked into Colosimo's New Theatre Restaurant, at 22nd Street on the South Side; the site had played its part in Chicago's history, having originally been owned by one of the city's notorious vice lords. Red's band took up a four-shows-a-night residency sharing billing with Billie Holiday and a couple of variety acts. But this was one of the most troubled periods in

Billie's life, and the club owners were reported as being 'not too happy about her presence'.[19] She was not offered an extension of her 8-day contract (26 April–4 May) and moved back East, where two weeks later she was arrested for narcotics offences. Coincidentally, in a candid interview published in the 22 April 1947 issue of *New Masses*, J.C. Higginbotham spoke on the subject of drugs, saying, 'Let us put an end to the common belief that music and marijuana are synonymous.' But this statement was only a subsidiary part of the article's main theme, racial prejudice. Under the headline 'Some of My Best Friends Are Enemies', Higgy attacked what he called 'the "look how liberal I am" group, who try to cover up their deep rooted prejudices against all minorities by deliberately seeking to mingle with colored musicians'.

Red's band finished their month-long contract in Chicago and moved on to Detroit where they appeared at the El Sino Club. The band clicked at this venue and played a series of return bookings there. Gradually club dates in other cities started to materialize, as did some prestigious theatre bookings in a show headlined by film actor Eddie 'Rochester' Anderson, first at the Regal, Chicago, in July 1947, then at the Apollo, New York, in August 1947.

While in New York the band did a session for the independent Apollo label, waxing four polished sides, including a version of 'Shanty in Old Shanty Town' for which new lyrics had been devised that likened the shanty to an outdoor lavatory with three seats of different sizes. Red's personality gives the questionable lyric undeniable charm, and though the record did not sell well, those who heard it never forgot it. As a result it became one of Red's most requested numbers over the years. 'Mr Wamp Walks' is a sophisticated blues theme, which is neatly performed by an ensemble that has Red using a Harmon mute. The resultant sound is not unlike the closely scored small groups that Count Basie was later to occasionally record with, and has little resemblance to the earlier plangent recordings by Red's band. Stovall delivers a profusion of ideas in a laid-back fashion, then Red (still using a Harmon mute) takes a restrained but satisfying solo allowing Higgy's purposeful blowing to create an effective contrast. Red takes the vocal on 'Old Fool, Do You Know Me?', and shares some casual dialogue with Higginbotham, who plays the only solo on this track. 'My Melancholy Baby' like 'Shanty' is given some alternate lyrics and emerges as 'My Alcoholic Baby'. The B side of 'Shanty' was reserved for 'Bill's Down Beat', a bright 32-bar theme that features Stovall's flowing alto sax playing. Red and Higgy share a chorus, all three soloists benefiting from the swinging, buoyant rhythm section. Again, neat phrasing is the hallmark of the band's performance, and they achieve a standard that is worthy of the John Kirby Sextet at its best. Bizarrely, the two 'jokey' sides from this session ('Shanty' and 'My Melancholy Baby') were issued pseudonymously on another label as being by 'Fatso'.

Red's band played another New York theatre date at Loew's State, then returned to Chicago for a 'Battle of Jazz' (versus a small band featuring Flip Phillips, Bill Harris and Dave Tough, plus a Gene Ammons group) held at a giant roller-skating hall, prior to fulfilling bookings in Kansas City during September 1947. Later that month the band returned to Boston, a city where they enjoyed a durable reputation thanks to their various appearances at the Ken Club. This time they played at the Savoy Café on Massachusetts Avenue, a club where Sidney Bechet had achieved a good deal of success in the mid-1940s. It proved to be a venue to which Red's band often returned during the coming years.

Mass viewing of television was still a thing of the future, but some jazz was being featured on the growing number of channels, with Eddie Condon's Tuesday night *Floor Show* on WPIX being one of the pioneering efforts. Red Allen appeared on this show, and on various televised concerts during the late 1940s. He was still a star name with jazz followers, as was Higginbotham, but the trombonist, instead of being voted number one in the popularity polls, was now placed tenth, with Red's band not even gaining a place in the combo section. Most musicians pay scant attention to poll placings and Red Allen was no exception, but both he and Joe Glaser realized that the voting was an indication that neither Henry 'Red' Allen nor J.C. Higginbotham were 'in' names with jazz fans, and therefore the chances of the two men being featured at top New York clubs were slender. The answer was to take work on a less glamorous circuit in other cities, playing at venues like the El Sino in Detroit and the Dome Club in Minneapolis. At such clubs they conjured up their old magic and at the Dome they broke the attendance record on a night when the temperature dipped to 20°F below. They also did well at the Astoria in Baltimore, the Continental in Milwaukee and the Falcon in Detroit, but they could never find the right venue in Chicago that would enable them to recapture their popularity of yesteryear. They played at the Silhouette Club, the Brass Rail, the Blue Note, and the North Side Tailspin without creating a riot, but they kept working. Personnel changes were few and far between, but by the summer of 1948, Johnny Pate (from Chicago), then 24 years old and the baby of the band, was on bass. Red would not take any job that he felt was demeaning for his musicians. In Chicago he observed his old friendly rival, New Orleans trumpeter Lee Collins, entrapped year after year at the Victory Club on North Clark Street, where he played for seven nights a week from 7.30 p.m. until 4 a.m. At midnight Collins was usually allowed half an hour for 'lunch' but even this break was not always granted and pianist Dick Wellstood remembered seeing Collins playing through the whole session, eating sandwiches on the bandstand. Venues like the Tailspin Club did not have drape curtains at the back of the stage, but at least the crowd was always enthusiastic and the playing hours reasonable. By this time Red always drove his own Cadillac (having changed from a Buick Roadmaster in the late 1940s). One night he offered to drive Lee Collins to the Victory Club, and on the way he gently asked Collins if there was not a less arduous place for him to work, adding that he would do his best to help him find a new locale. Collins declined the offer, and said with sadness in his voice, 'I'm in a routine that I can't get out of', adding somewhat ominously, 'The people I work for wouldn't like it at all if I said I was leaving'.[20] When Collins eventually did leave Chicago he enjoyed considerable success in California and in Europe. From the summer through to the autumn of 1949 Red's band too worked mainly on the West Coast, including a return to San Francisco.

Red's contract at most of the clubs he worked at was for the duration of a week, sometimes with an option that allowed the clubowner to extend the run, but Red preferred not to take that sort of deal. He was happier knowing some months in advance where he was going to be playing. It needed careful planning to keep the engagement book reasonably full, but Red always liked to visit New Orleans once a year (usually at Mardi Gras Carnival time) in order to see his mother and father. His 1949 visit coincided with a very special event – the crowning of Louis Armstrong as the 'King of the Zulus'. Red was delighted to be in New Orleans at that time, particularly as he'd taken his son Henry III with him. Together with Red's father, they found space on a balcony and cheered as loudly as anyone when the float carrying the crowned Louis passed by.

10

METROPOLE MAGIC

Louis Armstrong's All Stars went from strength to strength in the early 1950s, with Joe Glaser being swamped with offers to book the highly mobile sextet from promoters and impresarios throughout the world, but enquiries for Red Allen's band steadily diminished and Glaser's staff had to work increasingly hard to keep the group working regularly. During 1950 the band continued to play in various cities such as Minneapolis, St Paul, Kalamazoo, Milwaukee, Detroit and Chicago, but it was difficult for Red to maintain a stable personnel when there were large gaps in the date sheet. Don Stovall left in the late spring of 1950, and his place was taken by alto saxist Bill Adkins; Stovall was disillusioned in seeing his income going up and down like a yo-yo, and decided to settle for a steady day job in New York. Soon afterwards bassist Johnny Pate (who later enjoyed success as a composer) left to join violinist Eddie South's Trio. Various pianists were used in the band, including Jimmy Phipps.

Coincidentally, at the very time that Red's sextet was experiencing difficulties in finding steady engagements, another renewal of interest in traditional jazz was stirring, with special attention being shown toward veterans who had been featured on classic jazz recordings. As a result, Red began to be booked as a guest star at various weekend jazz sessions (or jazz 'bashes' as they were also known) held at two venues on Second Avenue, New York: the Stuyvesant Casino (near 9th Street) and the Central Plaza (between 6th and 7th). Sometimes Red fronted a pick-up band comprising former colleagues, and occasionally he was part of Fletcher Henderson's New Dixie Stompers, a group organized by his one-time leader that revived the name of a unit he had led in the 1920s. Red's reunion with Fletcher Henderson also involved him in appearing with that leader in a show called *The Jazz Train*, which opened at Bop City (49th and Broadway) on 15 September 1950. The revue was an attempt (by director and writer Mervyn Nelson) to present a history of jazz by staging a series of musical presentations in different locomotive carriages. Henderson wrote the music, and J.C. Johnson, another important figure from early jazz, wrote the lyrics. Dancers and singers were backed by a big band that was full of jazz stars, including Red Allen, Claude Jones, Tyree Glenn, Eddie Barefield, Lucky Thompson and Jimmy Crawford. Red was also featured in one of the sketches, playing the role of Louis Armstrong.

Unfortunately no recordings were made of this three-shows-a-night enterprise, which turned out to be a short-lived venture. A *Billboard* reviewer noted, 'Performers could get snow blindness from staring at the white cloths covering the empty tables'.[1] The production closed when Bop City folded in early October, but it was revived at the same venue (by now renamed the Paradise Club); even so the reprise ended in mid-November when the show ran out of customers. Red again worked with Fletcher Henderson at the Stuyvesant Casino on 17 November 1950 as part of an all-star line-up that included the two fiery cornetists Wild Bill Davison and Rex Stewart, plus the legendary sousaphone player Cyrus St Clair. This was one of the last occasions that Fletcher ever played in public. He briefly led a sextet in December 1950, then suffered a stroke that ended his playing career – he died in late 1952.

Red's income fell when he began making himself available for these New York weekend sessions, but in having no travelling expenses, or hotel charges, he was not that much worse off. His finances were considerably improved by a US District Court case brought on his behalf by Joe Glaser in 1950. It concerned the marked similarity between a currently successful song, 'Rag Mop', and Red Allen's 'Get the Mop' (recorded by Red in 1946). Joe Glaser's International Music publishing company took Hill and Range Music to court and filed a suit asking for an injunction, damages and an accounting of profits.[2] The case was settled out of court for what was described by *Down Beat* as 'a substantial payment plus a financial interest in the song'.[3]

Red was gladdened by the outcome of the case and celebrated by taking Pearly May to Louisiana for a vacation, but their stay there was shortened by a telephone call from their son in New York. In that July 1950 conversation Henry III relayed the news that he had enlisted in the US Marine Corps in order to serve in the Korean War. His parents immediately ended their visit to Algiers and returned to New York where Red vented his considerable anger by remonstrating with his son, 'Ain't there enough fools over there getting killed? Are you out of your mind?'[4] But Red soon calmed down and subsequently spoke with pride about his son's service achievements in Korea during 1951 and 1952. Initially, after Henry III had completed his boot-camp training he was stationed at a naval unit in Earle, New Jersey, and Red, after he finished his night's work at a New York club, willingly drove his son back to this base in the early hours of the morning. Red always spoke of his son with great affection: 'I love my son, and I guess my father loved me'.[5]

Most of Red's playing in early 1951 was done at Lou Terrassi's Hickory Log club at 154 West 47th Street, New York. There he led a small band consisting of Big Chief Russell Moore on trombone, Kenny Kersey on piano, Arthur Herbert on drums and Buster Bailey on clarinet. Buster was ill for part of the booking at Terrassi's and tenor saxist Bob Dukoff deputized for him. During this period, 16-year-old clarinettist Kenny Davern played his first gig with Red Allen at an American Legion Hall in Queens. Looking back, Davern remembered that Red was full of encouragement, 'Red was absolutely colour blind, if he liked someone's playing he didn't care whether they were black or white, and he was as helpful as he could be with young musicians'.[6] During the following years Davern played many gigs with Red; on one in Brooklyn (with Ed Wilcox on piano and Sonny Greer on drums) the clarinettist was impressed by Red's ability to take in a situation with the merest of glances. Red observed that Sonny Greer was, with glass in hand, loudly recounting events from his illustrious past. Red did not mind this but was vexed to realize that Sonny's anecdotes were being oiled by a ceaseless flow of alcohol, and this was before the band had played a note. When they got on to the bandstand, Red soon told the audience about Greer's successful years with Duke Ellington. He then announced a drum feature on 'Caravan', which Red tapped in at a breathtaking tempo. Chorus after chorus tumbled out of the drums but Red showed no signs of wanting the piece to end. Gradually the drumming got slower and slower until it came to a complete halt. Red gave a wry smile and then shouted out, 'Take it, Sonny!' Greer, suitably chastened, later apologized to Red for getting drunk before a gig.

On another gig, this time at the Central Plaza, Kenny saw Red deal with Jo Jones, a master percussionist, who could also be a model of awkwardness. Jones was behaving badly and the trumpeter retaliated by telling pianist Cliff Jackson, trombonist Jimmy Buxton and Davern that they were to stay with him and follow whatever musical twists and turns he took. Red then played the most involved rhythmic phrasing that Davern had ever heard. The trumpeter surpassed his reputation for superimposing rhythms and, in crossing and re-crossing the beat deliberately, he completely bewildered the great Jo Jones who ended up playing the hi-hat cymbal on the first and third beats (instead of the second and fourth). Red, affecting surprise, turned to Jones and said, 'You know what you did?'[7]

Red and J.C. Higginbotham had temporarily ceased working together. Higgy went off to Cleveland, where he led a band featuring his brother Bob on trumpet; from there he moved on to Boston, playing long residencies (often with his own band, which at one time featured Rex Stewart) at the Hi-Hat, at the Paradise and at the Savoy Café. When Lou Terassi's club went on to its summer schedule of three nights a week (Thursday, Friday and Saturday) Red went to California (in July 1951) to briefly deputize for an ailing Marty Marsala at the Hangover Club in San Francisco. Soon afterwards Red took Pearly May to Louisiana to resume the vacation that had been interrupted a year earlier. Red's place at Lou Terrassi's was taken by Buck Clayton.

Red's visit to New Orleans and Algiers allowed him the chance to see that his father (who had suffered a mild stroke) was increasingly frail, but he still continued to administrate his brass band's itinerary. Red borrowed a trumpet and proudly marched in his father's band, and he also enjoyed a playing reunion with clarinettist George Lewis and his old friend, drummer Paul Barbarin. These three, together with Jim Robinson (trombone), Alcide Pavageau (double bass), Lester Santiago (piano) and Lawrence Marrero (banjo), visited the WDSU studios in August 1951 where they recorded material for Joe Mares and Rudi Blesh that was originally issued on the Circle label.

Here Red does revert to an earlier style, or rather he plays in a way that combines traits from his past and present endeavours in creating a lead that does not sound incongruous alongside the work of his two older front-line partners. Red plays vigorously but economically on the first chorus of 'Darktown Strutters' Ball'; on the second his phrasing is a little more flamboyant but neither Lewis nor Robinson seems fazed, even though Red here and there introduces notes (such as flatted ninths) which would not figure in their improvisations. Lewis plays a typical bittersweet chorus, then Robinson counters with a ruggedly expressive solo. Red re-enters and blows resolutely through three ensemble choruses, steadily getting busier but still marshalling a robust front-line, which is vigorously underpinned by the sound of Alcide Pavageau's slapped string-bass. Paul Barbarin takes a four-bar drum tag, a device more often used by New York Dixieland line-ups than by New Orleans ensembles, and this contributes an effective ending to the piece.

On 'Hindustan', Red sketches out the bones of the melody by phrasing sparsely, then (coping with what sounds to be a poor instrument) pianist Lester Santiago creates a careful solo which is followed by an unshackled chorus from Red, during which Jim Robinson's trombone offers some effective, complementary musical asides. Lewis's solo is full of spirit and aptly prepares the way for the give-and-take of the final ensemble. The two takes of 'St James Infirmary' reveal many differences, both in the band's playing and in Red's singing of the lyrics – on one version he humorously inserts the name of the session's instigator, Rudi Blesh, by singing 'God bless her, Rudi Blesh her'. George Lewis's backing of Red's vocal is admirably delicate, but the mood changes as Red mounts a grandstand finale in which he employs a device that was to play an increasing part in his playing, namely the way he created a growling effect without using a mute. He did this by making a rasping sound in his throat and linking this with rapid tongue articulations (known as flutter-tongueing). It is not a pretty effect, but one that was (on occasion) mighty effective. 'Some of These Days' again shows the sparser side of Red's playing, and, whether consciously created or not, some of the variations he plays sound slightly reminiscent of lines that Bunk Johnson might have played. Lewis and Robinson again blow worthy solos, but in the background Lester Santiago's chordal progressions seem to be too simplified. The front-line achieve a nice rapport in the final chorus and combine well to produce an unspectacular ending that sounds appropriate and effective.

Red and Pearly May returned to New York where Red resumed playing club gigs. He also played sessions for Bob Maltz at the Stuyvesant Casino and made many appearances at the Central Plaza. Lots of Red's fans attended the weekend Central Plaza sessions and were delighted to have the opportunity of talking with him, whereas in the ambience of a night club they might have felt shy about approaching him. Red was happy to discuss jazz during his intermissions, but was just as pleased when the subject was sport, and particularly so if the guest shared Red's love for certain teams: the Mets (baseball), the Knicks (basketball) and the Cleveland Browns (football). By this time in his life Red enjoyed the odd glass of beer, and an occasional bourbon or sherry; in later years he sometimes drank whisky. At the Central Plaza the exuberant weekend audiences encouraged the bands to eschew subtlety. The most requested numbers were old traditional 'war horses', but at least promoter Jack Crystal (father of film actor Billy Crystal) was letting the crowd hear top-class musicians at reasonable prices: the slogan was 'one dollar fifty to get in, and absolutely nothing to get out'. Pianist Ralph Sutton, who often played there, offered a description of the place: 'Everyone yelled and stomped and nobody listened'.[8]

Red often worked with pianist Willie 'The Lion' Smith during this period. Later, drummer James 'Sunny' Murray, then a youngster, played some of his first New York gigs in bands that featured the two veterans. He recalled, 'Red and Willie had a thing as to who was the leader of the band, and drummers got bugged because with one cat you had to play one thing, with the other you had to play another. I tended to listen to Red Allen more because he liked the bass drum broken up – or none at all – where Willie liked it steady. But Red could play, like an earlier Fats Navarro, that way of long timing.'[9] Red and 'The Lion' had their squabbles but their friendship survived and the pianist later booked Red's band to play at his golden wedding party.

Red was willing to take on all sorts of work, including gigs with the young modern drummer, Max Roach, at the Apollo Bar on West 125th Street. Recalling this booking Red said, 'One time I followed Charlie Parker into a club, working with Max Roach's Band. When Parker's engagement finished I replaced him, but it didn't throw me.'[10] Writer Peter Clayton summed up Red's reputation as a forward-thinking improviser: 'He was a modernist before the term was invented'.[11] Guitarist Lawrence Lucie added to this viewpoint in surveying his early days with Red, 'He was a real spiritual player. He ran changes, sort of like an early Clark Terry…there were lots of notes played scalewise which sounded like the kind of modal playing a lot of the modern guys got into years later.'[12]

In the early 1950s Red was still on Joe Glaser's books as a bandleader so offers still came in for his band to play in other cities. The influx of these opportunities was small compared to the frequent and regular bookings that Red had fulfilled in the 1940s, but whenever possible Red took an organized band to these out-of-town engagements, rather than using a pick-up group. In late 1951 he led a strong line-up at the Silhouette in Chicago, consisting of J.C. Higginbotham (back in the fold), Buster Bailey, Sonny Greer on drums, Al Williams on piano and a local bassist. Red occasionally used tenor saxist Skinny Brown in his band during the early 1950s. Red's band returned home for Christmas, then played a residency at the Savoy in Boston early in 1952. Any pleasure that Red felt at again being in demand was totally eclipsed by the death of his father, Henry Allen Sr, on 11 January 1952, aged 75. Although he had been in fragile health for a year or more, his passing greatly affected Red. He travelled to Louisiana, and at the wake held at his father's house on Lamarque Street, West New Orleans, he met up with many musicians who had played regularly in the Allen Brass Band. The funeral was a big affair, with four bands, and Red was visibly moved when someone pointed out that his father had led a brass band for longer than anyone else in the history of New Orleans.

Red returned to New York and fulfilled all the engagements he was booked for, but offstage he was full of sadness and it was to be some months before his zest for life returned, though none of his audiences were aware that anything was amiss. Red continued to play regularly at Central Plaza. He also took part (representing the old school) in a 'Hot Versus Cool' series of concerts. In these presentations a small band of 'modernists' played alternating sets with a 'traditional' jazz band prior to the entire cast assembling on stage for what invariably turned out to be a shambolic jam session. The concept had a brief burst of popularity, mainly on the East Coast, but few fans went back for a second helping. Red shared the stage with Charlie Parker on a couple of these concerts (organized by tenorist Jerry Jerome). In the summer of 1952 Red's band played another booking at the Silhouette in Chicago, this time with Big Chief Russell Moore taking the place of J.C. Higginbotham; Buster Bailey was again on clarinet. The band's year ended by again returning to the Savoy in Boston, but there was still no sign of a boom in bookings. Red wasn't forgotten by his fellow professionals or by his devoted fans but his name rarely appeared in any music magazines. Red occasionally guested with various small jazz bands, and on a couple of these dates in 1952, he shared the limelight with singer Lee Wiley, at the Rustic Lodge, North Brunswick, New Jersey, where bassist Bill Green led the resident band. Red kept himself busy by playing at private engagements, which included barmitzvahs, publicity launches and hotel dances, but these 'ordinary gigs' mingled with more prestigious bookings, as in late August 1953 when both Red and Sidney Bechet guested for a week with Lucky Millinder's Orchestra at the Apollo Theater. Red was featured on his old showcase 'Ride, Red, Ride', and he also played a couple of numbers with Bechet.

By 1953 Bechet was resident in France and out of touch with the American jazz scene. As a result he asked Red to recommend suitable musicians to accompany him on his temporary return to the USA; Red willingly drew up a list for the visitor.

The shortage of work for the band meant that Red sometimes took bookings for the group that he might have turned down in busier times. For a 1953 residency at the Spa Club in Baltimore, Maryland, Red's group was billed as 'Henry "Red" Allen and his Dixieland Band'. When a writer visited that club, Red was keen to point out that this billing was not his idea:

> I must explain about the Dixieland billing. That word is now good box office, but when we go downstairs you'll see we just play old tunes in a nice jamming style. We don't have a strict two-beat drummer.[13]

The writer, noticing that the musicians took their drinks at a separate service bar, commented, 'Race relations have not advanced overly in this Southern city'.[14]

Red's percussionist on this job, Sonny Greer, was certainly not a two-beat drummer. Others in the band were trombonist Herb Flemming, Prince Robinson (a former star of McKinney's Cotton Pickers) on clarinet, and pianist Al Williams. For economic reasons the band often had to dispense with using a double bassist, but for a Caribbean booking during this period, the band added bassist Lloyd Trotman (and used Eddie Barefield on reeds, in place of Prince Robinson). Pearly May did not often travel with the band, but she was delighted to be on that trip to Bermuda. The decline in media interest towards Red continued and, when a tribute to the late Fletcher Henderson was published, Red's name was not even included in a long list of that bandleader's famous ex-sidemen; however, things were about to change dramatically.

Ben Harriman, manager of the Metropole, a large bar situated on Seventh Avenue (close to Times Square) had watched with interest the growing audiences at various New York venues that featured quasi-Dixieland and mainstream small groups. The Metropole, which had existed as a 'Gay '90s' bar on the northeast corner of 48th Street and Seventh Avenue, moved a couple of doors along and began functioning as a live music bar. Harriman got advice from Joe Glaser's Associated Booking Corporation on the availability and fees for various jazz musicians. Trumpeter Jimmy McPartland was one of the first approached, and he quickly rounded up a small group which began playing at the Metropole in April 1954. Red Allen was offered the chance to lead a band that alternated with McPartland's group, and he accepted, with alacrity, the five-nights-a-week schedule.

McPartland, about to leave for a trip to Europe, soon handed over the reins of his group to Bud Freeman, who in turn was replaced by Wingy Manone. Red's group held steady and it was soon obvious to the management that Allen's presentation, his appealing vocals and his outgoing stage personality were exactly what the customers wanted. As writer Sinclair Traill summed it up, 'He makes it his business to see that his audience are having a good time, but never lets them lose sight of the fact that it is jazz they are listening to'.[15] The music magazines soon got wind of the excitement being engendered at the Metropole and Red's name began appearing again in various columns. *Down Beat* (of 28 July 1954) mentioned Red Allen and Wingy Manone sharing the Metropole residency, 'When they do "The Saints" together, Armageddon sounds almost here.' Something special was needed to fill clubs during an era that marked a mushrooming of growth in the ownership of television sets – in the USA sales rose from 3 million to 20 million sets during the period 1950 to 1954.[16]

The success of the Metropole's new policy was instant, and soon the management decided to increase its live music schedule to include afternoon sessions. A large pool of freelance jazz musicians began working there, and regular trios and quartets took shape to fill the demand. Among those who worked there regularly were: Tony Parenti, Big Chief Russell Moore, Pee Wee Erwin, Tony Scott, Zutty Singleton, Louis Metcalf, Marty Napoleon, Cliff Jackson, Oliver Jackson, Charlie Shavers, Joe Thomas and Dick Wellstood. Wellstood only worked occasionally with Red Allen, but he enjoyed the experience immensely; he was once asked how backing Red compared to working with cornettist Bobby Hackett, and replied, 'Bobby is like a watchmaker who positions every screw, every ratchet, every jewel, perfectly; but' (and here came a pregnant pause) 'to tell the truth, I'd rather play with Red Allen.'[17]

Red tried whenever possible to use the same line-up during his early days at the Metropole: Herb Flemming on trombone, Buster Bailey on clarinet, Claude Hopkins on piano and bassist Lloyd Trotman (whose place was soon taken by the return of 'Buster' Moten). For a while drummer Cozy Cole was featured with Red as a special guest, but the usual drummer with the band was Eddie 'Mole' Bourne. Red enjoyed an especially happy social relationship with Buster Bailey, a delightful man, who was blessed with an outstanding technique on clarinet. Buster was never a jazz giant, but he was always musically correct, and had the gift of following a pianist's wrong chords so skilfully that the audience remained totally unaware that a musical disaster had been averted. He modestly summarized this accomplishment by saying, 'I can't whip 'em so I joins 'em.'[18] Red was always loyal to his musician friends, and regarded recordings he made with them in the same way he might have treasured a snapshot of them. He said, 'I never think in terms of great players. Some guys can play an awful lot and others play less but are friends of mine, which evens things up.' It was a theme he returned to again and again, particularly if he was asked to compile a merit league of great jazz musicians. One such question brought the reply, 'A certain trumpeter may not be the greatest, but there's something there I like. Another trumpeter is good, but I just don't like his personality.'[19] Red summed up his attitude when he told me, 'My favourite records feature my favourite people'.[20]

The Metropole's management took a tolerant attitude to the use of substitute musicians; they were not paying the top rate and were willing to grant 'leave' so that musicians could play important gigs or go on overseas tours. The wage scale differed considerably but the average would be about $100 a week with double for the leader – not a great deal but the regularity and frequency of the bookings compensated. Because drinks were expensive in the Metropole, most of the musicians spent their intervals across the street in the Copper Rail, where drinks were cheaper and the regulars were granted a weekly 'tab' by the owner, Fred Infield. The atmosphere there was friendly and the soul food (cooked by Della) was said to be the best in town.

Many of the Metropole's musicians had the sad task of attending the funeral of the vastly under-rated jazz trumpeter, Oran 'Hot Lips' Page, who died in November 1954, aged 46. Red Allen, together with Roy Eldridge, Emmett Berry, Jimmy McPartland, Louis Metcalf and Ed Lewis, acted as pall bearers and later played at a big benefit held at the Stuyvesant Casino. Lips was not one of the Metropole regulars, and his health had begun to fail just as the club blossomed, but he surely would have been in his element at that venue. Many jazz trumpeters, including Red Allen, Roy Eldridge and Dizzy Gillespie, were wary of duelling with Lips in a jam session, and on one memorable occasion Red was taken apart by the tornado force of Page's playing. Dan Morgenstern recalls that it was a night when Red's nickname could have applied to his face after the musical mauling he received from Lips, but Red bore no long-term grudge and wept at the news of Page's passing.

Business boomed at the Metropole, and dozens of musicians were employed during the course of a week, to play in afternoon and evening shifts; the doors were left open so that the music would draw in casual customers and passing tourists. The star of the evening presentations was undoubtedly Henry 'Red' Allen, whose group, originally billed as the Giants, became known as the Metropole All Stars. A dozen or more years of tavern work throughout the USA had honed Red's showmanship and developed his adroit gift of coaxing an audience into accepting and enjoying a blend of honest-to-goodness jazz, participation songs and flag-wavers.

Ben Harriman, a short figure who always walked with his hands behind his back, supervised the Metropole, sometimes assisted by his son, Lonnie. Harriman left the musical organization to the leaders of the various groups, and it was up to the bandleaders to make sure that standards remained high, and up to each musician to fix his own substitutes – all the musicians and the leaders were paid direct by the Metropole. Later, trumpeter Pee Wee Erwin became the official con-tractor for the Metropole, responsible for booking musicians and collecting the Musicians' Union tax. The two longserving bartenders were Sol and Morty Dacks, who later went off to run their own club. Another bartender was Otto, whose huge presence ensured that the customers never caused trouble. Jack, the floor manager, saw to it that the sets ran on time, and upstairs in the office the secretary Geraldine did the administration and kept the accounts.

A lively example of the 1955 musical goings-on at the Metropole was recorded for the Bethlehem label, featuring Red Allen's band and a group led by Charlie Shavers (including trombonist Frank Rehak and reed player Eddie Barefield). The two groups combine to create a wild, atmospheric version of 'When the Saints Go Marching In'; it might have been wonderful to behold but, in the cold light of later listening, it sounds chaotic. As the number ends Charlie Shavers sums up the confusion by asking humorously, 'Which way did they go?' Allen's band play a brief version of 'Buddy Bolden Said' and, complete with a near jovial vocal from Red, they then launch into an untidy blues, 'Kiss the Baby', which serves to introduce each member of the band; it later became one of the band's big production numbers. The best item from the date is a duet between Red Allen and Charlie Shavers entitled

'Trumpet Conversation'. Compère Al 'Jazzbo' Collins's spoken comments take the form of a bystander's narration in which he encourages the two trumpeters to take part in a musical combat. Red and Charlie had already rehearsed the routine, but each of them improvises a series of 4-bar and 8-bar exchanges that never become frantic; this interplay raises the number above the status of a novelty offering. The Metropole was later blamed for being the birthplace of a new blend of raucous jazz, but the brash approach had started to form earlier, at the Central Plaza sessions in particular, where an unremitting barrage of hoary traditional tunes (sprinkled with occasional ballads such as 'Body and Soul') formed the staple offering.

'Kiss the Baby' became an unofficial anthem at the Metropole, gradually developing into an elaborate routine that not only served to introduce each member of the band but also stimulated some good-humoured audience participation. Red would spot a couple in the audience and jovially ask the fellow to 'Kiss the Baby', and usually, after some persuading, a peck on the cheek was planted. Red pretended to be offended, saying 'That's not much of a kiss', which usually resulted in the couple sharing a more fervent embrace, then Red would shout gleefully, 'Now you're working'. It was all innocent fun, and if a man was there with two women, Red went through the usual routine then invited the fellow to 'Kiss the Spare', which always produced guffaws of laughter from the trio being addressed, and from everyone in the bar.

In August 1955, for the first time in years, Red entered the recording studio as part of a small band. He was a member of a pick-up sextet assembled by Tony Parenti (though the sides were later issued under both Parenti's and Allen's names); most of the participants were Metropole regulars. Parenti's unhesitant clarinet is featured on three trio numbers, but on the remaining tracks the solos are shared out democratically, usually in the same order. Pianist Hank Duncan's bold two-handed playing creates several worthwhile, no-nonsense solos but his accompaniments (based on relentless um-cha, um-cha figures) tend to put a ball and chain around the soloists' efforts. Even the sterling efforts of Milt Hinton on double bass and George Wettling's nimble, crisp-sounding drumming cannot eliminate the plodding effect. Several of Red's solos border on the brilliant, being full of daring phrases, some eccentric, all of them ingenious. The tone is acrid, the dynamics effectively ranging from a whisper to an exuberant shout. All of his ideas sound spontaneous and impressive, particularly on 'Maryland, My Maryland', 'Bill Bailey' and 'Careless Love', but on several tracks the contrast between the artistic economy of Red's lead playing in the opening choruses and his frantic assaults on the melody during the final ensembles creates a frustrating unevenness; as ever, his majestic approach to playing the blues (on 'Vieux Carré') compensates. Trombonist Tyree Glenn is classy throughout, even though he is dusting off phrases he used on previous occasions.

The music created is a memento of the Metropole's 'house-style'. There were no rules that the last chorus of any up-tempo number had to be loudly played, complete with a bewildering surfeit of notes, but these tactics soon became the standard procedure for Red's band; it was like a musical equivalent of Gresham's Law where good money is chased out by bad. Soon the Metropole's audiences and its management seemed to feel short-changed if the decibels (and the front-line's blood pressure) did not rise dramatically during the final stages of any fast numbers. Even so, it was the position of the Metropole's stage that caused the musicians more woe than any other aspect of the venue, situated as it was, up behind the bar. The steep elevation posed its own problems but in the narrowness of the bandstand area the musicians had to play spread out in a line, making it difficult to achieve an internal balance. For Red Allen it was a hark back to his early days in New Orleans where it was common for bands to play in a single line when working in dance halls. At the Metropole, eye contact between the musicians was a problem, though it could be achieved by reflections from the large mirror opposite the bandstand; unfortunately a time-lag often occurred as the sound echoed off the walls and the mirror, but the old professionals devised their own methods of combating the difficulties. The Metropole soon established itself as a rendezvous for white-collar workers who wanted to take a few drinks before going home, and for out-of-town con-ventioners who wanted an hour of two in the lively, convivial atmosphere. Hard-core jazz fans were in the minority but the number of converts grew, initially drawn in by the amplified sounds that bombarded part of Seventh Avenue.

Business at the Metropole thrived. An upstairs section was opened, and jazz giants such as Lionel Hampton, Gene Krupa and Illinois Jacquet were featured as special attractions. Woody Herman's big band played several residencies at the Metropole, the musicians achieving a swinging cohesion by watching drummer Jake Hanna's hi-hat cymbal in the mirror.[21] The musicians' working hours at the Metropole were long, usually from 8 or 9 p.m. until around 3 a.m. (later on Fridays). Bands alternated by playing sets lasting 30 or 45 minutes, usually changing over on the same number, with the oncoming musicians replacing the incumbents by joining them in a jam session. Red Allen was not above employing gamesmanship in this changing-of-the-guard routine. He would choose a well-known number, but he would play it in a very unusual key, making the musicians who were about to take over struggle to find appropriate notes as they joined in. This ploy did not endear him to the musicians in the other group. Bassist Bill Crow was part of one of these uneasy changeovers:

> Henry 'Red' Allen was a powerful trumpet player, a member of the old New Orleans school of combative jazzmen. He challenged all comers, not content until he had established his supremacy. I got to watch him at close quarters while working at the Metropole with Sol Yaged, opposite Red's band. Sol and Red played alternate sets, and twice during the night we had to play a 'jam session' set combining both bands, with a double rhythm section. On the first of these Red immediately threw down the gauntlet. 'What is that you've got on Sol?' he signified, peering at Sol's tuxedo with exaggerated disdain, 'You look like a waiter'. 'What do you want to play?' Red demanded. Sol suggested a tune we all knew, 'After You've Gone'. 'Okay, "After You've Gone" in B natural' Red snapped, calling a key he hoped Sol would find uncomfortable. He stomped it off quickly, before anyone could demur. After an ensemble led by Red's exuberant melody line, we all played choruses, feeling our way through the unusual key. Red waited to solo last and was ready for us. Standing with his shoulder blades pressed against the back wall of the narrow bandstand, he pumped a continuous stream of swinging, belligerent jazz through his horn. As he played he began marching in place. As he continued shifting his weight from one foot to the other, his sizable shoes began to carry him forward, an inch at a time, so that by the end of his last chorus his feet protruded halfway over the edge of the stage. With his mouthpiece jammed against his leathery embouchure Red pointed his trumpet over the customers' heads and bounced the last notes of his chorus off the mirrors on the back wall, winding up with a screaming high B. Dripping with sweat he accepted his applause like a fighter who had just KO'ed his opponent.[22]

The Metropole crowd responded to Red's personality almost as much as to his playing and singing. As one visitor observed, 'They either applaud or drink up and go'.[23] At the Metropole Red introduced the old New Orleans tactic of repeating a number (or part of it) when he felt the crowd's applause justified a reprise – and sometimes as a ploy to whip up what had been a sporadic response. Red's excellent memory, and his friendly manner toward the customers, soon built him a coterie of new fans, many of whom became personal friends. Some were locals, but many were out-of-town people who began making the Metropole an automatic port-of-call whenever they returned to New York. Red made it his business to wave at them from his vantage point on the bandstand, greeting them individually during his intermission, asking about their families, the new house or the new job, enquiries based on the vast amount of information he had stored away in his mind. Dan Morgenstern felt that Red's public relations exercises sometimes interfered with his music-making: 'He'd start a solo and get a groove going, and then abruptly jerk the horn away from his chops to yell "Hey, good my man!" to greet a fan who'd just walked in'.[24]

Red's arrival at the Metropole was usually spectacular. He drove up in his Cadillac, parked it temporarily outside the Metropole, then flamboyantly threw the keys to an attendant who went off to park the vehicle for the duration of Red's gig. Then, weather permitting, Red would don a maroon dinner jacket on the sidewalk and stride into the club. The Cadillac was still religiously replaced by a new model every other year.

Kenny Davern, then a young up-and-coming clarinettist who often played at the Metropole, retains many memories of those days:

Red Allen was the most dynamic musician I ever worked with. I tried to fathom out how he managed to win over what was, at times, a really rough crowd. I watched him work at the Metropole, he'd pick a couple and sing 'Kiss the Baby' to them, they'd soon start smiling and pretty soon everyone was in a good mood.[25]

Saxophonist Steve Lacy, recalling his early days, spoke of his first professional gigs with musicians such as Red Allen, Pee Wee Russell and Vic Dickenson:

All those guys were fantastic. These are the guys that made me want to play in the first place. It was a thrill just to have the privilege of being allowed to play with them at the time because I was just a kid and they were living legends. It has to do with their sounds mostly, their manner of playing.[26]

Ride, Red, Ride

The young Davern, Lacy and trumpeter Dick Schwartz were listening to the music at Minton's Club, when, to their amazement, Red made a bold entry into this bastion of jazz experimentation. The trio on the bandstand were an avant-garde threesome, with the pianist performing with his head only four inches away from the keyboard. Red jumped up onto the small stage, slammed down his alligator-skin case, pulled his trumpet out and began playing 'Rosetta'. The trio changed step and began backing Red, who followed his trumpet solo with an exuberant vocal chorus. The place erupted, everybody cheered and yelled, Red smiled, put his trumpet away and marched out. It was, as Kenny Davern said, 'A Red Allen happening'.[27]

11

EUROPEAN DÉBUT

Personnel changes within Red's group at the Metropole were few and far between. Bassist Buster Moten left to work with Wilbur De Paris's Band and was replaced by Arvell Shaw, Rufus 'Speedy' Jones occupied the drum chair for a while, as did 'Sticks' Evans, but a major switch occurred when J.C. Higginbotham rejoined Red. After spending some while in Boston, Higgy returned to New York in early 1956 and played gigs at various venues, including Central Plaza, but then let it be known that he would like to rejoin Red's band. Unfortunately, the old magic that had existed between the two brassmen never quite materialized again. Higgy could still whip up excitement occasionally, but somehow the inner fire had been doused, and on a social level his relationship with Red developed a certain formality, partly caused by Red having to fulfil the duties of a bandleader in getting all the musicians back on stage on time, and sober. British pianist Colin Purbrook visited the Metropole on an occasion when Higgy was late back on the bandstand. Red gave him a hard look but made no attempt to reprimand him; instead he went into a number that featured the trombone, and each time Higgy shaped up to finish his improvisations, Red called out, 'Carry on! Carry on!' Higgy got the message. There were worse scenes, and photographer-writer Jack Bradley twice saw a well-oiled Higginbotham fall from the bandstand, which at the Metropole was about five feet high – mercifully the trombonist was uninjured.

It was sad to see one of the greatest of all trombonists in a sorry state, but it was usually all too obvious when Higgy had overdone the tippling; his friendly disposition remained unaltered. Red undoubtedly retained his admiration for Higgy's playing: 'I must say that when he's in shape, a guy like J.C. Higginbotham is a rough man to beat. Higgy, on form, is a most flexible player. He had everything, power, excitement and flexibility.'[1] But the telltale use of the past tense seemed to indicate Red's inner feelings. In 1972, when Higgy gave his candid recollections of his long-time musical partner, his comments were mostly unflattering. In this interview (conducted by Donald Byrd, Jimmy Owens and Leonard Goines) Higgy's observations about Red Allen included such comments as, 'He always felt he could play better than anybody else', 'At the Copper Rail, in front of Buster Bailey and me, he said "I'll admit I'm an Uncle Tom to make a dollar"', 'I knew what Red was going to play anytime, and he knew what I was going to play so we understood each other. But other than that... He had a funny disposition.'[2]

One suspects that money was at the root of most of the Allen-Higginbotham problems. Higgy was not only a carefree spender, he was also a hard bargainer who never seemed content with his earnings, even when he was on top rates, and this was one of his big problems in dealing with Joe Glaser in the 1930s. In the early 1940s, at Café Society Downtown, he went direct to the club's owner, Barney Josephson, to get a raise, but Red intervened (as was his right) and said, 'I'm the leader. Give him what I say.' The fact that Higgy quoted Red's words 30 years later (during his 1972 interview) shows that he had long brooded over the incident.

Nevertheless, Higgy's presence on the bandstand at the Metropole added another star musician to the line-up, and enhanced the band's prestige. In July 1957 they were featured at the Newport Jazz Festival (then in its fourth year), where Red fronted Buster Bailey on clarinet, Higgy on trombone, Claude Hopkins on piano, Arvell Shaw on double bass and Cozy Cole on drums. After two numbers the band were joined by Jack Teagarden on trombone and vocals, then trombonist Kid Ory replaced Teagarden for a version of 'Muskrat Ramble' before all three trombonists were featured together on 'High Society'. The guest stars were late additions to Red's set; they were originally scheduled to be part of Louis Armstrong's onstage birthday celebrations, which formed part of the evening presentation, but Louis, angry at being told not to feature his singer Velma Middleton, decided not to amend his repertoire to include a musical reunion with Teagarden and Ory. On this occasion all efforts by Louis's long-time manager, Joe Glaser, couldn't pacify Armstrong, so Glaser asked Red to accommodate the guests within his set. Red agreed to do this – Glaser was, of course, his agent too – but the musical results were a mixed bag.

Red's band was announced by the Voice of America's radio jazz compère, Willis Conover, who pointed out that everyone in the group (except Claude Hopkins) had worked regularly with Louis Armstrong. The band then launched into a spirited version of 'Struttin' with Some Barbecue', with Red soon showing that his chops were in fine shape. Claude Hopkins's blending of stride piano and block chording fill out a couple of choruses, then Higgy, radiating endeavour, blows fiercely but haphazardly. The star of the proceedings is definitely Red Allen, who sounds exciting and inventive. Buster Bailey makes several excursions into his thin-sounding high register, but does not stoke anything combustible into the proceedings; Arvell Shaw's huge-toned, vigorous bass playing reinstates the earlier mood and the band romp into a spirited finale. A reprise built more on strength than subtlety showcases some emphatic drumming which is topped by the front-line's call-and-answer finish. Cozy Cole's tom-toms introduce a medium-paced version of 'St James Infirmary', complete with a less-than-serious vocal from Red, which bristles with several of his stock exhortations, including 'Make 'em happy', 'Way down, Way down' and 'Very nice'.

These two numbers were followed by Red's introduction of Jack Teagarden. Red first reminded the audience that J.C. Higginbotham was a 'natural great' before saying that Teagarden's arrival meant there were 'two kings on one throne'. Jack comes on stage and says how nice it is to be working with 'Allen and his wonderful group', then puts his trombone to his lips and purrs the melody of a beautifully phrased 'China Boy', which is backed by Red's subsidiary but ingenious counterpoint. Teagarden sings 'Basin Street Blues', again backed by Red's deft ideas, then plays an immaculate solo which inspires Red to construct a chorus that is devoid of grandstanding effects but highly effective. Teagarden then announces 'The daddy of all the tailgate trombonists, Kid Ory', allowing Ory to thrust his way into his own composition 'Muskrat Ramble', on which he blows a series of sturdy phrases with an infectious enthusiasm. Ory sings a vocal then again adds his inimitable sound to the lively ensemble. On the final number of the set, Higginbotham, Teagarden and Ory combine spiritedly on an untidy version of 'High Society'. Through lack of rehearsal there is some bumping of notes on the trio strain of the tune, but none of these collisions are fatal to the performance and the audience react approvingly. Buster Bailey's best moments of the session occur during his relaxed, low-register solo.

If anyone at this time feared that Red's inventiveness and artistry were in danger of being destroyed by his continual involvement in tavern Dixieland, the issue of a 1957 Allen-led All Stars album provided instant refutation. Though the line-up is Metropolish, the music is devoid of Dixieland standards (except 'St James Infirmary'). Red's All Stars consisted of Buster Bailey, Higgy, Cozy Cole, Lloyd Trotman, pianist Marty Napoleon, guitarist Everett Barksdale and the enormous jazz talents of tenor saxist Coleman Hawkins. The up-tempo numbers 'Ride, Red, Ride', 'Love Is Just Around the Corner' and 'S'Wonderful' are exciting without becoming frantic and even though 'Ride, Red, Ride' has some lively singing by the band (and studio guests) the exuberance never gets out of hand, even in the mettlesome finish, and all the subtle nuances of Red's voice and his brilliant trumpet tone are faithfully recorded. Red sings a version of 'St James Infirmary' that is devoid of hokum; the bonus here is Higgy's bold trombone solo. Red hardly ever used a mute at this stage of his career, but he does so in playing the melody of his own blues composition 'Algiers Bounce'. The string of 12-bar choruses on this number seem to be somewhat self-contained, so one never gets the feeling that a mighty climax is pending; nevertheless there is no shortage of good ideas. The bouncy 'Ain't She Sweet' has an ingeniously timed vocal from Red – and some stomping trumpet-playing. Coleman Hawkins's chorus is nonchalantly delivered but is still full of high-class improvisation; the overall effect conveyed by the sound of the ensemble is of happy, free-wheeling jazz. Hawkins moves up a couple of gears on 'Love Is Just Around the Corner', pumping out a series of stirring phrases that contain a rhythmic energy that surges into the rhythm section – a fine example of a soloist inspiring his accompanists.

Admirable though the rapport is on the swifter numbers, the great moments from the session occur on the slow ballads, with Red Allen's playing surpassing anything he had recorded for years. Tonally, rhythmically and harmonically, Red proves that he was still capable of being in the forefront of jazz exploration. If the playing on 'I've Got the World on a String', 'Sweet Lorraine' and 'I Cover the Waterfront' had been created by a young recording débutant it would have been hailed as the decade's most interesting and satisfying marriage of old and new jazz concepts. Gunther Schuller described Red's work on 'I Cover the Waterfront' as 'one of the most magnificent extended trumpet solos of that or any other period'.[3] On each of these ballads Red demonstrates his amazing ability to superimpose new time signatures on the four-in-a-bar accompanying patterns, blowing a flurry of rubato phrases that link up with the rhythm section at pivotal points in the song's structure. The fluffy-edged tone with which these ideas emerge from the trumpet bolsters the feeling of relaxed mastery, and the perfectly controlled inclusion of the lowest notes in a trumpet's register (as on 'Sweet Lorraine') show that Red never needed to fly into the stratosphere to command attention. Harmonically there is no devised system; Red lets his imagination take his fingers on to notes that sometimes sound jagged, but these daring excursions are breathtakingly original. Martin Williams effectively summarized the trumpeter's remarkable achievements when he wrote, 'Allen united the plaintiveness of a blues man and the lyricism of a fine ballad player'.[4]

A much less satisfying album under Red's leadership (entitled *The Dixiecats*) was recorded in May 1957. As the album title suggests, the tracks are made up of Dixieland favourites, but the overall feeling is similar to that created by transcriptions made by jazzmen during radio's golden years, where the usual rule was 'safety first' rather than wild abandon. The musicians are mostly Metropole regulars, the one outsider being tenor saxist Abraham 'Boomie' Richman (incidentally the only white musician on the date). Richman's work is skilful and reliable, albeit bland, and though his solos are well constructed they never engender a feeling of genuine excitement. Pianist Willie 'The Lion' Smith adds his eccentric talents to the group, but despite having played on innumerable sessions with Red he does not seem at ease when accompanying the complicated rhythms that are scattered throughout Allen's solos – on 'Royal Garden Blues' Smith seems to be hanging on for dear life. The Lion's pianistics are featured on 'Wolverine Blues', where he demonstrates an unusual path through the tune's chord changes by following his own harmonic signposts. Arvell Shaw's playing is, as usual, artistic and powerful, while Buster Bailey's clarinet work again exemplifies his professionalism. Trombonist Tyree Glenn adopts a tailgate role on several tracks and creates some appropriately fruity sounds on 'Tin Roof Blues'; elsewhere his smoother phrases make pleasant listening, as do his humorous 'quotes' such as the transplanting of a phrase from 'Lullaby of Broadway' into 'Muskrat Ramble'. Red, who rarely used quotes in his solos, has some fine moments on the album; his tender blowing on 'Tin Roof Blues' is touching, and on 'Royal Garden Blues' he is in fine, exploratory mood, whereas on 'Basin Street Blues' (which he had probably played once too often that week), he almost sounds flippant. The biggest disappointment of the date was the surfeit of untidy concluding ensembles, many of them uncohesive to the point of chaos.

Ride, Red, Ride

In December 1957, a star-studded assembly of jazz musicians gathered to rehearse for *The Sound of Jazz*, a television show that was part of CBS's 'Seven Lively Arts' series. On 5 December recordings were made (and issued) featuring a similar line-up to the one that assembled three days later for the hour-long live transmission of the programme (aired from 5 to 6 p.m. Eastern Standard Time). The producer and director relied on the expert guidance of writers Whitney Balliett and Nat Hentoff in the selection of this stellar cast, which included Count Basie, Billie Holiday, Lester Young, Roy Eldridge, Gerry Mulligan and Jimmy Rushing. Red Allen's two feature numbers, 'Wild Man Blues' and 'Rosetta', employed a marvellous line-up: Rex Stewart on cornet, Vic Dickenson, Pee Wee Russell, Coleman Hawkins, Nat Pierce on piano, Milt Hinton on double bass and Jo Jones on drums. Guitarist Danny Barker did not take part in the recording session but was on the televised show. Red Allen and Rex Stewart were good friends but this did not eliminate an air of competition between them. Each man stirs the other into producing dramatic solos, with Rex summoning up reserves of energy and daring to blow a series of fierce, high notes on his cornet. Vic Dickenson, Coleman Hawkins and Pee Wee Russell all parade their unique sounds on both numbers, but despite each of these musicians having a markedly individual tone the overall sound makes an eminently satisfying blend. The sounds of the television show were later also issued on record and they demonstrate the consistency and brilliance of both of the studio performances.

The transmission of *The Sound of Jazz* delighted jazz fans, as did a series of Art Ford's Jazz Party programmes, relayed on WNTA Television (and on FM radio). Throughout 1958 Red and Higgy (plus various other New York-based jazz stalwarts) played on several of these shows, alongside guest instrumentalists and singers. During this same period the Metropole All Stars were featured on a series of Armed Forces Radio Service shows transmitted from the Metropole. The All Stars consisted of permutations of regulars including Red, Higgy, Buster Bailey, Sol Yaged, Coleman Hawkins, Willie 'The Lion' Smith, Claude Hopkins, Gene Ramey, Eddie 'Mole' Bourne, Lou Stein, Milt Hinton, Cozy Cole and Vic Dickenson (it was Dickenson who made the observation, 'I wish I had Rockefeller's money and Henry Allen's memory'[5]).

Red, as one of the Coleman Hawkins All Stars, participated in a Soundcraft recording session in August 1958, which was (very unusually) originally issued as a reel-to-reel tape. The subsequent longplaying record was called *The Sweet Moods of Jazz*; the music it contained greatly pleased Red and he told British writer G.E. Lambert that he regarded the date as being one of the most satisfying sessions of his entire career. Most of the tunes are taken at medium tempo, and utilize uncomplicated arrangements (devised by Larry Clinton); everyone sounds admirably relaxed. Earle Warren, usually an alto-sax specialist, plays clarinet on this session and does so with skill and feeling. Pianist Marty Napoleon provides sparse and thoughtful keyboard accompaniment, allowing the soloists to stretch out unhampered by obtrusive arpeggios. Bassist Chubby Jackson (the former Woody Herman star) plays energetically and musically, and fashions a particularly ingenious solo on 'Lonesome Road'. George Wetting on drums again proves that his percussion skills were a fertile combination of technical élan, strength and swing. Coleman Hawkins creates several superfine solos, seemingly without expending much effort; nevertheless his improvisations are models of musical form. Red Allen, for his part, continues to explore and fortify the musical tunnels he had been digging for years, creating softly blown angular lines and skilful re-adjustments of the melody on 'Mean to Me', 'Lonesome Road' and 'Sleepytime Gal', often using a minimal vibrato; on 'Tea for Two' he used a cup-mute throughout. Red's solos contain a whole gamut of tonal effects and shadings, but none of them are gimmicky; there is a slight rush of blood to the head in 'All of Me', but the session is notable for its lack of agitation and musical stampede.

Any comparison between the *Sweet Moods* date and one that produced *Dixieland Jazzfest* for the same company (on 16 December 1957) proves invidious. The assembled talent is just as noteworthy: Red Allen, Coleman Hawkins, J.C. Higginbotham, clarinettist Sol Yaged, bassist Milt Hinton, drummer Cozy Cole and Lou Stein on piano, but this album has Metropole written all over it. The parade of old traditional warhorses includes 'Bill Bailey', 'The Saints' and 'Battle Hymn of the Republic', all ridden hell-for-leather. Red Allen proved on countless occasions throughout his career that he could summon up musical inspiration in the most unlikely circumstances, but, on some of the Dixieland dates of the 1950s and 1960s, try as he may he cannot lift the offerings up beyond a run-of-the-mill rating. In an attempt to inject novelty into over-familiar material Red added a new effect, blowing half-valved notes in the upper register, producing a squeezed-out squeal that, when repeated often, rapidly loses its enthralling quality. J.C. Higginbotham was candid enough to admit that he was not by nature a Dixieland player; 'Dixieland tunes, they have special notes, but Red would teach me. That's the way I learned to play Dixieland, during the intermissions he'd take me upstairs (at the Metropole) and tell me.'[6]

Red's Metropole routine was interrupted by occasional outside excursions; among them some studio sessions where he sang on a series of trial jingles for Ballantine's Ale. He and the band guested at a Carnegie Hall concert in February 1958, and in another interlude Red took part in poetry-with-jazz recordings featuring Langston Hughes. Four months later, in July 1958, Red and his Metropole cohorts collaborated with Hughes for appearances at the Stratford Shakespeare Festival held in Ontario, Canada. Red had a devoted coterie of fans in Toronto as a result of his occasional appearances there. He also continued to work for the Connolly Brothers in Boston; he played for them often at the Savoy Café, but in later years he appeared at their Stardust Room (in the Roxbury district). Red also took his own pick-up bands out to locations close to Manhattan, usually collecting those musicians who wanted a lift at a point near 145th Street and 8th Avenue. Kenny Davern took advantage of Red's offer of a free ride and was pleased to note that dozens of people tooted their car horns as a sign of recognition as soon as Red got out of his Cadillac to supervise the loading of the instruments. One of Red's long journeys in the summer of 1958 was a drive down to New Orleans to visit his mother, who was then 75 years old.

One unusual 1958 record date (under Claude Hopkins's name) featured an all-star musical cast (including Red and Charlie Shavers on trumpet). This album, *The Music of the Early Jazz Dances* is a series of painstaking arrangements of compositions from around the turn of the century, none of which offer scope or space to the improvising skills of the participants.

A big upheaval in Red's working routine took place in July 1959 when he flew to Los Angeles to make an album with Kid Ory's Creole Jazz Band. This West Coast recording (for Norman Granz's Verve label) was a preliminary to the European tour that Red did with the Ory ensemble from September to November 1959. Commenting on the record date, Red said, 'Norman Granz flew me out to Hollywood on my day off from the Metropole. I left at 9.45 in the morning, was recording with Kid Ory by 3 p.m. and in the air again by 11.30 that night. It was my first experience of the jet plane.'[7] Although Kid Ory and Red Allen had first worked together in King Oliver's band in 1927, their paths seldom crossed during the subsequent 30-year period, and the sides made at the Newport Jazz Festival in 1957 were their only recordings together. The cohesiveness of their 1959 album belies their previous lack of contact and gives the impression that Red was a regular member of a well-organized unit, but not the least of Kid Ory's gifts was his ability to be a supremely effective bandmaster. On the session there was no attempt to perform tunes associated with the 'New Orleans golden era'; instead a catholic selection, consisting of well-known standards and some Swing Era hits was the order of the day. 'Come Back Sweet Papa', originally recorded by Louis Armstrong's Hot Five, was revived, as was another number that was linked to Armstrong's early career. This curio, 'Keep off Katie's Head', was the original title of a tune that the young Louis sold cheaply only to see it earn huge amounts in royalties for other people as 'I Wish I Could Shimmy Like My Sister Kate'. One suspects that Louis would not have been overjoyed to learn that Ory claimed composership for this particular recording. The opus provides Ory with his one vocal on the album, although his performance, which has a certain roguish charm, is recited rather than sung. This track's best musical moments come from Red, who creates a daringly timed break in the first chorus, following it with some suspended notes that give the initial impression of hanging right into the next measure, but, at the last split second, Red nonchalantly clips them back into place.

There is no doubt that Kid Ory had the gift of imprinting his musical personality on almost all of the sides his latter-day bands recorded. Despite personnel changes the overall feel of various Ory dates is markedly similar. It would be unfair to describe Allen's recordings with Ory as 'Red Under Wraps' since the trumpeter was allowed to play his solos in any way he chose; nevertheless there is sometimes a feeling that the tracks are coming off a factory line (admittedly one that produced high-class products). This air of repetition is exacerbated by having all the solos in the same order: clarinet, trumpet, trombone, piano, with occasional double bass solos and strummed rhythm features for guitarist Frank Haggerty. Bob McCracken was a competent jazz clarinettist, who had also worked with Louis Armstrong's All Stars and with Jack Teagarden, but his solos here never rise beyond a certain emotional plateau, and the counterpoint he plays to Red's lead occasionally sounds flummoxed. His best moments are the low-register solo on 'I Got Rhythm' and his lively work on 'Come Back Sweet Papa' (reminiscent of Don Murray), but in general he does not sound inspired. Red had angled for the young Kenny Davern to do this session and the tour.

Ride, Red, Ride

Pianist Cedric Haywood, whose wide experience included working with Lionel Hampton, Illinois Jacquet and Sidney Bechet, gives good support throughout the date. He was an unfussy pianist, whose jaunty accompaniments supported rather than cut across a soloist's lines; his rolling solo phrases were played with great assurance, and although he was not in the top league of jazz musicians he was consistently effective. Drummer Alton Redd was not a musical experimenter, and once he got locked into a heavy offbeat pattern he usually stayed put, no matter what was happening around him (though he claimed that he was commanded to take this approach by Ory). Redd's 4-bar tags are crisp and definite without being spectacular and his vocals ('Some of These Days', 'Lazy River' and 'Ain't Misbehavin'') are noted for their rugged enthusiasm.

Kid Ory's massive contributions to early jazz are indisputable. He was not only a pioneer but also a prime performer, whose role within Louis Armstrong's Hot Five and Jelly Roll Morton's Red Hot Peppers during the 1920s showed by example the perfect method of playing tailgate trombone. His ingeniously timed thrusts and apt glissandos, delivered with an attractively robust tone and propulsive rhythms, created a role model for countless trombonists. He recaptured some of his early musical flair in the 1940s (when he returned to regular playing after a long lay-off) but by the time these recordings were made he had settled into a patriarchal role in which he often seemed to be caricaturing his own past achievements. However, it must be taken into account that he was in his seventies at the time of his recording with Red, he had been seriously ill the year before, and was suffering from hearing problems. Nevertheless Ory's rich, fruity tone was still apparent, and is shown at its best in his renderings of the melody on 'Some of These Days' and 'Tishomingo Blues', but he was not always successful in carrying a tune, as he shows in a series of near-misses on 'Tuxedo Junction'. Ory still had the knack of blowing decisive, punchy lines (as he does on 'I Got Rhythm') but often his solos sound like a compendium of phrases he had originated long ago. He made no attempt to find subtle harmonies, and even though he starred on the original of 'Come Back Sweet Papa' he seems uncertain of the chords on the verse of this recreation. To his credit, his knack of drilling musicians of disparate styles (and talents) into producing admirably cohesive ensembles would alone place him among the most important figures in the history of traditional jazz.

Throughout the album Red is accorded the lion's share of the solos. There are traces of Metropole 'growling and grandstanding' and a few moments of wildness, but restraint is the order of the day, certainly when Red is leading the ensemble. He hovers around the melody to good effect on 'San', 'Come Back Sweet Papa' and 'Lazy River', and his excursions into his low register sound warmly emotive; when he moves high he does so with surety and power. On 'I Got Rhythm' he plays one chorus with a straight mute then drops the mute and continues to blow, creating a powerful open solo. There are no indifferent moments from Red, but perhaps only 'Honeysuckle Rose' shows him at his best, yet even an 'ordinary' middle-register solo, such as on 'Ain't Misbehavin'', could not have been created by any other jazz trumpeter. Such was Red's individuality.

Meanwhile plans for the transatlantic tour went ahead, with shrewd Ory realizing that the European jazz audiences would bay with pleasure at hearing Red's originality live, so throughout their travels together the bandleader made no effort to curtail Red's blowing or his showmanship. Just before Red left New York for Europe (on 14 September 1959) he was delighted to greet the famous New Orleans veteran bassist Wellman Braud, who journeyed over from Brooklyn to the Metropole to wish him bon voyage. Although Kid Ory had toured Europe with his band in 1956 (which included pianist Cedric Haywood), this was Red Allen's first transatlantic trip. Red was delighted to discover a dedicated clique of his fans in each city that the band visited. He was not unrealistically modest, but was genuinely surprised by the number of people he met who could discuss many of his recordings in detail. He said at the time, 'It seems that all over Europe youngsters have come up to me with books full of old photographs of me that I don't have myself. They take to jazz like a kind of religion. I feel honoured.'[8] In Austria Red was almost moved to tears when he saw (on the wall of Fatty George's Jazz Club in Vienna) a large blown-up photograph of his father, Henry Allen Senior.

The group, billed as Kid Ory's Creole Jazz Band, began its tour in Germany on 17 September 1959. Most of the venues were concert halls, in which the band played two shows, one starting at around 6 p.m. or 6.30 p.m., the other at 8 p.m. or 8.30 p.m. The band did not base its programme exclusively on material from their recent recordings; instead they played a wide range of old traditional jazz favourites including 'Savoy Blues', 'Wolverine Blues', 'Muskrat Ramble', 'Panama' and 'High Society'. One of the highlights of the tour was the band's appearances at the Salle Pleyel in Paris (on 4 October 1959). Happily one of these French concerts was filmed and later issued on video. While in France Red had planned a visit to Sidney Bechet's grave but the hectic touring schedule did not allow time for such an excursion. Not long before Red came to Europe he had played at a memorial tribute concert to Bechet, held at New York's Carnegie Hall.

After a successful tour of Sweden and Denmark the band flew to England, arriving on Monday 12 October 1959. Kid Ory chose to make the journey from Scandinavia by sea, and together with his wife, Barbara, and his five-year-old daughter, Babette, sailed into England two days later. Ory was met at London's Liverpool Street railway station by bands led by Terry Lightfoot and Mickey Ashman; touched by this gesture, Ory sang enthusiastically with the welcoming musicians. Lightfoot's band was the support group on most of Kid Ory's British dates. Lightfoot remembers it as a happy tour:

> For most of the jobs we all travelled together in a big band-bus. It was like a dream come true, being on the road with musicians who were part of jazz history. Our first date on the tour was at Cambridge and we set out very early, so much so that we decided to stop for while en route at the small town of Baldock. Red Allen didn't want to waste a minute of his first trip to England so he got out of the coach and started exploring the place. I remember thinking at the time, 'what if a life-long jazz fan was out strolling in Baldock and saw Red Allen doing some shopping, he wouldn't have believed his eyes'. Red was very friendly and forthcoming, and Ory was approachable, he had a dressing room separate from the band, but he didn't seem to mind if anyone knocked at the door for a chat.[9]

Terry Lightfoot's trumpeter then was Alan Elsdon, who was delighted to sit with Red on the tour bus:

> Red never got drunk, but he liked to sip sherry from a bottle of Harvey's Bristol Cream. He never warmed up for long before a gig. I wanted to learn as much as I could about Red's approach to harmony, but I soon found out that he didn't go in for elaborate theories. He believed in mainly using his ears, and advised me to try and hear a phrase before I played it, saying 'If it sounds okay, it is okay'. He blew a King Super Symphony trumpet (incidentally the same model that Harry James used) and his mouthpiece didn't have a name on; I asked him about this and he said, 'It came with the horn'. There was no trouble at all on that tour, but I felt that

Ory was a real disciplinarian. He had those piercing eyes, and I got the impression that the drummer Alton Redd was terrified of him. Alton explained to us one day that the heavy offbeat he played was as per Ory's instructions, apparently Ory was going deaf and he needed to hear an emphatic offbeat. The only times I saw Red get irate was when people came up to him and *only* wanted to talk about Louis Armstrong, Red definitely found this a bit hard to take, but he was great with all of us and when we joined in with the Ory band for a jam session finale, usually on 'Maryland', we were absolutely delighted.[10]

Wherever the Kid Ory band (tuxedo clad on stage) appeared in Britain they were given a tumultuous welcome. Ory got his fair share of applause but the really vociferous adulation was for Red Allen. The response was entirely merited; every phrase that Red blew radiated adventurous dexterity, but just in case the audience seemed hesitant about clapping, Red encouraged a response by shouldering his trumpet like a rifle, or by playing one-handed, stretching the other hand out over the footlights as though he was willing to shake hands with everyone in the audience. These eye-catching displays, linked with Red's extraordinary improvisations, ensured that the audience did not remain silent for long. Even the most dedicated and serious jazz fans were not dismayed by these flamboyant gestures. They took it as proof indeed that great New Orleans jazz musicians could also be master showmen.

Red never hogged the limelight. When his colleagues were soloing he stood in the shadows, his countenance grave or joyous, depending on the mood of the song, but when it was his turn to solo he made sure that all eyes were on him. He had a light, springy way of marching to the centre of the stage, knees slightly bent, with just a hint of a pigeon-toed gait. As soon as he reached the right spot he took up a stance by placing his feet wide apart, looking as well-balanced as a champion boxer; incongruously his trousers were usually hoisted up to show his socks clearly. For his solo on 'Maryland', Red regularly played one-handed, lifting his other arm and pointing a finger dramatically skywards. Kid Ory, ace bandleader that he was, seemed to enjoy these capers as much as anyone. He could plainly see that Red Allen's playing and his gestures were helping to sell a band that had deficiencies. Ory smiled benignly as Red took charge of the show by performing his Metropole-styled vocal version of 'St James Infirmary', complete with audience participation.

Ride, Red, Ride

Whenever Red Allen spoke of the man who was temporarily his nominal boss, he always referred to him as 'Mister Ory', seemingly without sarcasm or malice. Someone asked Red why it was that Kid Ory was staying at London's expensive Savoy Hotel while his sidemen were booked into a much less glamorous address in West London. Red replied without hesitation, 'Mister Ory chooses to spend his own money in his own way. All I know is that he is paying me exactly the figure I asked for, and I'm comfortable.'[11] It is safe to assume that Ory was paying Red a considerable sum, because, as Ory pointed out in a subsequent interview, the salary that Louis Armstrong and Joe Glaser offered Ory to relinquish his own band to join the Louis Armstrong All Stars was less than Ory was paying Red Allen on this tour of Europe.

The British jazz critics, most of them thrilled to be hearing and seeing Ory and Allen live, were full of enthusiasm, but a more wary assessment of this tour was written by Canadian Dick Lazenby, for *Coda* magazine: 'Red Allen is a fine but inconsistent soloist, but unfortunately not a traditional line-up lead man. Just when one despaired, he would offer a properly blown chorus then spoil it with a tasteless ride-out.'[12]

Red was determined to enjoy himself offstage as well as onstage and even before the tour officially opened at the Regal Cinema in Cambridge on Friday 16 October 1959, he was out and about in London. On his first night in London he went to hear Acker Bilk's Band playing at the famous jazz club situated at 100 Oxford Street. On the following night. he was persuaded to sample his first glass of bitter. Unlike most Americans Red took to the warmish, bubbleless brew immediately and although he was never a heavy drinker he became well acquainted with the taste during his stay in Britain. It was while he was going through his initiation that I first met him in an old pub close to Oxford Street. I almost got off on the wrong foot with Red (which was a difficult thing to do). Red loved to talk relaxedly about the many jazz musicians with whom he had worked, but his reminiscences rarely dwelt on other trumpeters, even those that were his friends. It was as though the fierce competition he had encountered as a young man in New Orleans (and in New York) caused him to evermore regard all other trumpeters as rivals. No sooner had I been introduced to Red than I asked, 'And how is Joe Thomas these days?' Looking back I can only surmise that my enquiry was born of nervousness. A thousand questions about Red's career preceded it in my mind, yet somehow this random query had tumbled out. I've always admired Joe Thomas's full-toned melodic trumpet-playing, but his work meant much less to me in comparison to

Red's monumental achievements. Red eyed me with a semi-suspicious curiosity then said, quite formally, 'Joe Thomas is going pretty good'. He then looked sideways at the person who had just introduced me as a devout collector of Red Allen's records, and abruptly changed the subject.

At that moment someone suggested that Red might like to visit the Marquee Club (then situated below a cinema in Oxford Street) to hear Humphrey Lyttelton's Band. A pack of us trooped into the club with Red and heard some passionate recreations of tunes that Red had recorded with Luis Russell's Band thirty years earlier. Red was very impressed by Humph's tribute and the performance remained firmly in his mind for a long while (as we shall see later). From the Marquee Club the entourage went into a pub in nearby Poland Street where Red insisted on buying everyone a drink. He exuded goodwill far beyond the call of public relations and as the evening wore on I managed to say a few sentences to him that were not connected to the work of other trumpeters. The earlier incident had left no scars, and Red willingly and expansively answered my questions. When I congratulated him on his extraordinary memory he tapped his forehead and said, 'The elephants, you know' and laughed.

Trombonist Dicky Wells, who had worked alongside Red in Fletcher Henderson's Band, was also in London at this time (with Buck Clayton's Band). Wells decided to call on the offchance at Red's hotel, but Red was out sightseeing so he left a note under Red's hotel room door, which the hotel maid picked up. When Red returned she told him about the message. Red, by now in a hurry to get on the band bus, and not wanting to undo his overcoat to get his spectacles out, asked her to read it out to him. The maid opened the note and relayed the words 'Hey Blondy. Why the fuck don't you stay home?' Red hurriedly said, 'Here, give me that. That sounds like a friend of mine.'[13]

The Ory Band's tour was successful but gruelling. A two-shows-a-night routine took the group to many British towns and cities, including Portsmouth, Birmingham, Newcastle, Sheffield, Leicester, Brighton, Liverpool, Bradford, Bristol, London and Glasgow (where they shared the bill with the Clyde Valley Stompers). Max Jones, writing in the *Melody Maker* about a London date, was full of praise for Red Allen's work, describing him as 'the hero of the event' and commenting how admirably he had adapted to Ory's methods. Max wrote that Ory's 'Savoy Blues' solo was 'punched out with the finesse of a shipyard riveter', but acknowledged that 'Kid Ory, blowing what he has blown for years, is still a tailgate master'.[14] McCracken's clarinet-playing did not cause Max to throw his beret in the air; instead he politely observed that this musician's ensemble work was 'almost discreet'. Despite commenting on the occasional raggedness of the band, and its tendency to speed up, it was plain that overall Max greatly enjoyed the occasion, as did, it seems, almost everyone who attended the concerts. Critic Charles Fox admitted he was apprehensive when he first heard of the Ory-Allen pairing, but said of Red 'years of cavorting at the Metropole has not really dimmed his spirit at all'.[15] Many fond farewells were said when the band left Britain on Monday 2 November 1959 to play more dates in Europe before returning to the USA.

12

FOUR'S COMPANY

After his return from Europe, Red was soon back leading his All Stars in the downstairs section of the Metropole (usually sharing bookings with Sol Yaged's Quartet). By this time Red's long association with J.C. Higginbotham was virtually at an end. Trombonist Ricky Nelson took Higgy's place at the Metropole, but left after a few weeks to join Bob Scobey's Band. His replacement, Frederic 'Keg' Johnson, stayed for an equally short period and was then followed by Jimmy Buxton. Later Henderson Chambers filled the gap for a while, and Herb Flemming acted as a standby.

Sammy Price was often on piano with Red's group, but he was becoming increasingly involved in local politics, making steadfast efforts to gain a seat on the New York Assembly. His zeal for electioneering landed him in trouble. *Down Beat* of 4 February 1960 reported that Price 'recently received a summons for using a microphone on 125th Street'. Claude Hopkins played on many of the Metropole dates when Price was absent, but then Red began using Bob Hammer as his regular pianist. Price did however find time to play on five tracks of a recording that Red Allen's Orchestra made for Norman Granz's Verve label in late 1960. The album was incongruously titled *Red Allen Plays King Oliver*. The billing was inappropriate because only four of the items recorded – 'Canal Street Blues', 'Someday Sweetheart', 'Baby, Won't You Please Come Home?' and 'Yellow Dog Blues' – were associated with Oliver. It was a wasted opportunity because Oliver's repertoire contained a good deal of excellent, unusual material. As it was, the band ended up by trotting out another album that contained typical Metropole fare.

Sammy Price's playing is commendable, and Red sings audaciously and effectively on 'How Long Blues', as well as playing powerfully on

'Snowy Morning Blues' (albeit with a surfeit of growling). His trumpet work and his vocalizing are splendid on 'Baby, Won't You Please Come Home?' – the best track on the album. The nadir of the session (perhaps of Red's entire recording career) is a 'Dixie Medley', consisting of brief, fast versions of 'Dixie', 'Marching through Georgia' and 'Battle Hymn of the Republic', all linked together by snare drum interludes. The medley resolves into a long version of Paul Barbarin's composition 'Bourbon Street Parade', in which Bob Hammer reveals (as he does elsewhere on the album) that he was a competent pianist, but nothing more, and Buster Bailey, never wanting for technique, adopts a Tyrolean style of playing. There are some effective moments: Red's melodic muted work on 'Someday Sweetheart', his stark solo on 'Canal Street Blues' and his ingeniously timed vocal on 'All of Me'. Milt Hinton plays forthright bass throughout, but Herb Flemming's trombone work sounds too contented to be stimulating. Sol Hall's drumming never gets in the way, but the rhythm section fails to jell, a fact that is highlighted by foolishly fast versions of 'Ballin' the Jack', 'Bill Bailey' and 'Fidgety Feet'.

The Metropole gradually adopted a changing policy during 1960, with Red Allen's group being occasionally rested, their place being taken by star bands such as the Dukes of Dixieland and groups led by Jack Teagarden and Turk Murphy. In the upstairs section Gene Krupa's Quartet became something of a fixture. The Metropole management began splashing out big money to book various orchestras, including those led by Lionel Hampton and Woody Herman. Joe Glaser's Associated Booking Corporation was still acting as Red's agent, and in that year's *Down Beat Combo Directory* the personnel of the Henry Allen Quintet was listed as Henry, Buster Bailey on clarinet, Jimmy Buxton on trombone, Sammy Price on piano and Solomon Hall on drums. However, by the summer of 1960 the group was being listed in the Metropole's advertisements as Henry Allen's Giants. To confuse things further, the band was billed as Red Allen's All Stars for its July 1960 appearance at the Newport Jazz Festival.

Late in 1960 the former Fletcher Henderson and Don Redman trombonist, Benny Morton, became a regular part of Red's group at the Metropole. Morton always retained the highest opinion of Red Allen as a musician and as a person. Looking back, he said:

A point I want to emphasize is that Red Allen made the Metropole job. The whole jazz life of the place, such as it was, was owed to him. He stayed seven years, and that speaks for itself. He had such an entertaining personality, which going along with the music, created audience participation. And, of course, he worked hard. I've seen a one o'clock Sunday lunchtime when there's been six men at the bar, but Red would arouse them with chatter and so on, before we even started playing. Yes, Red made is possible for all who came after: Krupa, Hampton, Woody Herman, Cannonball Adderley and the rest. Some of them making three times the money he got, but if his music hadn't been successful there wouldn't have been a job. He made all that big money possible. If he hadn't done what he did, Hampton would never have looked inside the place.[1]

In 1961, by mutual consent, Red and Joe Glaser rescinded the agreement that gave the exclusive rights for Red's musical services to the Associated Booking Corporation. So when *Down Beat* published its 1961 *Combo Directory* Red's quintet was billed as being 'Independent' and not represented by any particular agency. This meant that Red himself could seek work anywhere, which he did, aided by the acumen and panache of Sammy Price (once more back in the fold). The *Combo Directory* gave an unvarnished appraisal of the Quintet: 'it avoids being ordinary if only because of Allen's exceptional abilities. It can be dull enough though as had been evident during the ten years it has been playing at New York's Metropole.'

In January 1961 Red took time off from the Metropole to work for two weeks as a single in Boston; later that year he also did solo dates at the Town Tavern in Toronto. He did not mind how 'modern' his accompanists were, as long as they played the right chord changes; he elaborated on this:

> As for rhythm sections adapting to a soloist. I don't go for that. I like a rhythm section to play as *they* do. If they've got three or four in a rhythm section it's better for me to try and join them than for them to try and join me, with four different minds. If they've been playing something for a few years and then right overnight they have to change for me – I don't think that's right. If everybody is a good musician I think it comes out all right.[2]

Occasionally things did go wrong. While working in Cleveland with a local rhythm section Red suddenly felt he had to curtail a number so he shouted out 'George Washington' which, in the parlance of a New York jazz musician, meant 'Go to the tune's bridge now' (the bridge being the third eight-bar segment of a 32-bar tune). Unfortunately the musicians did not know the expression and went back to the beginning of the chorus, producing temporary chaos. When Red wanted to describe harmonies that were downright wrong he called them 'Brooklyn chords'.

Red and Sammy Price (who often described himself as Red's manager) soon discovered, in attempting to get bookings for the band, that many club owners now shied away from hiring a sextet or a quintet because they felt that the attraction of the unit rested mainly on Red's playing and singing. The amount of money offered was virtually only enough to employ a quartet, so Red began working with Sammy Price on piano, Franklin Skeete on double bass and Jerry Porter on drums, and only occasionally leading a bigger line-up. In cutting down to a quartet Red was following in the steps of several Swing Era trumpet stars who were enjoying success with a four-piece set-up, notably Jonah Jones. Jonah's quartet was enjoying huge album sales and long residencies at the Embers on New York's East Side. Red's quartet occasionally played at this night club in the early 1960s; a review in 1961, commenting on his performance there, said, 'This indeed is a different Allen from the one on the Metropole bar, a more rewarding and satisfying jazz artist'.[3] In 1961 Red was delighted to attend a ceremony where he was presented with a *Playboy* poll award by Dizzy Gillespie. Red worked out new formats for his smaller line-up, but one senses he was trying to console himself when he said, 'Quartets are pretty good for travelling. Then they're good for financial reasons. Clubs won't pay for bigger bands – if they could cut you down to a single they'd be happy.'[4] One of the venues that provided recurring successes for Red's new four-piece band was the London House, Chicago. Their summer 1961 booking there was reviewed in *Down Beat* by Gilbert M. Erskine:

Chicago's London House is, like the Embers and the Roundtable in New York, one of those places where the talk is usually louder than the music. Most musicians react to such surroundings with different degrees of detachment. But Red Allen, somewhere along the way, has learned to cope successfully with this, and he does so without compromising his music.

Physically, Allen is a massive man. On the bandstand, towering over everyone, he leans over and pelts the audience with rhythmic shouts and roars, compelling attention and making conversations all but impossible. The net effect is that the crowd is drawn into each performance and is constrained to make a response.

The quartet features a variety of tunes from the back years of jazz and will play almost anything from the traditional and mainstream schools. Of all the recent trumpet quartets, this is easily the most interesting.[5]

Certainly the new line-up allowed Red to sprinkle his programme with class ballads such as 'Autumn Leaves', 'Tenderly' and 'Lover, Come Back to Me', but old traditional favourites were also well represented. In the autumn of 1961 Red made a well-paid journey to the musical past by being part of a 'New Orleans Band' featured in a television programme entitled *Chicago and All That Jazz*. The show, scripted by William Nicholas, attempted to present a history of jazz developments in Chicago, and allowed Red to work again with Kid Ory; Buster Bailey was on clarinet, Lil Hardin Armstrong on piano, Johnny St Cyr on banjo, Milt Hinton on double bass and Zutty Singleton on drums. Other star-studded groups took part, including one that featured Bud Freeman, Jack Teagarden and Pee Wee Russell. The end result was a brave attempt to condense a complex story into simple terms, but a feeling of truncation affects the music, and some of the performances seem absurdly brief (the version of 'Doctor Jazz', complete with a vocal from Mae Barnes, lasts for less than two minutes). 'Jelly Roll Blues' is the best offering by the 'New Orleans Band', opening with Lil Hardin Armstrong recreating the introduction originally devised by the tune's composer, Jelly Roll Morton, and then following the Red Hot Peppers' 1926 arrangement, with Buster Bailey affectionately paying homage to the clarinet part that Omer Simeon played on Morton's recording. Red Allen blows softly as he revives George Mitchell's phrasing of the verse, but when Red adopts the role of a musical ogre the lilt of the original recording is totally lost. He makes a satisfactory job in presenting his own slant on Louis Armstrong's 'Cornet Chop Suey', but this is only a 35-second vignette. Red and Buster Bailey are briefly and neatly featured on 'Heebie Jeebies', but the massed bands' version of 'Tiger Rag' is jarringly discordant.

Red's quartet continued to operate regularly through 1962 and 1963, playing several further residencies at the London House, Chicago, and fulfilling club dates in New York, Cleveland and Indianapolis. Sometimes Red and Sammy Price went out as a duo, and in the spring of 1962 they played a two-week booking at the Colonial Tavern in Toronto, sharing billing with Bud Freeman. Although the Allen-Price musical partnership was very successful, socially they shared a love-hate relationship. Red's lips didn't exactly curl when he mentioned the pianist, but he always referred to him simply as 'Price' (in a way that did not radiate much warmth). In his autobiography Price spoke of their association:

> I was working with someone who understood me and knew that I kidded a lot but most of the time I meant what I said… I stayed with Red eight years… Red was my best friend and I considered myself his best friend. He was hell to get along with musically because he was so sensitive, but I got along with him by telling him I made him sound good.[6]

Sammy Price's multifarious business interests combined with his political activities often curtailed his availability to play musical dates, and as a result pianist Lannie Scott began doing some of Red Allen's work. In its 1962 combo listing, *Down Beat* continued its campaign of candour in listing Red's group: 'In recent years Red Allen has been rediscovered by critics as the best of the last of the red-hot trumpeters. When he's good he's very good, even if some of his groups are horrid.' Lannie Scott and Sammy Price continued sharing Red's work, and each made separate trips to Chicago for the quartet's London House residencies; the group was featured on various broadcasts from that club, some of which were later issued on albums. The balance is indifferent on most of these 'air-shots', Franklin Skeete's double bass playing is almost inaudible and the sound of Jerry Potter's cymbals adds an obtrusive 'sound-wash' to the proceedings. There is also some 'wow' on the piano and Red occasionally steps 'off-mike'; nevertheless it is a fair portrait of the quartet at work in a club that did not cater exclusively for jazz fans. Red encourages the crowd and often uses his trademark exhortation 'Make him happy!' to get them applauding the solos. He also generously sprinkles the word 'Nice' throughout the programme.

The material used by the quartet covered a wide area. Following his appearance in the *Chicago and All That Jazz* TV show, Red took to using a neat arrangement of Morton's 'Jelly Roll Blues', which was issued on the 'air-shots' album. Sammy Price wisely makes no attempt to copy Jelly Roll Morton, creating instead some fine rolling piano playing that demonstrates his skilful, sturdy left-hand work. Red does not blast his way to a climax here and is similarly restrained on a tight arrangement of 'Aunt Hagar's Blues' (to which Red had been re-introduced during his European tour with Kid Ory); however his playing exuberance is unchecked on an imaginative version of 'Lover, Come Back to Me'. Lannie Scott was also featured on some of the Chicago broadcasts and plays well on a faster than usual version of 'Satin Doll', on which Red's solo is full of interesting gaps where he deliberately pauses for dramatic effect. The quartet's version of 'I Want a Little Girl' is a little too ornamental, but Lannie Scott shows that he, like Sammy Price, was a versatile pianist. Some of these Chicago performances are run-of-the-mill (by Red's standards) but it must be remembered that, for the musicians, this was an ordinary working night, which to their surprise was later issued on record. Had Red known this in advance he would not, one feels, have included the inappropriate and showy version of 'Hava Neguila'.

In contrast, the material recorded by Red's quartet (Scott, Potter and Skeete) for a Prestige-Swingville session in June 1962 was carefully selected. Critic Martin Williams was present at the recordings and in his long summary of the day's events he noted that Red's mood was one of nervous apprehension – he was often like this on recording dates, but the tension usually provided a creative source of energy. The musicians arrived at 12.15 p.m. (45 minutes early) at Rudy Van Gelder's New Jersey studios, and Martin Williams overheard drummer Jerry Potter say 'Early, this group is always early' with a half-smile that did not exactly reveal his feelings on the matter. While the sound engineer set the microphones in place, Franklin Skeete and Red Allen took it in turns to play piano. Williams commented 'Nearly everyone plays some piano and enjoys it, but it is frequently surprising to outsiders'.[7] Red's particular apprehension about this session caused him to refrain from excessive flamboyance and wild blowing, and instead (without losing his sense of daring) he concentrates on developing ideas within his improvisations, adding some deft light and shade to his musical sketches.

This period marked the height of the trumpet-and-rhythm-section popularity, and although Red's quartet did not set out to replicate the musical approach with which Jonah Jones's Quartet achieved huge record sales for Capitol, the medium-bounce treatment given to 'Just in Time' show they were well aware of Jonah's method. But Red Allen's playing, with complex improvisations likely to surface at any time, did not make him a contender for mass popularity. 'Just in Time' seems to have been a concession, and for most of the session the quartet plays in a straight-ahead fashion. It is no exaggeration to say that Red created hundreds of musical ideas on this date. He had really settled into the quartet format by this time and makes no attempt to force the pace by overblowing and adding wild effects. He adds his open growling in moderation and uses his fingered trills sparingly, sounding totally assured throughout.

The session opened with a fast version of 'Cherry', complete with a frisky and ingeniously timed vocal. Red's trumpet floats over the sprightly rhythm section, pouring out cascades of original phrases. Someone in the recording booth said, 'I wonder if he could repeat himself if he tried', and a little later Rudy Van Gelder remarked that maybe they should have recorded everything, including the warm-ups and run-throughs, such was the flow and calibre of the improvisations.[8] A rich vocal graces 'I Ain't Got Nobody' and on a subtle version of 'Sleepytime Gal' Red demonstrates how he could suddenly add a soft edge to his tone. This cashmere effect is in absolute contrast to the fiercely blown blue notes that Red injects into a re-make of his early composition 'Biffly Blues'. Lannie Scott plays delicate piano here but lets loose vigorously during his four choruses on 'St Louis Blues', and here Red's timing of the melody provides a totally new look at one of the most recorded of all jazz themes. On 'Nice Work if You Can Get It', Red again leaves plenty of space between his phrases, resolving the tune's interesting harmonic changes by using deft, economical lines. Here, as through most of the session, Red works mainly in the middle register, and on 'There's a House in Harlem for Sale', he enriches his sombre notes with an eerie flutter-tongued effect that germinates into an open growl. By late afternoon the session was over and Red had created an album that is one of the most fertile of his latter-day efforts. It was not wildly acclaimed on initial release, but remains a fine example of the trumpeter's extraordinary powers of invention.

In the autumn of 1963 English trumpeter Keith 'Cuff' Billett, on his way to New Orleans, stopped over in New York. Armed with an introduction from clarinettist Willie Humphrey, he telephoned Red Allen. Red took down the address of Cuff's hotel and said that his son, Henry III, would soon be round to pick him up. Cuff, unaware that Red's son was a policeman, was startled when a patrol car rolled up to deliver him to Red. Red delighted Cuff by playing recordings from the 1930s, such as 'Dinah Lou' and 'Rosetta', and blowing along with them note for note. He then invited Cuff to blow an accompaniment to the sound of these old 78 r.p.m. recordings, and after listening appreciatively he said, 'Learn how to do it, but don't do it. Go away and be yourself.'

Cuff was enthralled to meet someone whose playing he had so long admired, and later said, 'I felt there were two Red Allens, one who put on an entertainment front for on-stage and public performances, and the other who was quiet and thoughtful, quite happy to sit and chat relaxedly, making no attempt to be up-front or to take charge'.[9] Red was a firm advocate of learning through listening and said on another occasion, 'There ain't no books that can really tell you how to play jazz'.[10]

Very few jazz musicians of Red's era collected jazz records, but he was an exception. Pearly May commented on this:

Henry had a large collection of records. I couldn't even begin to number them, but they filled four big racks. Many musicians came to our home through the years. They didn't play there, because we lived in an apartment, but they would spend hours listening to jazz records. It seemed like white musicians were always his friends. They'd come up to the house too.[11]

After Kid Ory's 1959 concert in Zurich, the Swiss writer Johnny Simmen sat down in his apartment with Red and pianist Joe Turner (who was then working in Switzerland);

Joe wanted to be sure that Red knew how Joe Turner sounded on record. Red was sitting there grinning with joy and congratulating Joe on every record I played. Joe was tireless that night and always came up with a new idea of what we should hear and they were all Joe Turner records! Red enjoyed all of them, then he said, 'Turner, we've heard your records and they sounded wonderful but now I wanna hear a few of mine, because Johnny seems to have a few that I haven't got'.[12]

Red's close interest in his recordings highlighted yet another difference between him and his sidekick J.C. Higginbotham; when Simmen later asked Higgy whether he too was interested in his own discs the trombonist replied, 'I never bought any. I made them and forgot about them.'[13] Simmen got on well with Red and with Higgy, whom he described as being 'intelligent and witty, except when he had been drinking too much'.

Throughout 1963 Red's quartet played further bookings at the Metropole (with Ronnie Cole on drums in place of Jerry Potter). The management were not slow to observe that Red's return brought back customers who had not visited the bar in a long time, and accordingly they gave Allen a series of dates that stretched into spring 1964. Drummer Barry Martyn visited the Metropole during this period:

> In 1964 I was on tour with Kid Thomas. We had a night off in Bridgeport, Connecticut, so I suggested to Tom that we go into New York. He was pleased with the idea and got all dressed up. We caught the train in and decided we'd go to the Metropole to see Red Allen. Someone must have told Red that Kid Thomas was in the house because he made a big shebang about it from the stage and when the intermission came he sat down with us and he and Kid Thomas began talking about the old days. But neither of them mentioned the celebrated occasion when they had battled against each other for the prize of a leather satchel. I thought how much I'd like to hear them talk about that so I brought the subject up by saying 'Is this the first time you've met since you had that cutting contest?' Red affected not to remember anything about this, but Kid Thomas said he didn't think they had met since then, but neither of them elaborated and the conversation went on to other things. By then about ten people had gathered around to hear what these old guys were talking about, so Red became expansive while old Tom just sat listening; then Red said something to one of the crowd about his father having the greatest brass band in New Orleans. Suddenly Tom piped up, 'I worked in your daddy's band and it wasn't too good.' Well, I thought that Red might explode, but actually he sat there calmly and then said 'Maybe it wasn't that good, but it was history', and both men chuckled.[14]

Barry Martyn soon returned to the Metropole and saw Red working there with his quartet, which had Sammy Price on piano and a young bassist and drummer. Red was playing opposite Woody Herman's Big Band, who were on stage when Martyn arrived:

> I think this must have been one of Woody's noisiest bands. They finished their set and on came Red and the rhythm section. He absolutely took the place over and in no time at all he had all the people hollering and cheering, and the crowd let it be known they didn't want Woody Herman's Band to go back on. It was just about the most remarkable scene I've ever witnessed in my years as a

musician. It was a perfect example of showmanship and New Orleans jazz winning over audience.[15]

The Metropole bookings were not continuous so Red was able to take engagements in other cities. One long trip was in the offing, namely Red's first solo tour of Britain.

13

TRIUMPHANT TOURS

Red's first British tour wasn't organized by any of the big European agents, but was the brainchild of two officials of the Manchester Sports Guild (L.C. 'Jenks' Jenkins and Jack Swinnerton), who wanted a top jazz name to help them commemorate the tenth anniversary of their Jazz Section. What started out as a pipe-dream for the jazz-loving committee members of the Guild turned into reality and in April 1964 Red arrived in Manchester to begin a four-day residency, appearing each night with a different group, first with Alex Welsh's Band, then with the Al Fairweather-Sandy Brown All Stars, followed by Bruce Turner's Jump Band and finally Humphrey Lyttelton's Band. Red travelled via London, where his arrival at Heathrow Airport was greeted with some lively music playing by a contingent of British jazzmen, including clarinettist Wally Fawkes and trumpeter Ken Colyer. Early on Thursday 16 April he caught the train to Manchester and startled two bowler-hatted travellers by warming up on trumpet in the first-class compartment.

Red could not wait to play his first gig in Manchester, and at a press conference organized at the Sports Guild on 16 April, he unzipped his trumpet bag, got out his instrument, and happily sat in with the musicians who were providing background jazz for the reception. First Red played with an eleven-piece Count Basie-inspired group, joining in on 'Splanky' and 'Peace Pipe', then he blew enthusiastically with the Art Taylor All Stars (alongside their trumpeter Doug Whaley). Everyone was thrilled by Red's display of keenness and musical daring, and when he had finished blowing, even hardened hacks who had attended hundreds of press receptions were totally charmed by his friendliness. When he was complimented on his versatility, he chuckled and said, 'Oh man, we play 'em all, we play 'em all'.[1] Red was a publicist's dream, sparing time to answer mundane questions put to him by the non-jazz press and being equally patient as discographers plied him with queries about recordings he made over thirty years before.

The first three of Red's engagements at the Manchester Sports Guild were hugely successful. After a brief rehearsal with each of the separate bands, Red relaxed, then re-emerged to play and sing in a truly dynamic way. His programme varied each evening but was generally based on jazz standards such as 'Yellow Dog Blues', 'Just a Closer Walk with Thee', 'St James Infirmary', 'Canal Street Blues' and 'The Saints' mixed with numbers specifically associated with him, including 'Rosetta', 'Patrol Wagon Blues', 'Biffly Blues' and 'Rag Mop'. Steve Voce, reviewing Red's Manchester dates for *Down Beat*, wrote:

> Some of his extraordinary effects were on display – the heavy-vibrato growl, the muted effects created without a mute, and the intricate precision of his rapid-fire fingering. Without pandering to the audience Allen involved them in his vocals and created the highly volatile atmospheres that built up at each session. It can be said that he has done more constructive work for British jazz in his short stay than several 16-man groups have done during more intensive tours.[2]

Red poured out vast amounts of energy – and skill – on the bandstand, but, after midnight, at the end of the gig, he would happily sit on a bar stool while a cluster of his followers fired questions about King Oliver, Fletcher Henderson, Luis Russell, etc. The only less than ecstatic evening was on Red's fourth booking on which he was accompanied by Humphrey Lyttelton's Band. The contretemps that developed caused Lyttelton particular disappointment because he had championed Red's playing for many years. Humph's pianist, Eddie Harvey, was also well acquainted with Red's work and, during his earlier days as a trombonist, he had learnt many of the Allen-Higginbotham discs note for note. The rehearsal went smoothly, with Red telling the band, 'Just you play your way, and I'll be with you.'[3] But on the gig itself incidents occurred that created a storm in a teacup that kept swirling for months. Lyttelton described the scene: 'It became obvious that something was wrong when Red began interrupting all the piano solos by calling in another soloist'. Just before Red took this action, Humph's redoubtable baritone saxophonist, Joe Temperley, had aired a band catch-phrase 'We're moving up' just as Red, in giving the audience a verbal summary of jazz history, had mentioned the year 1929. The band had adopted the expression from a Willie 'The Lion' Smith recording, and began using it as a standing joke, whether it was relevant or not to any particular situation. Unfortunately Red Allen immediately assumed that the comment was a hint that he was dwelling in the past. Humph recalls, 'Red, momentarily losing his temper, started to harangue the band over the microphone, stating "I can move up on you guys anytime"'.[4] Red also suggested that pianist Eddie Harvey was not playing the correct chord sequences. The result of these outbursts was an acrimonious session, with the resultant tension being transmitted to the audience. Soon afterwards Humph described the evening as being 'probably the least enjoyable experience in fifteen years of band-leading'.[5] Years later Humph learnt that a local trombonist had told Red that the Lyttelton band members felt that his playing was not modern enough for their tastes, which was certainly not true. However, with this seed implanted in his mind Red was vulnerable to an imagined slight. However, things were patched over at the end of the session and handshakes exchanged.

On the following weekend Humphrey Lyttelton's Band had again been booked to accompany Red, this time at the Marquee Club in Wardour Street, London. Red might still have been smarting over the previous events but his professionalism (and that of Humph's band) triumphed and some wonderful jazz was heard. The earlier incidents might have been forgotten but for a detailed review by G.E. Lambert in the June 1964 issue of *Jazz Journal*. In the July 1964 issue of the same magazine Lyttelton replied to the report, pointing out that Red 'was shouting for chords which Eddie Harvey was actually playing at the time'. Back in New York, Humph's reply was brought to Red's attention. It revived his earlier anger, so much so that a caustic letter bearing his name appeared in the September 1964 *Jazz Journal*, which ended 'We movin' up my man Humph. I may move to England'. Some while later I discovered from Red that this letter had actually been sent by Sammy Price (who had heard all about the incidents from Red). Nevertheless, the contents of the letter must have been suggested (or even dictated) by Red because it contained a reference to an evening five years earlier when Red had heard Humph playing Luis Russell numbers (something which Red, with his extraordinary memory, would not have forgotten). Happily the two trumpeters were reconciled during Red's next visit to London, and Lyttelton celebrated the occasion by taking Red out for a Chinese meal at Leon's Restaurant.

After concluding his 1964 four-night residency at the Manchester Sports Guild Red moved off to play dates in various parts of England, accompanied on most of them by Alex Welsh's Band; an exception was the concert that an old friend of Red's, Allan Gatward, organized at the Central Hall, Westminster, London, on 1 May. Gatward, a frequent visitor to the USA, never failed to link up with Red during his business trips to New York, and a firm friendship developed. The line-up for the London concert consisted of a pick-up band, billed as 'Henry "Red" Allen and his All-Stars', and featured Red, Sandy Brown on clarinet, Mac Duncan on trombone, Johnny Parker on piano, Diz Disley on guitar, Jim Bray on double bass and Terry Cox on drums. On the rest of this tour Red had been featured with established bands, but here his task was to unite a line-up that had never played together before. It was a joy and an education to see Red rehearse these musicians; he radiated encouragement and gently corrected any wrong notes, occasionally walking over to the keyboard to demonstrate a particular harmonic progression. He swiftly got everyone into shape and made sure that they all felt at ease. Unfortunately the hall's acoustics were poor and much of the afternoon's work was wasted as the sound of the band bounced around the walls of the ancient building. Undeterred, Red put on a magnificent show, and his personality turned the atmosphere of a vast place into that of an intimate club.

During his brief stay in London, Red attended a party given by some of his most dedicated fans, including record-shop owner Doug Dobell, John Kendall, Eric Saunders and Ray Bolden. Someone surreptitiously recorded part of this happy gathering and Red can be heard blowing his trumpet in tandem with the sound of some of his most celebrated recordings, proving that he had remembered arrangements recorded thirty years before (including 'Limehouse Blues', 'Big John's Special', 'Happy Feet', 'Jersey Lightning' and 'Panama'). Red was fascinated by Cockney rhyming slang and said the only time he had encountered anything similar back home was when veteran New Orleans musicians used the name of an old notary, Henry Clay, as a substitute for the word 'pay' in asking the question 'Have you got your Henry Clay yet?'

During the late stages of the tour Red played a return date at the Manchester Sports Guild with Alex Welsh's Band. The gig ended with presentations to the visitor, a silver tea service inscribed for Red's wife Pearly May (from the Sports Guild) and a pewter tankard for Red (from the Alex Welsh Band). Red was quite overcome when receiving these gifts and responded by saying it was the greatest night of his life since he joined Luis Russell's Band in the 1920s.

Red's final date of the trip occurred on 5 May when, together with Alex Welsh's Band, he recorded two prestigious 'Jazz 625' programmes at the BBC's Shepherds Bush studios in London. Trumpeter Alex Welsh sat out for several of the numbers when Red was backed by Roy Crimmins on trombone, Al Gay on clarinet and tenor sax, Fred Hunt on piano, Jim Douglas on guitar, Ron Mathewson on double bass and Lennie Hastings on drums. The band were in top form and the music provided a worthy climax for Red's tour. He flew back to New York the following day, leaving behind a farewell message that left his British fans in no doubt as to how much he had enjoyed his stay: 'I had the time of my life… it has nothing to do with finance, it is a feeling that you're wanted, that helps a guy so much. Very, very nice!'[6] Bandleader Alex Welsh summarized the tour: 'Red Allen played wonderfully well, but kept within himself during the first three nights. But the fourth night – once he'd settled down and tested us – he cut loose and frightened the life out of us.'[7]

Red was too much of a professional to feel a sense of anticlimax when he returned to his New York haunts. Word of his success in England reached the Copper Rail habitués via Steve Voce's enthusiastic review in *Down Beat*. Red took the tankard that Alex Welsh's Band had given to him down to the Metropole and proudly showed it to the customers and to fellow musicians. The Metropole had again re-vamped its policy with Red now being advertised as leading the house band (Gene Krupa's Quartet maintaining the upstairs residency). In July 1964 Red took part in a Carnegie Hall tribute to his old friend Eddie Condon.

News of Red's triumphs in Britain seemed to awaken the critics, and in 1964, for the first time ever, Red was listed in the International Jazz Critics Poll; but the most remarkable acknowledgement of Red's talent, and probably the most praiseworthy piece ever written about him, came from another trumpeter, Don Ellis. Headlined 'Henry (Red) Allen is the most avant-garde trumpet player in New York City', Don Ellis's praise filled a page of the *Down Beat* issue of 28 January 1965. It began:

Everytime I have gone to the Metropole to see Henry 'Red' Allen during the past two or three years I have said to myself 'It can't be true. He must just be having a very good night. All those wild things he is doing must just be lucky accidents. After all, he's been around almost as long as Louis, and it is simply impossible that he could be playing that modern.' Well, a few weeks ago, after hearing Red on a slow Tuesday night with only a handful of people in the club – I became convinced that Red Allen is the most creative and avant-garde trumpet player in New York.

What other trumpet player plays such asymmetrical rhythms and manages to make them swing besides? What other trumpeter plays ideas that may begin as a whisper, rise to a brassy shout and suddenly become a whisper again, with no discernible predictability? Who else has the amazing variety of tonal colours, bends, smears, half-valve effects, rips, glissandos, flutter tonguing, all combined with iron chops and complete control? What makes all this even more incredible is the fact that he does all this within a 'mainstream' context and with a flair for showmanship that appears to keep the squarest entertained.

Don Ellis commented further on Red's presentation, saying 'His patter between sets is hilarious and, again, never quite predictable', then he returned enthusiastically to further analysis of Red's trumpet work:

It is phenomenal that he is still one of the most exciting, creative jazz players of all time. There are countless 'influences' on Red's style no doubt, but he is able to use these in a completely original way and still create within the style. He is one of the major jazz improvisers, in the truest sense of the word. Other trumpeters may be able to play faster and higher than Red (though his facility and range are remarkable), but no one has a wider scope of effects to draw upon, and no one is more subtle rhythmically and in the use of dynamics and asymmetrical phrases than Henry (Red) Allen.

Not long after that review appeared, Red's group played a brief season at Mushy Wexler's Theatrical Grill in Cleveland, Ohio, where a huge blow-up of the Don Ellis article was put on display. Ellis himself was an excellent musician who at that time was experimenting with unusual time signatures; the fact that he praised Red so emphatically considering they hardly knew one another was a remarkable gesture, and one that naturally pleased Henry a good deal.

Life at the Metropole was about the same as usual when Red returned from Cleveland. His group was again back to the quartet format, with

Sonny Greer temporarily on drums, and with Chuck Folds on piano in place of Sammy Price. Occasionally the group was augmented into a sextet, but regardless of size it was advertised again as the Metropole's 'house band'. However things were soon to change. Details of the venue's new policy were given in the *Down Beat* issue of 1 July 1965:

> The latest New York club to go discotheque is the Metropole. However the Times Square jazz landmark will continue to book name band attractions to work opposite live rock-and-roll groups and a line of frugging girls. The long-time house band led by trumpeter Henry (Red) Allen is out.

Jazz musicians never considered the Metropole to be an ideal venue; however, Red, like the true professional he was, had buckled down and always gave of his best there, making sure that the dozen people who made up a typical Tuesday late-night gathering heard as much good music as did the weekend throng. As a result Red gained many new fans, and introduced hundreds and hundreds of people to live jazz during his 12-year tenure. Red was quite sad to end what was sometimes a gruelling residency, and knew that he would miss seeing many of the regulars who had become his friends. His wife, Pearly May, summed up the situation: 'He loved working there. Everybody would come along and see him there. He'd made a lot of friends there – he used to say "I never made a million dollars but I made a million friends".'[8]

Red's long-time colleague and close friend, clarinettist Buster Bailey, simply shrugged his shoulders when he was told about the demise of the Metropole as a jazz venue. Like Red, he had grandchildren and he was happy at the prospect of spending more time with them. However in July 1965 Buster was offered the well-paid post of clarinettist in Louis Armstrong's All Stars, so he went back on the road again. Distance did not stop Bailey from continuing his regular practice of telephoning Red Allen for long conversations. He retained the Fletcher Henderson Band's nickname for Red, and if Pearly May picked up the telephone she would hear Buster's sing-song voice asking 'Is Blondy there please?' Red kept in touch with many of his ex-colleagues, going right back to riverboat days (corresponding regularly with pianist Burroughs Lovingood). He was happy to join the 'Friendly Fifty Club', a social organization for senior musicians that restricted its membership to fifty. Among this élite club's rollcall were two saxophonists who had worked with Red in Luis Russell's Band, Charlie Holmes and Greely Walton. Red kept loosely in touch with Luis Russell, who had retired from full-time music in 1948 to open a store in Brooklyn. When this began to lose money he managed a club in the same area, and later became a part-time chauffeur until his death in 1963.

Red's own grandchildren, Alcornette (born 1954) and Juretta (born 1959), were a central part of his life. When their father, Henry III, left the US Marines he became a policeman and served for 23 years (until retiring in 1980). For part of that time he was based at Harlem's 32nd Precinct and often did shift work. Red helped out by delivering the two children to school (no matter how late he had been working), later collecting them and taking them to the Prospect Avenue apartment before returning them to their home four blocks away. The kids loved seeing their grandfather roll up at school in his Cadillac Eldorado, knowing that there would usually be some sort of treat in store for them. Red even arranged for Alcornette to celebrate her fifth birthday at the Metropole, where the band joined in the party spirit by playing 'Happy Birthday' as the youngster shared out her cake.

Besides helping to tend the grandchildren Red also found time to take the family dog, White Fang, for regular walks. The Allen family had a series of White Fangs, the first having been bought for Henry III during his childhood after he had been thrilled by a movie about Jack London's heroic canine. The original pet was a Samoyed-husky, but during the 1960s the White Fang in residence at 1351 Prospect Avenue was a white German Shepherd dog.

The 'buzz' that Don Ellis's article had created was still reverberating around the bars where New York jazz musicians gathered (the Copper Rail also put a blow-up of the *Down Beat* article in its window). The renewed interest in Red's work stirred the King instrument company (whose trumpets Red had played for years) to take a special advertisement in the music magazines, which read:

Red Allen's trouble is that people keep re-discovering him. This has been going on for 40 years, so it probably doesn't bother Red as much as it bothers the rest of us who've always known he's a great artist.

When Red sensed that his days at the Metropole were numbered he took a two-week booking for his quartet at the Blue Spruce Inn, situated at the east end of Long Island's Roslyn Bridge. Jazz attractions such as

Teddy Wilson and Jimmy and Marian McPartland had preceded Red by working at this celebrated restaurant. The booking materialized when David Metzger (who had become a fan of Red's at the Metropole) persuaded the management to hire the quartet. Metzger's enthusiasm about Red's suitability for the venue proved to be entirely justified – the group's initial two-week booking was soon extended into a two-month residency. The quartet began their evening's work at 7 p.m., playing for dinner, then after a break they performed brief sets that took them to a midnight finish. The main snag to music-making was the restaurant's proximity to the local firehouse; when the fire siren went off next door, the band had no option but to stop playing. Fortunately there were no conflagrations or false alarms when the quartet did a series of live test recordings at the club in June 1965 (which were later issued on the Merritt label); the line-up was Red, Benny Moten on double bass, George Reed on drums and Sammy Price on piano (for most of the tracks).

Although Red usually drove Sammy Price out to the Blue Spruce Inn gig, some of these journeys took place in silent animosity; they had one of their periodic disagreements just before this test recording session began. David Metzger observed the contretemps:

> Red had an argument with Sammy over a Harlou button Sammy was wearing. I heard Red asking him to take it off saying that they were musicians and not politicians. Red was quite annoyed and when they started to record the first set, Lannie Scott was at the piano and not Sammy. Later Red relented and used him in either the second or third sets.[9]

Despite the indifferent acoustics of the restaurant, the results proved that it was worthwhile for a major recording company to set up a full-scale live recording; the trial attempt contained some fine moments including a fast, thrilling 'Caravan' and an almost tender 'Crazy Blues'. Soon after the test session, recordings were made there for CBS. The producer was Franklin Driggs, a jazz collector of many years standing, who captured Red Allen almost at his latter-day best. Even so there was another show of animosity between Red and Sammy Price. According to Price the two had been involved in a spat during the previous weekend, which led to the pianist saying, 'Red, I'm getting sick and tired of you again, so I gotta go'. Red took Price at his word and booked Lannie Scott for the recording session; Price recalled his reaction:

> I knew that he would get Lannie Scott to go in as substitute. But I also knew that Lannie didn't know the tunes: he hadn't been playing with Red for eight years. So this Monday night I went out. I got in my car and said 'Well, I might as well go help this turkey out', meaning Red. When I walked in, John Hammond and Frank Driggs were there with Red. And Red said to John Hammond, 'Here's the politician now'. And I said 'Well, Red. Come on man, I came out to make you sound good.' So we made 'Feeling Good'.[10]

It seems as though Red's enormous successes in Britain had stimulated his confidence and his musical imagination, for he was in top form for this date and sounding completely at ease. 'Cherry', a particular favourite of Red's during this period, is taken at a fast clip, and Red's trumpet work and his debonair vocal seem to defy musical gravity, contrasting effectively with Sammy Price's purposeful stride piano-playing. Red sings Jelly Roll Morton's 'Sweet Substitute', displaying a fine insight into his old hero's work; the plaintive trumpet-playing conveys rich emotion but a jarring note is created by the quasi-dramatic ending. Red's vocal on 'Trav'lin' All Alone' owes little to Lady Day's version but unfortunately veers towards a disappointing orderliness. Sammy Price comes into his own on 'Yellow Dog Blues' which leads into a wild vocal from Red on 'How Long Blues', one that moves close to being a pastiche; again a raucous ending seems unnecessary. However, Red is at his most charming on 'You're Nobody Until Somebody Loves You', where his warm vocal conveys a marvellous sense of enjoyment, and his trumpet solo, accompanied only by a 'walking' bass, is full of lovely melodic twists and turns. Red's charming projection of this song emphasizes what a pity it was that he never got the chance to work the Las Vegas rooms where Louis Prima enjoyed such success (and huge fees).

Red's own composition 'Siesta at the Fiesta' has a strong performance from Sammy Price and a very positive bass solo. The title track 'Feeling Good' (from the musical *The Roar of the Greasepaint*) opens with some atmospheric, ostinato piano figures. Red absorbs the mood of the song's unusual structure and blows the minor-keyed melody with the same dramatic intensity that he imparts to his long vocal; in fact his trumpet-playing takes second place here, and only takes over for the final growling cadenza. 'Patrol Wagon Blues' rocks along steadily, with Red's trumpet sounding convincingly sombre. Overall 'I'm Coming, Virginia' is disappointing, though Price's piano-playing rolls along mightily and Red's trumpet-playing sounds pleasingly flamboyant, but the arrangement (which lasts for over 8 minutes) consists of a surfeit of key changes and a series of false endings. These reprises get wearisome and the listener is left with a feeling of anticlimax. Nevertheless, when surveying his entire career, Sammy Price selected this track as his own favourite recorded performance. 'Gee, Baby, Ain't I Good to You' is evocative though brief, and 'Rag Mop' shows how quickly Red could get an audience to join in with his singing.

Red's feud with Sammy Price kept replenishing itself, and months after the Blue Spruce recording Red's English friend, Allan Gatward, noticing how terse the two musicians were with each other, asked what was wrong with Price. Red growled his answer, 'Too many badges'.[11] Allan Gatward was based in London but spent a good deal of time in New York, where (at that time) he was a paper-bag salesman, touting for export orders. He took up Red's kind offer to show him around Harlem, where by luck, they met former world heavyweight champion boxer Joe Louis on 125th Street. Joe Louis knew Red and they greeted each other warmly. Red, who always liked to be expansive in his introductions, onstage or off, waved his hand and with a flourish said 'Meet Allan Gatward, he controls the paper trade in Europe'. The great boxer looked suitably impressed. On another jaunt Allan went out with Red to Princeton University where Red led a pick-up band (which included Kenny Davern and a weary J.C. Higginbotham) that played at a class reunion. Davern had good cause to remember the sequel to that gig:

> I was working at the Cinderella Club in New York and Red kindly called there to pay me for the Princeton gig. Now, the Cinderella was in a very narrow thoroughfare. Red turned up in his Cadillac and left it outside while he came in to pay me. Nothing could get past and all hell was let loose, but Red remained totally relaxed and cheerful and nonchalantly got into the Cadillac and drove off.[12]

Triumphant Tours

Red continued to work at the Blue Spruce Inn after the recording session, and on one of his dates there David Metzger had particular reason to be grateful to him. Metzger brought some rare 78 r.p.m. records to the restaurant for Red to autograph, but when the cardboard folder was opened it was discovered that one of the batch had been broken during the journey. Metzger was naturally upset but next night Red showed his generosity by bringing in his own copy of the rare Vocalion disc to replace the broken record.

14

A VALIANT FAREWELL

The Blue Spruce Inn residencies, and other gigs that Red played, ensured that his chops were in good shape when he played at the 1965 Monterey Jazz Festival in California. On 19 September Red was featured on stage with Dizzy Gillespie, Clark Terry (on flugel horn) and Rex Stewart (who borrowed a trumpet to take part in this assembly of jazz giants). Writer Whitney Balliett, who was at the event, felt that Red 'cut' the three celebrated musical combatants with whom he shared the stage. Balliett wrote eloquently about Red's triumph at that Sunday afternoon concert. He began by noting that Allen got off to a poor start:

> His solo was strained and full of fluffs and his generally ebullient almost vaudeville stage manner was distracted and uncertain. The next number was even less complimentary. In the middle of it, Gillespie and Terry, joined by the singer Jon Hendricks, broke into some nonsense singing; Allen, who is one of the redoubtable jazz singers, was unaccountably left at the back of the stage, his trumpet swinging idly from crossed hands, a bleak smile on his face. When Allen played again, after a slick, technically perfect Terry number, he suddenly became himself. His characteristic long melodic lines had become airborne and his tone had taken on its usual crackle. It was a slow blues and in it he constructed three august choruses, sang as many more in a soft, husky high voice, then closed the number with a climactic, high-noted chorus. That night, Allen, who had arrived from New York just the day before, flew home. Little else in the weekend matched him.[1]

A Valiant Farewell

Down Beat concurred with Balliett's assessment, noting that 'Allen sang and played beautifully on a slow blues'.[2] On Red's return to New York he played a series of gigs in small clubs and taverns, then did a couple of weeks at L'Intrigue with pianist Ronnie Ball and bassist Jimmy Rowser. Guest appearances in Providence, Rhode Island, and in Brooklyn helped fill the engagement book, as did a series of East Coast college dates. One intriguing idea put to Red came from jazz historian Richard B. Allen, who suggested that the Luis Russell Band be re-formed. Luis Russell had died in 1963 but Red, Higgy, Charlie Holmes Albert Nicholas, Greely Walton, Paul Barbarin and Pops Foster were all alive and well. Unfortunately the plan never achieved fruition. When there was a sizeable gap in between his gigs Red usually found some-where to sit in; he was not bothered about the style of the resident group and happily blew a couple of sets with clarinettist Tony Scott at a New York club. Red was also always willing to play at benefits for fellow musicians. Together with a team of his ex-Metropole colleagues he took part in a fundraising event for the ailing pianist Pete Johnson.

By this time almost all the details of Red's next visit to Britain had been finalized. This time the wide-ranging 1966 tour was under the auspices of the powerful Harold Davison Agency and organized by Jazz Horizons (a company headed by agents Jack L. Higgins and Jim Godbolt). Except for two of the dates Red was accompanied throughout the tour by Alex Welsh's Band. The 18-date itinerary took Red to most parts of England; a few of the gigs were theatre concerts, but the bulk of the engagements were in large jazz clubs or in ballrooms. Trombonist Roy Crimmins was no longer with Alex Welsh's Band and his place was taken by Roy Williams, who was delighted at the prospect of working with Red:

When I was first introduced to Red Allen I looked at that creased, solemn face and I thought to myself, 'I hope we get on okay', but when he smiled the sun came out and I knew everything was going to be fine. The tours we did together are among my happiest memories. He was an adorable man, and such a wonderful player. He joined in with all the band fun and developed a special liking for Mitchell and Butler's bitter, and he loved fish and chips. Our drummer Lennie Hastings wore a wig, which, when the mind took him, he used to throw into the air. When Red saw this caper he was convulsed with laughter. We finished our gig in Redcar, Yorkshire, and went back to our hotel where the owner had laid out some sandwiches for us. A big fire was burning and he kept the bar open for us, so we all gathered around and sang our party pieces, Red sang 'Ol' Man River', but instead of doing it in a jazzy way he sang it straight and it was terrifically moving.[3]

Red was a model of affability throughout this tour, but this did not mean that he invited anyone to take advantage of him. The slightest hint of racial prejudice was immediately countered. Dan Morgenstern dwelt on this when he wrote, 'He had real good old-fashioned manners, very courteous, but, in spite of Higgy's claim, not in a Tomming way'.[4] On this same theme, Albert McCarthy said, 'He was devoid of racial attitudes, though it was obvious that he would stand up for himself if the need arose'.[5] Red's son, Henry III, summed up his dad's personality when he said, 'You didn't gorilla him'.[6] On one of the 1966 tour engagements someone set up recording microphones without asking permission. Red immediately insisted that he would not play a note until they were removed. On another occasion, a few days later, someone sauntered up to Red and said, without any grace whatsoever, 'Why don't you play some Louis Armstrong numbers?' Red affably enquired which Armstrong numbers the man was thinking of, and was boorishly told that Louis had recorded a number called 'Cornet Chop Suey'. Red politely replied, 'I'm sorry my man, we won't be playing that selection tonight', whereupon the man said 'I don't suppose you could play it any night'. Red gave the interloper a fierce look and said, 'I've had the pleasure of recording that number, and if I wanted to I think I could play it in every key, but I have my own repertoire and I won't be playing it for *you*'. Red uttered this last word in triple volume, making the inquisitor jump out of his skin, prior to departing hastily. Red's reply was not of course designed to denigrate Louis Armstrong; on a gig in Bath a well-wisher approached and said, 'Red, you're greater than Louis Armstrong'. Red, close to anger, replied, 'Don't say that, don't ever say that! Louis is the King.' One night Red, in a reflective mood, said, 'I can see the point of people like Louis who want to go on playing. I liked everything that Louis did, and still do.'[7]

Rex Stewart was scheduled to re-visit England later in 1966. Although I greatly admired his cornet-playing I had never spoken to him, having previously found his apparently fierce demeanour quite daunting. When I mentioned this to Red, he laughed out loud and said:

No. Rex is a great guy. I know you two would get on fine. I'll give you a note for him, and this will give you an excuse to start talking. Now if you had asked me about Cootie Williams, I couldn't guarantee what his mood would be like when you said 'Hello'. I saw him recently at a festival and said, 'Let me buy you a drink, Cootie.' He blew up, saying, 'Don't you know I'm not drinking?' I said, 'Okay, sorry I bothered you', but my mind went back to the time when he and Ella Fitzgerald were having a scene together and Cootie used to get so drunk that Ella regularly had to carry him home.[8]

Whenever Red had spare time in London during that tour he linked up with writer Albert McCarthy, who had been commissioned by publishers Cassell & Co. to tape Red's autobiography. McCarthy's task was to question Red and then arrange the reminiscences in chronological order, eventually presenting the transcription as a finished manuscript; at Red's request the book was to be called *Make Them Happy*. Unfortunately the project was never completed, although an excerpt from the tapes, covering Red's early years in New Orleans, was eventually published in Albert McCarthy's magazine *Jazz Monthly* in its February 1970 issue.

On one of the gigs on the tour, in late February 1966, Red and Alex Welsh's Band played a concert at the Empire Theatre, Sunderland, sharing the bill with the New Orleans All Stars, a group that featured several of Red's old friends, including trumpeter Alvin Alcorn, trombonist Jimmy Archey, clarinettist Darnell Howard, pianist Alton Purnell, drummer Cie Frazier and bassist Pops Foster. British trumpeter Keith Smith, who had organized the All Stars' tour, was also featured within its line-up. Smith recalled the occasion, saying, 'It was just fantastic to observe Red enjoying an unlikely reunion with guys he hadn't seen for years. You could tell they were all thrilled to see him.'[9]

During the last few days of the tour Red and Alex Welsh's Band played in Crawley, Sussex. Red was back in London before midnight; there was no thought of an early night, and instead he went and sat in with Stan Tracey's Trio at Ronnie Scott's Club, where his ebullience won over a crowd, many of whom were previously unfamiliar with his work. He enjoyed the experience and humorously told the audience that they must not get the impression that he was doing an audition. The penultimate date of the tour was a Sunday afternoon gig (with Alex Welsh's Band) at Douglas House in West London. This venue was a club for American servicemen who could sit, drink and chat with their buddies during a weekend furlough. It was not an ideal audience for Red as few of those present had any idea who he was; the ceaseless babble of conversation remained unabated as the band played their first number. Red loved this kind of challenge and immediately got to work on the audience, not by firing the heavy artillery of his singalong routines, but subtly, by playing pianissimo solos. Sinclair Traill once wrote that Red 'without the aid of a mute can play a solo within an inch of your eardrum', and he certainly demonstrated this gentle skill to the soldiers and airmen gathered at Douglas House. He got down off the bandstand and strolled from table to table whispering open-trumpet phrases to young ears that had never before been charmed by improvisation. He blew so softly and with such control that within minutes the entire audience became appreciatively silent, totally absorbed in Red's music. It was an unforgettable scene.

Red retained a lively interest in sport and, if asked, could reel off the achievements of long-retired boxers and baseball players, but I never heard him boast about this – or anything else. In March 1966 when Red played at the Six Bells, a famous old pub in the Chelsea district of London, someone there asked him if he could put him in touch with Cassius Clay (as the great Muhammad Ali was then called). He must have repeated the question half-a-dozen times, and eventually his persistence led Red to say, 'Gee, you must really admire the guy'. The man exploded with rage, 'Admire him? I hate him, he can't fight. I want to get near enough to give him a good hiding.' Red didn't bother to argue; we left there and then. In the taxi ride back to Red's hotel, Red could not stop laughing at the man's audacity, but his chuckling was interspersed with a lilting, chronological summary of all of Ali's fights going back to his early triumph at the Rome Olympics. Finally he said, 'That stupid guy would have lasted eleven seconds in the ring with the champ, one on his feet and ten on the canvas'.[10]

This British tour was an eye-opener for Red. He was regularly asked to autograph a wide variety of his albums, and despite having three or four of his own compositions on them he soon realized that he had not received any royalties for these foreign issues. Whenever possible he purchased a copy of the offending record so he could take it back to New York and broach the relevant publisher about the money owed to him. Later he told me the results of his enquiries: 'They said they had been trying to get the money to me, but I kept changing my address'. Red snorted derisively as he recalled his answer: 'Man. I've lived at the same address for 25 years, and I've got no plans to move.'[11]

A Valiant Farewell

Having made a few guest appearances at Jimmy Ryan's Club in New York after leaving the Metropole, Red was invited in the spring of 1966, soon after his return from the UK tour, to join the house band at that famous club. However, this bout of full-time employment was short-lived. The roster at Ryan's was packed with jazz talent (Zutty Singleton on drums, Tony Parenti on clarinet, Cliff Jackson on piano, Max Kaminsky on trumpet and Marshall Brown on trombone), but socially the group was less than harmonious and Red soon left, feeling he could not work in an atmosphere of continual bickering. A more satisfying engagement occurred on 4 July 1966 when Red was featured in a 'Trumpet Workshop' at the Newport Jazz Festival alongside Ruby Braff and Clark Terry. It was a sweltering day, and during the rehearsals the musicians played in T-shirts or singlets – all except Red, who looked immaculate in his suit, collar and tie. Jack Bradley, there to take photographs, said to Red, 'Why don't you at least take your jacket off?' Jack later recalled, 'Red looked at me as though I had made the wildest suggestion possible. His New Orleans pride and his keenness to maintain standards kept him from even undoing the top button on his shirt, but I must say he looked so very sharp.'[12]

By this time British trumpeter Keith Smith had temporarily moved to New York and was happy to renew his acquaintanceship with Red:

He could not have been kinder. He showed me around and introduced me to all sorts of musicians. Took me to the Copper Rail and to Beefsteak Charlie's (opposite the Roseland Ballroom) where many of the veteran jazzmen gathered. Red took me to sit in at the Roarin' Twenties and generously gave up time to find me gigs. Through Red I played with Kenny Davern, Ed Hubble and Dick Wellstood out near Manasquan on the New Jersey coast. One night Red said to me, 'Let's go and see the damn fools'. Didn't know what he meant, but this was his expression for the Tony Parenti, Zutty Singleton and Cliff Jackson Trio which was working at Jimmy Ryan's.[13]

In late July 1966 Red decided that the gaps in his engagement diary would allow him to take Pearly May to visit his 82-year-old mother in New Orleans. Just to keep his lip in he played at Dixieland Hall, 522 Bourbon Street, on 31 July; on the following day he was interviewed on WYES-TV. Red returned to New York and carried on playing casual gigs and private engagements; he also worked briefly with clarinettist

Joe Muranyi on a series of Friday night gigs at Mike and Dave's Restaurant in downtown Brooklyn. During this period Red began to feel increasingly tired, whether he exerted himself or not. He contemplated going for a thorough medical check-up, but did not want anything to interfere with the plans for his next tour of Britain, scheduled to begin in mid-February 1967.

Red was still blowing well and remained determined not to curtail his playing routine. He was delighted to be offered the chance to record again with Pee Wee Russell (almost 35 years after they had combined so memorably on the Rhythmakers' sides). The get-together for these two supremely individualistic jazzmen took place in late October 1966 at the Massachusetts Institute of Technology in Cambridge, where they shared a concert date, backed by Steve Kuhn on piano, Marty Morell on drums and Charlie Haden on double bass. The music the group played on stage was used to illustrate a lecture on jazz by Whitney Balliett. Record producer Bob Thiele decided that the reunion between Allen and Russell was important enough to merit a release on his Impulse label, so he went ahead with plans to tape the evening; the end-results were issued as *The College Concert of Pee Wee Russell and Henry 'Red' Allen*.

Although Red had practised trumpet at his home prior to this concert date, he had played fewer gigs than usual in the run-up to the event; Red's method of keeping his lip in shape at this stage of his life was to play along with whatever music came on television. But muted practice within the confines of an apartment is only partially beneficial to a brass player, and regular blowing at full power is needed to ensure that an embouchure remains responsive in all registers. There was no question of Red's 'chops' caving in on the concert recording; he blows strongly and without making fluffs, but for the most part he deliberately avoids the upper register. The commendable rhythm section is more 'modern' than many of those that Red and Pee Wee had worked with, but this did not worry either of the two veterans, both of whom had always thrived on experimentation.

It was perhaps too much to expect that the reunion date would be as epoch-making as Red and Pee Wee's 1932 collaborations. One of the problems is the lack of rapid tempo, as almost everything the group play is on the slow side. On the theme of Thelonious Monk's composition 'Blue Monk', Red's timbre sounds curiously like that of the latter-day Louis Armstrong; here Russell plays a cleverly devised first chorus then takes off in a manner that makes him sound too eager to show that he was still a musical eccentric. Red blows some glorious low notes at the start of his three blues choruses, moving up methodically as he progresses through the 36 bars. The piano sustains the mood, then Charlie Haden picks up one of Red's phrases and develops it ingeniously. The group avoid the smooth route through 'I Want a Little Girl'; Russell's counterpoint to Red's lead is full of agitated phrases that give the impression of a cat on a hot tin roof; his fine solo is, by comparison, peaceful. Again Red makes no attempt to play high, but there is no lack of boldness in his low-register work, and he times the second eight bars miraculously. After a thoughtful piano solo, Red plays muted before climaxing the piece with eight bars of open playing.

After a neat piano introduction Red begins a charming vocal on 'Body and Soul', gracefully pitching the melody notes, and endowing each phrase with just the right amount of emotion. High notes are again absent in the trumpet solo but there is a burst of excitement as Red takes the rhythm section into a double-time interlude. They revert to the original tempo and Red reprises the vocal before being joined in the last eight bars by Pee Wee Russell. The ending is decidedly unspectacular but the trumpet's final note is effective enough. Red is absent from 'Pee Wee's Blues' but returns for John Lewis's blues '2 Degrees East 3 Degrees West'. The opening ensemble sounds scruffy, with Red and Pee Wee making an ineffective attempt to play the melody in unison. Piano, trumpet and clarinet all solo in a restrained fashion, but the ideas that surface do not develop beyond the fragmentary stage. 'Graduation Blues' is more spirited and contains some off-beat call-and-answer phrases between Red and Pee Wee. Red sings a bold chorus and exhorts Pee Wee to 'Carry on! Carry on!' but the best solo is played by Charlie Haden on bass. The finale of this piece highlights a clarion call from Red, and a fleeting revival of a Metropole-like *rallentando* ending. One feels that the audience were thrilled to see and hear these two remarkable musicians performing together, but the recorded results are really only snapshots and not in-depth portraits.

The two veterans shared the train journey up from New York and Pee Wee told Kenny Davern later that he could not help noticing that Red was looking very morose; he remained unconvinced when the trumpeter said that things were fine. Pee Wee tried a different approach by using a jocular expression he had quoted before to Red, 'Come on, Red, you can tell me. Didn't we fight our way out of all those East St Louis bars back to back?' This brought something of a smile to Red's face, but the frown soon returned and he said, 'Well, I've got bad news for myself. I think I've got the big one.'[14] Soon afterwards Red played at

Blues Alley, the successful jazz club in Washington, DC, run by clarinet-tist (and vibes player) Tom Gwaltney and his wife Betty. Red enjoyed the musical company but his condition worsened. He returned to New York where he was seen by Dr Arthur Logan (who was Duke Ellington's physician). Shortly after Christmas 1966 he entered the Sydenham Hospital in New York where he underwent surgery. Sadly the surgeon's task had begun too late and it was obvious from the first explorations that it was only a question of time before cancer of the pancreas proved fatal.

Displaying amazing fortitude, Red insisted on fulfilling his planned 16-day tour of the UK and sent word to his British agents to say that he was feeling fine and would arrive as scheduled on Wednesday 15 February. And so he did. I was the only one there to meet him at Heathrow Airport when his plane landed at around 7 a.m. As I strolled around the arrivals section on that bleak winter's morning I was suddenly filled with a sense of foreboding, and the first sign of Red that morning confirmed my fears. His usual brisk, swinging strides were replaced by a slow, weary trudge, his face was gaunt and his frame seemed to have shrunk alarmingly. I estimated that he had lost about sixty pounds in weight. As we shook hands Red averted his eyes, seemingly embarrassed by the drastic change in his appearance, then he said simply, 'I've lost a lot of weight, John.' All I could say was 'That can sometimes be a good thing'. 'Not the way I've lost it', he said quietly. Then suddenly the old trouper took over, he stroked the lapels of a light grey suit that he could not have possibly got into a year earlier, and said, 'Still I'm looking pretty sharp, eh?'

Red kept the jollity going for most of the taxi trip into West London, where his hotel was situated. The gloom descended when he spoke about the recent death of his old colleague, Edmond Hall. There was a long silence, then Red said, 'Of course I've been very lucky, they operated below my abdomen, so I'll have no trouble blowing the trumpet'. He looked sombre as he said this, but fortunately, at that moment, we reached his hotel. Red braced himself, as if to say 'This is where the tour really starts', and he never again referred to his health throughout the entire trip.

Those who heard Red for the first time during that last amazing tour could never have guessed that they were listening to a dying man. Once onstage Red somehow pulled energy and inspiration out of the air and was never less than magnificent. On his 16-day tour he was again accompanied by Alex Welsh's Band. Unfortunately, Welsh's reed-player Johnny Barnes had been seriously injured in a road crash a couple of weeks before Red arrived and his place in the band was filled on different occasions by Al Gay, Bruce Turner and Alan Cooper. Red made sure that he was part of the benefit date organized for Johnny Barnes. The tour itinerary included return trips to Manchester, Birmingham, Nottingham and Redcar plus three bookings at London's 100 Club.

Despite his debilitating health problems Red retained his sense of humour. After a gig near London we were being driven back to his hotel and passed several signposts for Putney (a district in south-west London). 'Ah', said Red, 'if only old Putney Dandridge knew that they'd be putting up signs for him in London Town he would have been so proud'. Red was weary but loquacious on these late-night return trips. During a random conversation I happened to mention that Wingy Manone had told me how the Mafia had always assisted his career, perhaps (Wingy surmised) because he helped them during his early days in New Orleans. Red forgot how tired he was and let out a loud, derisive hoot. 'Wingy help the Mafia!' he spluttered. 'Only way he could have helped them was by riding his bicycle and delivering them a ham sandwich.' But that conversation quickly took on a serious note as Red said, 'I keep reading that the Mafia is finished. Forget it. They will always be linked with anything that makes money, including the entertainment business. The mob were in New Orleans when I was a kid, and then a lot of them moved on to Chicago and organized clubs there, and that's one of the main reasons why so many musicians went straight from New Orleans to Chicago.'

At most times Red was extremely courteous and friendly to everyone, even when pedants tried to drag him into arguments by comparing the merits of various players. However I heard him squash one person who said that 'St Louis had produced more jazz trumpeters than New Orleans'. Much as Red admired musicians from that Missouri city he was not going to listen to anyone belittling his beloved home territory. Red said tersely, 'Okay buddy, you name me one good player from St Louis and I'll name you two or more from New Orleans'. Towards the end of the tour someone gave Red a photograph, taken a few days earlier, which showed him surreptitiously looking at his wristwatch on stage. Without a second's hesitation (and with a twinkle in his eyes) he said, 'Ah, you see my man, I'm not counting the minutes to the end of the gig, I'm looking at my watch to make sure the customers get full measure'.

Although this tour involved seven days in the north of England and Midlands, the rest of the dates were in the London area, but unfortunately no further tapings were done for Red's autobiography. Albert McCarthy later explained, 'I proposed to get Henry to fill in and enlarge certain parts of the autobiography, but an initial meeting convinced me that his health was such as to make this impossible'.[15] Nevertheless Red continued to make quips about various aspects of life. Trumpeter Max Kaminsky had recently published his autobiography, and carried a supply of the books to sell on gigs, successfully displaying some vigorous salesmanship. This high-pressure selling led Red to comment on 'those two great jazzmen, Bix Beiderbecke and Max Buy-der-book'.

When Red was in good health he really enjoyed his food – it was a pleasure to see him eat – but on this last tour he seemed to do little more than rearrange the food around the edge of his plate. One evening, prior to his playing at the 100 Club in London, Red came to our apartment for dinner. Before doing so he made my wife, Teresa, promise that she would not cook an elaborate meal for him: 'I just want some ham and melon, that's all', but even that lightweight snack was too daunting for his appetite.

Two of Red's Northern dates were at his old stomping ground, the Sports Guild in Manchester. His performances there were reviewed by G.E. Lambert who wrote of Red's playing, 'The swinging eccentricities of rhythmic placing and the beautiful melodic conception, and the great lyricism were as potent as ever'. Lambert described the second of the bookings as 'one of the finest evening's jazz heard at the Guild for some time'.[16] Neither Lambert nor the audience could have guessed that this was one of his last gigs. Red's final gig at the 100 Club was the last time I ever saw him play. It was an emotional experience for many of his friends because they sensed that this would be his farewell visit to Britain, yet it was a happy night because he played so superbly. On the final number he blew a long, daring coda, playing onehanded. A great roar of applause rang out, and, as I looked at Red he seemed for a split second to change into a young man. It was the only mystical experience of my life, and even now, as I write, I relive that eerie moment.

On the morning of Red's departure a small group of wellwishers gathered at his hotel in Queen's Gate, west London. Doug Dobell took photographs of Red and his admirers on the steps of the hotel, then Red, knowing I had to leave early to play a distant gig, called me aside and said in a very soft voice, 'Well, champ, this is it, this is it.' The pretence of survival was over, we shook hands, turned, then shook hands again, and I went off to play a gig of which I have no memory.

Red returned to New York a shadow of his former self. His son Henry III recalled that 'he became very self-conscious about his appearance. He wouldn't get out in front of the house if anybody was there, because he'd lost so much weight. He'd never been sick before. He couldn't understand it. Became more solemn.'[17] Red's sombreness increased when he learnt that his old New Orleans sidekick, Walter 'Fats' Pichon, had died in Chicago on 26 February, and the pain and suffering was made all the more unbearable when on 12 April Red's long-time close friend, Buster Bailey (who had only just returned from touring with Louis Armstrong), died in his sleep. Red's granddaughter Juretta said, 'He looked and acted as if he'd lost his best friend. I guess you could say he had.'[18] Then, to increase Red's sadness, Pearly May was taken to hospital. Red made one last call into the Copper Rail, close to the scene of his many triumphs at the Metropole. Jeff Atterton, then writing for the *Melody Maker*, saw Red leaving that bar and noticed he was carrying a bottle of whisky, an unusual sight. The end was desperately near and Red was soon admitted to the Sydenham Hospital where he spent his last hours before dying on 17 April 1967.

Mercifully Pearly May was not seriously ill and was out of hospital by the day of Red's funeral, 21 April. Louis Armstrong went to Prospect Avenue to offer his condolences in person to Red's widow, adding ominously that it would not be long before he and Red were together again.[19] Red's funeral Mass was held at St Anthony's Roman Catholic church in the Bronx. It was attended by scores of musicians, including his old colleague J.C. Higginbotham. Many who had worked with Red over the years were there, including Teddy Hill, Hilton Jefferson, Dicky Wells, Sandy Williams, Claude Hopkins and Zutty Singleton. Fellow trumpeters Charlie Shavers, Emmett Berry, Joe Newman and Joe Thomas attended as did bassists Al Hall and Hayes Alvis, drummer Slick Jones and saxophonist Harold Ashby. Saxophonist Ornette Coleman, then the leading avant-gardist, also attended, and it seemed fitting that he was paying respects to someone who in his day had been a beacon of jazz exploration. Those who gathered at the funeral could have made up a magnificent musical ensemble, but their playing skills were not required. Pearly May followed her husband's wishes, 'I was surprised when he told me not long before he passed that he didn't want any music at his funeral. He said he couldn't take those New Orleans music funerals. I never knew that. He didn't want it for himself.'[20]

To celebrate Red Allen's life a wonderful Memorial Concert was held on Sunday 4 June 1967 at the Riverboat (situated in the basement of

New York's Empire State Building). Dozens of musicians gave their services including Earl Hines, J.C. Higginbotham, Max Kaminsky, Louis Metcalf, Charlie Shavers, Tyree Glenn, Jo Jones, Jimmy Rushing, Yank Lawson, Wilbur De Paris, Red Richards and Sonny Greer. Dozens of others including Willie 'The Lion' Smith were ready to perform but could not be fitted into the overcrowded schedule. Louis Armstrong, booked elsewhere, sent a telegram that was read to the audience. Many people were turned away and over $5,000 was raised, half of which the Allen family immediately gave to the American Cancer Society. One of the organizers, Jack Bradley, felt that it was one of the biggest jazz benefits ever held.

The huge turnout was an indication of the love and esteem that musicians and the public felt for Henry 'Red' Allen. That affection and appreciation has never diminished; in fact he has posthumously gained many new admirers who hear within his work a perfect blend of tradition and exploration. Red's own words provided his epitaph: 'I have no fears about the future of jazz. This music can't die out while there are always new generations of musicians trying new things. I only hope that they also combine their innovations with listening to some of the players who have gone before them.'[21]

NOTES

CHAPTER 1
1. Richard Sudhalter's notes for Time-Life Records *Giants of Jazz* booklet (Alexandria, VA, 1981)
2. *Ibid.*
3. Whitney Balliett interview, *New Yorker*, 25 June 1966
4. V.J. Thiberville, Notary Public, Parish of New Orleans, 28 February 1944
5. *Jazz Monthly*, February 1970
6. *Jazz Journal*, September 1964
7. See *Waterfront Workers of New Orleans, Race, Class and Politics 1863–1923* by Eric Arnesen (University of Illinois Press, 1994).
8. *La Nouvelle-Orléans, Capitale du Jazz* by Robert Goffin (Éditions de la Maison Française, Inc., New York, 1946)
9. *Ibid.*
10. *Ibid.*
11. *Jazz Monthly*, February 1970
12. *Jazz Journal*, September 1964
13. *Jazz Monthly*, February 1970
14. *Jazz Masters of New Orleans* by Martin Williams (Macmillan, New York, 1967)
15. *Jazz from the Beginning* by Garvin Bushell (as told to Mark Tucker) (University of Michigan Press, 1988)
16. Conversation with the author, 1966
17. *Jazz Monthly*, February 1970
18. *I Guess I'll Get the Papers and Go Home* by Adolphus 'Doc' Cheatham (Cassell, London and New York, 1996)
19. *Jazz Journal*, September 1964
20. *Jazz Mentors* (a dissertation by Al Kennedy, New Orleans, Louisiana, 1996)
21. Letter from Al Kennedy to the author, 19 August 1997
22. *Melody Maker*, 26 February 1966
23. *Jazz Monthly*, February 1970
24. *Second Line*, Spring 1991, and *Jazz Monthly*, February 1970
25. Les Tompkins interview, *Crescendo*, February 1966
26. Hogan Jazz Archive, Tulane University, New Orleans; Harrison Barnes interview, 29 January 1959
27. Whitney Balliett interview, *New Yorker*, 25 June 1966
28. *Jazz Monthly*, February 1970
29. *Coda* magazine, September 1959
30. *Record Changer*, November 1947
31. Hogan Jazz Archive, Amos White interview, 23 August 1958
32. *Jazz Journal*, February 1960
33. *New Yorker*, 25 June 1966
34. *Jazz Monthly*, February 1970
35. *Record Changer*, December 1954

CHAPTER 2
1. Hogan Jazz Archive, Paul Barbarin interview, 27 March 1957
2. *New Yorker*, 25 June 1966
3. *Ibid.*
4. *Melody Maker*, 26 February 1966, and *Record Changer*, December 1954
5. *Call Him George* by Ann Fairbairn (Crown, New York, 1969)
6. Conversation with the author, 1964

7. Conversation with the author, 1965
8. *Ibid.*
9. *Jazz Monthly*, February 1970
10. Interview with Val Wilmer, *Jazz and Blues*, November 1971
11. Hogan Jazz Archive, Eddie Marrero interview, 11 October 1961
12. Hogan Jazz Archive, Bill Mathews interview, 10 March 1959
13. *Jazz Monthly*, February 1970
14. *New Yorker*, 25 June 1966
15. Hogan Jazz Archive, Leonard Bocage interview, 24 March 1972
16. *Ibid.*
17. Hogan Jazz Archive, John Casimir interview, 17 January 1959
18. *Ibid.*
19. *Jazz Masters of New Orleans* by Martin Williams
20. Hogan Jazz Archive, Clarence Vincent, December 1959
21. *Ibid.*
22. Time-Life, *Giants of Jazz* booklet, 1981
23. *Jazz Masters of New Orleans* by Martin Williams
24. *Jazz Monthly*, June 1964
25. Interview with Les Tompkins, *Crescendo*, February 1966
26. *Jazz Monthly*, February 1970
27. *Jazz Information*, 8 November 1940
28. *New Yorker*, 25 June 1966
29. *Ibid.*
30. *Coda*, November 1959
31. Conversation with the author, 1964
32. *Ibid.*
33. *Ibid.*
34. *New Yorker*, 25 June 1966
35. *Footnote*, Vol. 7, No. 3. Interview Joseph T. Rouzan
36. Harold Dejan comment 1997, relayed by Barry Martyn
37. *Footnote*, Vol. 7, No. 3. Interview Joseph T. Rouzan
38. *Jazz Journal*, February 1960, and *Jazz Monthly*, February 1970
39. Hogan Jazz Archive, Leonard Bocage, 24 March 1972
40. *Jazz Monthly*, February 1970
41. Time-Life, *Giants of Jazz* booklet, 1981
42. *Melody Maker*, 2 April 1966
43 *Ibid.*

CHAPTER 3
1. *Satchmo – My Life in New Orleans*, by Louis Armstrong and Peter Davies (London, 1955)
2. Sinbad Condelucci, letter to author, 1972
3. *Jazz Journal*, September 1964
4. Hogan Jazz Archive, Bob Watts, 28 February 1963
5. *New Yorker*, 25 June 1966
6. *Jazz Monthly*, February 1970
7. Hogan Jazz Archive, Captain Joseph Streckfus, 20 February 1958
8. *Saint Louis Argus*, undated clipping from files of Frank Driggs
9. Conversation with author, 1966, and *Jazz Monthly*, February 1970
10. Conversation with author, 1966
11. *Ibid.*
12. *Jazz Information*, 9 August 1940
13. *Pops Foster, New Orleans Jazzman*, as told to Tom Stoddard (University of California Press, 1971)
14. *Jazz Monthly*, April 1957
15. *New Yorker*, 25 June 1966
16. *Cadence*, June 1979
17. *The World of Swing* by Stanley Dance (Scribner's, New York, 1974)
18. *Pops Foster, New Orleans Jazzman*
19. Conversation with the author, 1964
20. *Ibid.*
21. *Ibid.*
22. *Jazz Journal*, September 1964
23. *Jazz Monthly*, June 1964
24. *New Yorker*, 25 June 1966
25. Time-Life, *Giants of Jazz* booklet, 1981
26. National Endowment for the Arts interview (1972) held at the Institute of Jazz Studies, Rutgers, New Jersey
27. *The Best of Jazz – Basin Street to Harlem* by Humphrey Lyttelton (Robson Books, London, 1978)
28. Interview with Johnny Simmen, *Coda*, Issue 163, 1978

CHAPTER 4
1. *Trumpet Story* by Bill Coleman (Macmillan, London, 1990)
2. *Ibid.*
3. *Ibid.*
4. *Ibid.*
5. Greely Walton, quoted in Frank Drigg's sleeve notes for Luis Russell album, CBS S 880 39
6. *Jazz Beat*, May 1964

7. BBC radio programme, 'Hear Me Talking to You', 1964
8. *Jazz Journal*, September 1964
9. Conversation with author, 1964
10. Lil Hardin Armstrong interviewed by Robert Levin, *Jazz 'N' Pops*, April 1957
11. *Baltimore Afro-American*, 18 January 1930
12. *Melody Maker*, 7 January 1956
13. *Jazz Monthly*, April 1957
14. *Melody Maker*, 7 January 1956
15. *Melody Maker*, 12 February 1966
16. *Pops Foster, New Orleans Jazzman*
17. *Cadence*, June 1979
18. *Down Beat*, 8 November 1962
19. *Cadence*, June 1979
20. *In the Mainstream* by Chip Deffaa (Scarecrow Press, New Jersey, 1992)
21. *Down Beat*, 30 January 1964
22. *Jazz Journal*, February 1960
23. *Rhythm*, December 1935
24. *New Yorker*, 25 June 1966
25. *The Best of Jazz – Basin Street to Harlem* by Humphrey Lyttelton
26. Conversation with the author, 1966
27. *Jazz Monthly*, June 1964
28. *Coda*, Issues 163, 178
29. *Melody Maker*, 7 January 1956
30. Hogan Jazz Archive, Monk Hazel, 16 July 1959
31. *Record Changer*, December 1954
32. *Jazz Journal*, September 1964
33. *The Swing Era*, by Gunther Schuller (Oxford University Press, New York, 1989)
34. *New Yorker*, 25 June 1966

CHAPTER 5
1. *The Second Line*, Winter 1978
2. Hogan Jazz Archive, Paul Barbarin, 28 January 1960
3. *Cadence*, July 1979
4. *The Swing Era* by Gunther Schuller
5. *Melody Maker*, 26 February 1966
6. Author's conversation with Keith Smith, 1997 and Frank Drigg's sleevenote for CBS S 880 39
7. *Melody Maker*, 7 January 1956
8. *Pops Foster, New Orleans Jazzman*
9. *Footnote*, Vol. 3, no. 5
10. *All What Jazz* by Philip Larkin (Faber and Faber, London, 1970)
11. *Ibid.*
12. Conversation with author, 1964

13. Conversation overhead by author, Paris, 1962
14. Earle Howard, letter to the author, 3 October 1969
15. Conversation with the author, 1964
16. *Swing Music*, November–December 1935
17. *Jazz Journal*, September 1964
18. *Melody Maker*, 22 July 1939

CHAPTER 6
1. *Hendersonia* by Walter C. Allen (Jazz Monographs, New Jersey, 1973)
2. *Ibid.*
3. *Crescendo*, February 1966
4. Time-Life, *Giants of Jazz* booklet, 1981
5. Smithsonian interview April 1975, copy held in the Institute of Jazz Studies archive, New Jersey
6. *The Swing Era* by Gunther Schuller
7. Conversation with author, 1967
8. *The Jazz Makers*, edited by Nat Shapiro and Nat Hentoff (Peter Davies, London, 1958)
9. Time-Life, *Giants of Jazz* booklet, 1981
10. *The Swing Era* by Gunther Schuller
11. Conversation with the author, 1965
12. *Coda*, June 1961
13. National Endowment for the Arts interview, 1972
14. *Melody Maker*, 2 June 1934
15. *Melody Maker*, 7 July 1934
16. *The World of Swing* by Stanley Dance
17. Conversation with the author, 1964
18. Conversation with the author, 1964
19. Conversation with the author, 1966
20. *John Hammond on Record* by John Hammond (with Irving Townsend) (Ridge Press, New York, 1977)
21. *Melody Maker*, 14 October 1933
22. *This Horn for Hire* by Pee Wee Erwin and Warren Vaché Sr (Scarecrow Press, New Jersey, 1987)
23. Time-Life, *Giants of Jazz* booklet, 1981
24. *Down Beat*, 8 April 1965
25. *The Street That Never Slept* by Arnold Shaw (Coward, McCann and Geoghegan, Inc., New York, 1971)
26. Time-Life, *Giants of Jazz* booklet, 1981

Ride, Red, Ride

CHAPTER 7
1. *New Yorker*, 25 June 1966
2. *Jazz Journal*, September 1964
3. Time-Life, *Giants of Jazz* booklet, 1981
4. *New York Age*, 15 August 1936
5. *Coda*, October 1962
6. *Record Changer*, December 1954
7. Time-Life, *Giants of Jazz* booklet, 1981
8. *Cadence*, July 1979
9. *Crescendo*, February 1966
10. *Ibid.*
11. Conversation with the author, 1964
12. Conversation with the author, 1956
13. Conversation with the author, 1964
14. *Metronome*, May 1938
15. Time-Life, *Giants of Jazz* booklet, 1981
16. *Coda*, November 1959
17. Time-Life, *Giants of Jazz* booklet, 1981
18. Hogan Jazz Archive, Captain Joseph Sreckfus, 20 February 1958
19. *Jazz Information*, 20 September 1940
20. *Jazz Journal*, September 1964
21. Conversation with the author, 1964

CHAPTER 8
1. *Jazz Information*, 25 October 1940
2. *Jazz Journal*, July 1992
3. *Jazz Masters of New Orleans* by Martin Williams
4. *Melody Maker*, 7 January 1956
5. *Coda*, November 1959
6. *Cadence*, July 1979
7. *Melody Maker*, 28 April 1956
8. National Endowment for the Arts interview, 1972
9. *Down Beat*, 15 December 1940
10. National Endowment for the Arts interview, 1972
11. *Jazz Information*, 25 October 1940
12. *Ibid.*
13. Time-Life, *Giants of Jazz* booklet, 1981
14. National Endowment for the Arts interview, 1972
15. *Down Beat*, 15 August 1941
16. *Metronome*, August 1941
17. *Down Beat*, 1 October 1941
18. *Jazz Monthly*, February 1958

CHAPTER 9
1. *Cadence*, July 1979

2. *Music Dial* (undated cutting)
3. *Bunny Berigan, Elusive Legend of Jazz* by Robert Dupuis (Louisiana State University Press, Baton Rouge, 1993)
4. *Down Beat*, 1 October 1942
5. Hogan Jazz Archive, Punch Miller, September 1959
6. *Down Beat*, 15 December 1942
7. *Queen of the Blues* by Jim Haskins (William Morrow, 1987)
8. Conversation with Johnny Simmen, Switzerland, 1959
9. *Down Beat*, 1 March 1943
10. *Crescendo*, February 1966
11. *Dizzy – to be or not to bop* by Dizzy Gillespie and Al Fraser (W.H. Allen, London, 1980)
12. *Buck Clayton's Jazz World* by Buck Clayton (Macmillan Press, London, 1986
13. Time-Life, *Giants of Jazz* booklet, 1981
14. *Jazz Monthly*, June 1964, and *Crescendo*, February 1966
15. *Jazz Monthly*, June 1964
16. BBC radio programme, 'Hear Me Talking to You', 1964
17. *Down Beat*, 3 June 1946
18. *New York Age*, 26 January 1946
19. *Down Beat*, 21 May 1947
20. Conversation relayed by Henry 'Red' Allen, 1967

CHAPTER 10
1. *Billboard*, 30 September 1950
2. *Down Beat*, 22 September 1950
3. *Down Beat*, 9 February 1951
4. Time-Life, *Giants of Jazz* booklet, 1981
5. *Jazz Journal*, February 1960
6. Conversation with the author, August 1977
7. *Ibid.*
8. *Loose Shoes* by James Shacter (Jaynar Press, Chicago, 1994)
9. *Cadence*, June 1979
10. *Crescendo*, June 1979
11. *Sunday Telegraph*, 27 February 1966
12. Time-Life, *Giants of Jazz* booklet, 1981
13. *Record Changer*, April 1954
14. *Ibid.*
15. *Jazz Journal*, June 1964
16. *Changing Channels* by A. Charren (Sandler, 1982)

Notes

17. Sleevenote by Marty Grosz, ARCD 19188
18. *Coda,* September 1967
19. *Jazz Monthly,* June 1964
20. Conversation with the author, 1964
21. *The Leader of the Band* by Gene Lees (Oxford University Press, New York, 1995)
22. *Allegro,* November 1987
23. *Melody Maker,* 14 March 1964
24. Letter to the author, 8 January 1998
25. Conversation with the author, August 1997
26. *Coda,* Issue 197, 1984
27. Conversation with the author, August 1997

CHAPTER 11
1. *Melody Maker,* 22 February 1966
2. National Endowment for the Arts interview, 1972
3. *The Swing Era* by Gunther Schuller
4. *Jazz Masters of New Orleans* by Martin Williams
5. *Jazz Beat,* April 1966
6. National Endowment for the Arts interview, 1972
7. *Melody Maker,* 17 October 1959
8. *Ibid.*
9. Conversation with the author, 24 August 1997
10. Conversation with the author, 19 September 1997
11. Overheard by the author, 1959
12. *Coda,* December 1959
13. *Melody Maker,* 7 November 1959
14. *Melody Maker,* 24 October 1959
15. *Jazz News,* 20 December 1961

CHAPTER 12
1. *Melody Maker,* 21 October 1967
2. *Crescendo,* February 1966
3. *Jazz News,* 26 July 1961
4. *Melody Maker,* 26 February 1966
5. *Down Beat,* 3 August 1961
6. *What Do They Want?* by Sammy Price (Bayou Press, Oxford, 1989)
7. *Down Beat,* 30 August 1962
8. *Ibid.*
9. Conversation with the author, 26 August 1997
10. *Jazz Journal,* September 1964
11. *New Orleans States-Item,* 29 August 1968
12. *Coda,* Issue 163, 178
13. *Ibid.*

14. Conversation with the author, 1998
15. *Ibid.*

CHAPTER 13
1. *Jazz Beat,* June 1964
2. *Down Beat,* 18 June 1964
3. *Jazz Journal,* July 1964
4. *Jazz Journal,* July 1964, and conversation with the author, 6 February 1997
5. *Jazz Journal,* July 1964
6. *Jazz Journal,* September 1964
7. *Melody Maker,* 21 November 1964
8. Time-Life, *Giants of Jazz* booklet, 1981
9. Insert notes for Merritt album 27
10. *What Do They Want?* by Sammy Price
11. Conversation with the author, August 1997
12. Conversation with the author, 6 August 1997

CHAPTER 14
1. *New Yorker,* 25 June 1966
2. *Down Beat,* 4 November 1965
3. Conversation with the author, 23 September 1997
4. Letter to author, 8 January 1998
5. *Jazz Monthly,* June 1967
6. Time-Life, *Giants of Jazz* booklet, 1981
7. *Melody Maker,* 26 February 1966, and *Jazz Monthly,* June 1964
8. Conversation with the author, 1966
9. Conversation with the author, October 1997
10. Conversation with the author, 1966
11. *Ibid.*
12. Conversation with the author, 14 December 1997
13. Conversation relayed by Kenny Davern, October 1997
14. Conversation relayed by Kenny Davern, 6 August 1997
15. *Jazz Monthly,* February 1970
16. *Jazz Journal,* April 1967
17. Time-Life, *Giants of Jazz* booklet, 1981
18. *Ibid.*
19. Conversation relayed by Henry Allen III, 1997
20. Time-Life, *Giants of Jazz* booklet, 1981
21. *Jazz Masters of New Orleans* by Martin Williams

SELECTED DISCOGRAPHY

COMPILED BY BRIAN PEERLESS

Henry Allen on CD

CDs listed are those that have the best sound to date. In some cases other issues exist but the transfers are not as good, or are inconsistent, e.g. Classics (F) have only been used where that is the only issue available. Their sound is perfectly acceptable, but could be better.

Information given in parentheses after CD title relates to recording dates applicable to Allen and/or other sessions not under his leadership that he played on.

All CDs cited are American unless indicated by the following codes after the label:

Au	Austria	Den	Denmark	Eu	Europe
F	France	G	Germany	H	Holland
I	Italy	Sw	Sweden	UK	United Kingdom

CD Title	Label & Number
Clarence Williams 1927	Classics (F) 736
Henry Allen & New York Orchestra Vol 1 1929–30 (+ Victoria & Addie Spivey 1929)	JSP (UK) JSPCD 332
Henry Allen & New York Orchestra Vol 2 1928–30 (+ Addie Spivey 1929-Alternates + Luis Russell Oct/Dec 1930)	JSP (UK) JSPCD 333
Luis Russell 1929–1930 (+ J.C. Higginbotham Six Hicks 1930/Louis's Song of the Islands 1930)	JSP (UK) JSPCD 308
Teddy Bunn 1929–1940 (Walter Pichon 1929)	RST (Au) JPCD 1509-2
Fats Waller & his Buddies (1929)	BMG (G) RCA BB ND90649
The Jelly Roll Morton Centennial: His Complete Victor Recordings (1930) 5 CD Set	BMG RCA BB 2361-2-RB
Jelly Roll Morton Volume 6 1929 (single CD with Allen titles)	Media 7 (F) MJCD 80
Crazy Clarinets – Raucous Reeds (all Wilton Crawley titles 1929–30)	Jazz Crusade (UK) JCCD 3019
Louis Armstrong Volume 6 St Louis Blues (1929)	Col 46996/ (Eu)467919
King Oliver Volume Two 1929–1930 (1930)	JSP (UK) JSPCD 348
Luis Russell Collection 1926–1934 (Lou & his Ginger Snaps/Orchestra 1930/1931)	Collectors Classics (Den) COCD-7

Selected Discography

CD Title	Label & Number
Don Redman & his Orchestra 1931–1933 (1931)	Classics (F) 543
Henry Allen Collection Vol 1 1932 (Jack Bland/Billy Banks/The Rhythmakers)	Collectors Classics (Den) COCD-1
Henry Allen Collection Vol 2 1932–1935 (The Rhythmakers (Jack Bland) & Orchestra)	Collectors Classics (Den) COCD-2
A Study in Frustration – The Fletcher Henderson Story (3 CD Set)	Col 57596
Henry Allen–Coleman Hawkins 1933 (+ Horace Henderson 1933)	Hep (UK) HEP CD1028
Fletcher Henderson 1932–1934	Classics (F) 535
Harlem Rhythm Vol 1 1933 (Fletcher Henderson Sept 1933)	EMI (F) Jazz Time 252 710-2
Spike Hughes & Benny Carter (1933)	Retrieval (H) RTR 790005 Jazz
Don Redman & his Orchestra 1933–1936 (1934)	Classics (F) 553
Fletcher Henderson 1934–1937 (1934)	Classics (F) 527
Benny Morton 1934–1945 (1934)	Classics (F) 906
Indispensable Fletcher Henderson & his Orchestra (1927–1936) (1934)	RCA (F) Jazz Tribune 743212 26182
Fletcher Henderson – Tidal Wave (1934)	MCA GRP 16432
Mills Blue Rhythm Band 1933–1934 (1934)	Classics (F) 686
Swing Street – Volume 1 (Buster Bailey 1934/ James P Johnson March 1939-2 titles)	Tax (Sw) Tax S-9-2
Mills Blue Rhythm Band 1936–1937	Classics (F) 731
Henry Allen Collection Vol 3 1935–1936	Collectors Classics (Den) COCD-13
Mills Blue Rhythm Band 1934–1936	Classics (F) 710
Putney Dandridge 1935–1936	Timeless (H) CBC 1-023 Jazz
Henry Allen Collection Vol 4 1936–1937	Collectors Classics (Den) COCD-15
Bunny Berigan 'Through the Years' (MBRB 5 Nov 1936)	Archives of Jazz (H) 3891192
The Quintessential Billie Holiday Vol 3 (1936–1937) (Teddy Wilson 1937)	Col CK 44048/ (Eu) 460820
Henry Allen Collection Vol 5 1937–1941 (+ Zutty Singleton Orch. 1940)	Collectors Classics (Den) COCD-23
James P Johnson 1938–1942 (1939)	Classics (F) 711
Rosetta Howard 1939–1947 (1939)	RST (Au) JPCD-1514-2
Trixie Smith Volume 2 (1925–1939) (1939)	Document (Au) DOCD-5333
Complete Lionel Hampton & his Orchestra Vol 3/4 (1939)	RCA (F) Jazz Tribune 743212 26142
Jazzin' the Blues (1936–1946) (Helen Proctor 1939/ Lee Brown 17 April 1940)	RST (Au) JPCD 1515-2

Ride, Red, Ride

CD Title	Label & Number
Blue Lu Barker 1938–1939 (1939)	Classics (F) 704
Lee Brown (1937–1940) (11 Jan 1940)	Document (Au) DOCD-5344
Jelly Roll Morton Last Sessions (1940)	Commodore CMD14032
Frankie 'Half-Pint' Jaxon Volume 3 (1937–1940) (1940)	Document (Au) DOCD-5260
Johnny Temple Volume 3 1940–1949 (1940)	Document (Au) DOCD-5240
Ida Cox – I Can't Quit My Man (1940)	Affinity (UK) CD AFS 1015
Complete Sidney Bechet Vol 1/2 (1932–1941) (1941)	RCA (F) Jazz Tribune ND 89760
Complete Sidney Bechet Vol 3/4 (1941)	RCA (F) Jazz Tribune ND 89759
Henry Allen Collection Vol 6 1941–1946	Collectors Classics (Den) COCD-24
Indispensable Artie Shaw Vol 3/4 (1940–1942) (1941)	RCA (F) Jazz Tribune 7432164142
Trumpet Royalty (Bill's Downbeat 1947)	Vintage Jazz Classics VJC-1009-2
Laughter from the Hip (Shanty in Old Shanty Town 1947)	Jass J-CD-20
George Lewis with Red Allen The Circle Recordings (1951)	American Music AMCD-71
Dr Jazz Sampler 1951–1952 (Baby, Won't You Please Come Home 1952)	Storyville (Den) STCD 6040
Dr Jazz 1951–1952 Vol 9 Henry 'Red' Allen from Central Plaza	Storyville (Den) STCD 6049
Lee Wiley – Music of Manhattan 1951 (1952)	Uptown UPCD 2746
Lee Wiley Rarities (1952)	Jass CD-15
Henry 'Red' Allen World on a String Legendary 1957 Sessions	BMG (G) BB ND82497
More of Best of Dixieland (China Boy – Newport 1957, Ory/Allen – Come Back Sweet Papa 1959, Ballin' the Jack 1960)	Phillips (Eu) 838 347-2
Jazz-Club Mainstream Trombone (St James Infirmary – Newport 1957, Ballin' the Jack 1960)	Verve (G) 845 144-2
Sound of Jazz (Studio 5 December 1957)	Col 45234/ (Eu) 465683 2
The Legendary Sound of Jazz Telecast (8 December 1957)	Bandstand (I) BDCD1517
Coleman Hawkins & Red Allen Standards and Warhorses (Soundcraft Sessions 1957/8)	Jass CD-2
Weary Blues with Langston Hughes, Charles Mingus and Leonard Feather (1958)	Verve 841 660-2
Jazz-Club Mainstream Dixieland (Ory/Allen – Ain't Misbehavin' 1959, Ballin' the Jack & Yellow Dog Blues 1960)	Verve (G) 845 149-2

Selected Discography

CD Title	Label & Number
Kid Ory (Ory/Allen – Tishomingo Blues 1959)	Giants of Jazz (I) CD53087
Kid Ory and Red Allen in Denmark (13 Nov 1959)	Storyville (Den) STCD 6038
Swing Trumpet Kings (Red Allen Plays King Oliver)	Verve 533 263-2

Henry Allen not on CD

Many of the later Henry Allen long-play recordings have yet to be transferred to CD, either in their complete form or even individual titles from the albums. Listed below are long-play albums falling in this category that are worth seeking out.

Album Title	Label & Number
Jazz at the Metropole – Red Allen/Cozy Cole/ Charlie Shavers (1955)	Bethlehem BCP-21/London (UK) LTZ-N 15010
Happy Jazz by Red Allen's All-Stars (1955)–10 inch also by Tony Parenti's All-Stars – 12 inch LP (no extra Allen titles)	Jazztone J-1030 Jazztone J-1215
Dixiecats featuring the Dixieland All-Stars (1957)	Roulette R25015/Col (UK) 33SX1080
Red Allen, Kid Ory & Jack Teagarden at Newport (1957)	Verve MGV8233/Col (UK) 33CX10106
Henry Allen Meets Kid Ory (1959)	Verve MGV1018/ HMV (UK) CLP1329
We've Got Rhythm – Kid Ory & Red Allen (1959) (MGV1018 & MGV1020 also issued as double album Henry Red and the Kid)	Verve MGV1020/ HMV (UK) CLP1422 Metro (UK) 2682 006
Henry Red Allen Quartet 'Live' at the London House Chicago Sept 15 & 22 1961	Fanfare 24-124
Mr Allen Henry 'Red' Allen (1962)	Prestige/Swingville 2034/Xtra (UK) 5032
Henry 'Red' Allen – Feeling Good (1965)	Col CL2447 (mono)/ Col CS 9247 (stereo) (UK) BPG 62400
The College Concert of Pee Wee Russell and Henry Red Allen (1966)	Impulse A9137 (mono), AS9137(stereo)/(UK) MILP509 (mono), SILP509 (stereo)

A comprehensive discography of Henry 'Red' Allen and J.C. Higginbotham has been compiled and published by Franz Hoffman, Gierkezeile 38, D-10585 Berlin, Germany. A solography of Henry 'Red' Allen, covering his recordings from 1927 to 1942, has been compiled by Jan Evensmo and Per Borthen, and published by Jan Evensmo, Granasen 73D, 1347 Hosle, Norway.

INDEX

Index

213

Index

Index

Index